D1171372

AMERICAN CATHOLIC EXODUS

American Catholic Exodus

Edited by
John O'Connor

Philip Berrigan, SSJ

Eugene C Bianchi, SJ

William Birmingham

Robert McAfee Brown

Dennis Clark

A V Krebs, Jr

Maryellen Muckenhirn, CSC

John Mulholland

Arlene Swidler

Frederick D Wilhelmsen

John O'Connor

CORPUS BOOKS

Washington – Cleveland

CORPUS PUBLICATIONS

Editorial Offices	*Sales & Distribution*
1330 Massachusetts Ave., N.W.	2231 West 110th Street
Washington, D.C. 20005	Cleveland, Ohio 44102

First Printing 1968

Printed in Great Britain

To Sara Lee

whose life is hope

Contents

Introduction

JOHN O'CONNOR

The Scot visitor to the United States, D W Brogan, once said the Catholic problem in America, from the political and social point of view, was one of segregation. But he also called the American 'a new man'.

Allowing for some dramatic exaggeration in the latter, let us admit that the 'new world' and the push to new frontiers did call upon men seeking new freedom and new development. The Catholic American, no less than his neighbor, answered this call. Moreover, let us admit Brogan hit the nail on the head with his observation that an indigenous segregation has been among the Church's problems—but not alone from the social and political point of view. It goes deeper than that: the segregation of the people who claim to follow Jesus Christ into a highly organized, well-policed, expansionist institution, governed in secret, and comfortably well off, is a theological problem, and American Catholics have finally taken notice of that and are doing something about it. They are seeking a new Church.

Franklin Hamlin Littell has noted that Protestants, too, have confused the Church's mission with organizational success; while Msgr John Tracy Ellis has insisted, rightly I am sure, that you cannot separate the story of the Church in America from the general story of America itself.

The American Catholic, in case you didn't know, therefore, is more American than Catholic. And the impact of World War II on

I

his ghetto isolation, the impact of the communications revolution and TV on his information (and his religious guardians' control of news and opinion), and the impact of rising costs on his financially desperate school system (which system at one time seemed absolutely vital)—all of these mesh with the story of the American people, a people quite complacent in their comfort, now caught in the whirl of revolutionary change.

Wherever Catholics of any awareness meet today the question comes up: what's new in the Church? Sooner or later the subject comes around to who has left lately. The papers haven't carried the story, but Father So-and-so has gone—not necessarily to get married; just up and left. A nun goes over the wall. Her family is all broken up for a while; but she's home, and that's that. A young man comes home from college and announces to hell with Sunday Mass—nothing ever swings in the parish church anyway, so why bother? The parents have a fit. A pastor, wrought and red-faced over press accounts of what he calls disobedient and defecting clergy, blurts out blame for the drop-off in confessions on the mass media. You talk to friends and find out that they have long since made up their minds on the birth control question, guided by what they believe to be fully informed consciences and a proven sense of responsibility and mutual love. Here are other friends who have made a strong moral judgment about the war in Vietnam, though the prayers of the faithful in their parish have been vague and designedly unspecific when petitioning for peace, and though their bishop has kept mum on the whole thing.

Then you sense that within this Church that at times you were sure was very, very dead, there is movement, signs of life. But this movement—which way, out, or ahead? Is it an exit, or an exodus?

What's been happening in the American Catholic Church, as everywhere else, is a revolution: everybody admits that. Pope John let the fresh air in, the breeze turned into a hurricane, and things are getting moved around, and not all according to some cleverly designed, paternalistic plan allowing for some adaptation in order to see the institution through. Not at all. The spirit of reform ran smack into the rigid resistance of vested clerical interests and frightened lay tribesmen who quake violently at the thought of giving up their security blankets.

The action has been so exciting that I asked a number of my knowledgable friends who know the scene to tell me what they saw. Their observations, I think, are acute and prophetical: if you want to know where the Catholic Church, USA, is heading, then read what they have to say.

You will find in this book a number of thinkers who have been battle-scarred in the front lines of their specialities. Generally, they represent what might be called a progressive point of view; only one represents a caution to this progressive thrust. They speak as individuals, none knowing what his collaborators saw and wrote.

Of the contributors, only one, Professor Brown, is not of the Roman persuasion, though of my friends, in and out of the cloth, this ordained Presbyterian minister is one of the most Catholic gentlemen and priestly Christians I know. Another, Professor Wilhelmsen, represents and presents a more reverential view of where we, the Church, have been. Perhaps the future will prove him right; certainly, it will approve his concern.

What we are seeing in America today is a gigantic walkaway. But where a Charles Davis or a James Kavanaugh has attracted attention to what they call their leaving of the Church, I think the character of the present action is not so much that people are leaving the Church, but that they are taking the Church with them. They feel they are the Church. What they are leaving behind, for the most part, are old forms, old structures, some old ideas and prejudices and postures, and, sad to say, some old men in moldy mitres. Church leadership, they feel, has been crushingly disappointing.

Where only yesterday Catholics were party-liners on many different fronts from patriotism to the pill, today they are scattered in a diaspora situation and are departing from official chancery lines to establish a plurality of views within one faith. Rather than being certain they had God cornered in a tabernacle, guarded by canon lawyers and the flashing blades of those plumed samurai, the Knights of Columbus, they set out in search of him, among their

neighbors, from whom they can learn, to whom they can extend a
hand, and with whom they hope to rehabilitate the earth. The old
ideas towards war, Protestantism, youth's education, the Negro,
nationalism, the religious life, the place of the layman, the status of
women, the importance and authority of the clergy—especially the
bishops—have been re-examined, hashed over, and held up to the
light. The result has been a breakthrough into a new and unknown land.

Blood, War and Witness

PHILIP BERRIGAN, SSJ

On Friday, 27 October 1967, we are entering the Customs House in Baltimore, Maryland, to deface the draft records there with our blood.

We shed our blood willingly and gratefully in what we hope is a sacrificial and constructive act. We pour it upon these files to illustrate that with them and with these offices begins the pitiful waste of American and Vietnamese blood ten thousand miles away. That bloodshedding is never rational, seldom voluntary. In a word, non-constructive. It does not protect life, but rather endangers it.

We wish neither notoriety, nor labels of martyrdom or messianism. We desire merely to stand for human life and a human future. We realize painfully yet clearly that what we intend goes beyond the scope of constitutional right and civil liberty, and is therefore not to be taken lightly.

We believe that war proves nothing except man's refusal to be man and to live with men. We say that man must end war, or war will end man. We deplore our country's hot and cold warring and its crime against the often unwilling and powerless bodies behind these files.

Thus we unite with our servicemen against their real enemies. We shed our blood as they do theirs. We disrupt our lives as the draft does theirs.

We quarrel with the idolatry of property, and the war machine that makes property of men. We confront those countrymen to whom property means more than human life. We assert that property is often an instrument of massive injustice—like these

5

files. Thus we feel that our discriminate destruction of this property is warranted in the interest of human life.

Nonetheless, we take every measure to protect the personnel here from hysteria or injury. We are content to remind them of their complicity in the untimely death of young soldiers, in the murder of innocent civilians, in the pain of parents and sweethearts. We ask their resignations.

We agree that America is the greatest manufacturer and salesman of violence in the world today. We feel this is so because power rests not with the people to whom it belongs, but with an economic, political and military cabal whose aims can tolerate neither foreign autonomy nor domestic freedom.

We charge that America would rather protect its empire of overseas profits than welcome its black people, rebuild its slums and clean its air and water. Thus we have singled out inner-city draft boards for special attention.

We love our country and celebrate its greatness. But our love cannot accept its evil with silence and passivity. We withstand that evil with our consciences and bodies and invite the punishment that this entails.

We state that any law which forces men to kill and to face death furthers war as surely as it encourages men to profit from war. We assert that Vietnam is a rich man's war and a poor man's fight—it is an unjust war backed by unjust laws of conscription, tax benefits and suppression of dissent.

We indict such law with our consciences and our acts. We appeal to Americans to purge their law, to conform it to divine and humane law, to apply it impartially, and to build at home and abroad with it. We reject law when it protects injustice, since it is then not law, but a travesty of it.

Law is therefore under judgment with the evil it shields. In light of this, we spurn any counsel that would bargain for our benefit within the law, and stand on our merits alone.

We seek neither to avoid detection nor to plan escape, but submit to apprehension and the consequences of our action.

We implore our countrymen to judge our stand against this nation's Judeo-Christian tradition, against the horror in Vietnam and the impending threat of nuclear destruction. Against finally, the universal longing for justice and peace.

We invite friends in the peace and freedom movements to continue moving with us from dissent to resistance.

We ask God to be merciful and patient with us and with all

men. We hope that he will use our witness for his blessed designs.

Seriously yours,
Rev. James Mengel, Thomas Lewis,
David Eberhardt, Fr Philip Berrigan.

What to call the above—vow or manifesto? No matter—it had no meaning until we did what we had to do. All of us emphatically agreed that there are worse things to live with than the Johnson Administration, our intervention in Vietnam, or a few years in jail. And I don't mean the possibility of Richard Nixon as next President of the United States. I mean one's impotence and cowardice, one's complicity in unimaginable, insane injustice. Make no mistake about it, America's guilt goes very broad and very deep to touch us all.

Our 'thing' was ridiculously easy. The security guard, who had armed himself just prior to 21 October (the National Mobilization in Washington), was providentially wandering about the building. A little jockeying with receptionists to validate our presence and we entered that obscene gallery where human lives were reduced to a neat economy of print and record: where forms and files held barely shaven boys in abeyance before the Department of Defense (it has called itself the largest educational complex in the world) schooled them in the bloody business of fratricide.

Trim secretaries looked up as we strode into their game preserve. They were as antiseptic as the cabinets they tended. Quite unconscious, they presided in stupid unconcern over the tools of death, like hens scratching away over a minefield. Yet here, the tools represented bodies. Men for all their sophistication, research and technology have not yet found a way to honor war without bodies, preferably eighteen and nineteen year olds. Many of the bodies represented were blacks whose value had soared under war. Their housing would symbolically improve here in these steel cabinets as they qualified for manhood in a white man's war. Later, it would improve further in service barracks, while their families continued to languish in Baltimore's rotting slums. Who dares maintain that war is hostile to progress?

We acted quickly and with relish. The blood we carried was the biblical symbol of life—we would exorcize these files by pouring our life upon them. We yanked open drawers, sloshed blood upon their contents, moved on and did the same. The secretaries fooled us by reacting with a certain animal courage—protesting first, then trying to deter us. We spoke to them as kindly as we could, attempted to give them statements and New Testaments. They would have none of this: statements were ripped, New Testaments thrown to the floor, and one particularly righteous woman bounced the scripture off Dave Eberhardt's head. It became apparent that certain energies had been freed and were now out of our control. Reflex followed like Pavlov's dog, and immeasurably more expressive.

A crowd gathered, but the police were slow coming, the FBI slower still. When the first nervous policeman came on the scene, Dave Eberhard befuddled him with the following: 'As a taxpayer, I want to protest the lax security around this place!'

The delay gave us time for more than humor. I reflected as I sat waiting: 'They are so incredibly sure of themselves, the system is so enormously smug and confident. It really believes in itself.'

Agent Hansen was the first to arrive from the Federal Bureau of Investigation. One glance warned him of unusual variations: blood on the floor, file cabinets yawning, two clergymen and two well-dressed laymen waiting composedly for arrest.

Therein began a relationship. The FBI, the Federal Marshals and the police assumed that we were civilized men, and so were they. Our standing told them this, if our actions did not. But within or without jail, they would give us impersonal respect and consideration. Good police-community relations. Nonetheless, all of us were aware that implicit in their attitude was an acute sensitivity to our political potential. We had made trouble for Selective Service and for the machinery of militarism which had begun this war, and which kept it refueled. We could make trouble for them as well. We had a certain following and allegiance behind us: there was the ponderous and vaguely understood power of the Church, plus the volatile stridency of peace communities around the country

In a word, we were establishment figures, and their attitude was enhanced particularly when it came to me. In their eyes, a priest seems to carry a certain aura about him, one never wholly extinguished by what he had done. The aura was partly clerical totem, partly establishment logic, manifested by police care of alcoholic priests and mild admonitions in face of traffic violations.

Nonetheless, take these men out of neutral ground and they revert to type, which is to say that they protect the values and goals of the system. Their explanation is the 'preservation of law and order'. But without realizing it, they are saying that 'our way of life must survive'. And this is not a debatable issue. If escape were the plan, they would pursue us relentlessly for what we had done. Our submission to arrest changed that fact not one whit: it merely made the case less messy for them.

A quick hearing that afternoon at the Federal Commissioner's office; the machinery could be slow or fast, depending on the need. The government, through its prosecution, went into phase one of the carrot and stick. It would treat us now with the utmost leniency, knowing that it would sacrifice nothing in doing so. Later, it would be in a better position to treat us as it willed. The US District Attorney, a former young Rhodes scholar named Stephen Sachs, offered us release on a personal recognizance bond of $1,000.

Such a move, once agreed to, would effectively smother our protest by making it clear that we refused consequences, all the consequences. Moreover, that we were now standing upon privilege, even as the men of power stood upon theirs. Up to that point, our only voluntary suffering had been indecisiveness, anguish over imponderables and the temporary shock of feeling very much alone. Hardly a noticeable counterweight to the terrible drama of suffering imposed by our country, hardly more than a diversion from America's central business, the enforcement of our will around the world.

The protest had to go on—we felt this very keenly—and it had to be continued as non-violent resistance. This meant using available tools to confront the fierce and systematized imposition of American myth, exploitation and militarism upon people near and afar. Even as before, we had to now ask ourselves: is there any human response to a dehumanizing technocracy, with its accepance of overproduction and overconsumption, its contempt of marginal people, its obsession with ideological excuses, its profound trust in force, its fears and insecurities—all the sick hangups of a people who had too much and wanted too much more? One could disassociate from such ruinous presumptions; one could voluntarily exile himself from such a society; one could fast in face of its extravagance and indulgence.

The reactions were curious. Those who were horrified at their unrecognizable country expressed joy and gratitude. Their letters and telegrams told us so. Those who had consented actively to Americanism at any price loaded us with frightened invective, or watched us anxiously for unpredictable or threatening acts. The Warden of Baltimore City Jail isolated us from the prisoners (he asked us with obvious fear if we felt belligerent and if we intended to disrupt his jail). The inspector of federal prisons came up from Washington to check out our physical strength and peace of spirit. The guards kept us under constant, nervous surveillance. We had to sleep in two beds visible from the corridor, while night and day, five huge lights kept up the inspection.

Apparently, we had decided upon an indefinable course, employing weapons as devious as they were untouchable. Social value and code told our jailers, the government and the public at large that nobody chooses jail. Rather jail chooses somebody because he had not been light and benefit to the Great Society, because he had not, in fact, conformed to the gut need of social machinery for faceless and anonymous consensus. Furthermore, nobody punished the stomach, unless perhaps one had an overweight problem or one's metabolism was at high pitch. Perversely, we had none of these liabilities, yet we accepted only liquids for nearly eight days. Before we left jail, anxiety over our fast reached an absurd point—blood pressure and pulse tests every four hours, even through the night. A few more days and they would have forced intravenous feeding upon us.

Only the prisoners accepted what we were and what we were attempting to do. Many thanked us with a shaming initiative of friendliness and genuine emotion. Why acceptance? Why gratitude? These men, nearly all black, reacted with unerring rectitude to a valid human relationship, just as unerringly to a false or superficial one. While foundering somewhere outside the Great American Dream, apparently helpless in the pit dug for them beneath our social ladders, they had learned justice through being deprived of it, learned love through not having any. One morning, after being excoriated by the duty nurse, their analysis of her problems did vernacular justice to the best Freudian diagnosis. They had met her kind before; they knew how to resist and to educate her. She soon felt her helplessness, and called them together to apologize.

The counts against them were several, counts administered with ruthless exactitude. They were black and they were poor, to begin with. Moreover, they had not responded with gratitude and docility to a white man's world; they had not bought what they could not buy and share. Somewhere along the line of being black, they had compared rhetoric against existence, finding existence real and rhetoric false. In answer, they had done the only thing they could do and keep their sanity—resist. Resistance had taken humanly diverse and rich forms—numbers, addiction, alcoholism, burglary, confidence schemes, assault. All had different experiences, different stories; all had the same conclusion. Theirs was a bum rap.

No doubt it was. Society had conspired against them. Society had decided that the only good nigger was a white man's nigger who would willingly follow Booker T Washington past that good man's centenary. Or any distance or time that would cushion Whitey from his guilt.

Our 'brothers', as Tom called them, sensed that their treatment was appallingly and psychotically wrong, not even good for Whitey. Survival suggested many directions but, obviously, Whitey's rules had to go, since Whitey lived them least of all. Whitey's whiteness, wealth, power, morality—all the fiercely held myth and sign of privilege—had to go. These were tearing the world apart and no longer could be tolerated. Our brothers had mothers, aunts and grandmothers who 'toted' from white homes to compensate the pittance received for cleaning, cooking and raising white children; they had ancestors—soldiers like Crispus Attucks or rebels like Nat Turner. They came honestly by protest, and it meant little that protest was labeled 'crime' by white overlords.

Rather, the point at issue with them was that such a society— racist, hedonistic, brutal, incomparably arrogant—could no longer qualify as a human society. Lemming-like, it had chosen orgy, sadism and flag to the death. Moreover, death would come from its own internal self, or it would come from the symbol of defeat— the very Bomb calculated to protect it. Meanwhile its victims, the best human resource in its midst, would protest, would testify against it, would fill its jails and anti-war parades, would pick its vegetables and fruit and struggle in its ghettoes—while rational men wooed its God, ran its churches, businesses and defense plants, deliberated in its halls of authority, sent its young men to kill and brimmed up the cup of death and doom. Perhaps to the point of no return.

The security we felt with men like these was very nearly absolute. Divine irony had given them the priceless revelation entrusted to 'little ones'—we were privileged to share it. We soon learned (perhaps we had sensed it before) that they were the people about whom Jefferson used to ruminate; they were the groaning masses favored by Christ; they were the majority who against incredible deceit and oppression had preserved human integrity while their masters foundered in delusion and self-destruction. They were the ones, we felt, who would have immeasurably more to say about the future of man than the Texan in the White House, or the Rocke- fellers, or any of the international barons.

Prison grapevines established the fact that we were there; TV collaborated it. Our first Sunday in jail, after taking a seat with Catholics gathered for a six a.m. Eucharist, the chaplain told them that two war protestors would worship with them, and that one was a priest. 'Yeh', said one huge black man, 'he's one of us!' The remark filled me with shame and something approaching despair. Because the fact is that I had not been one of them and was only learning gropingly that being other than one of them was an inexcusable mistake. It was not even good tactics or politics. I had talked at length with Dean Rusk, corresponded with Robert McNamara and Walt Whitman Rostow, consulted with Senators like Fulbright, Tydings and Brewster, debated Congressmen, State Department people and academic types all over the country— the so-called men of power. Any assumption that one must work with those who happen to have power, however they came by it, or however they use it, can compromise justice and one's integrity. Power is justified by its delegation and by its use. And in light of this, what have these men said to Vietnam as it is, or to the imperial ambition that caused it?

Carmichael and the SDS kids, Camilo Torres, Douglas Bravo, Che Guevara and the NLF were closer to the truth and to humanity than I, in the sense of following an imperative to go to the people and to embrace their cause. Their reasoning in doing so was neither subtle nor complicated; they merely responded to situations of injustice too monumental to be overlooked. Justice for them meant struggling for power, all the power belonging to the people. It meant, in effect, giving another some voice in his own life. The right to power was to them an immeasurably more powerful resource than the fact of power, particularly when the right was scorned, and the fact was unjust.

Being one with the people was to be one with two billion strong around the globe, fully two-thirds of humanity. They are 'the people' not only because they are most of men, but because the Gospel gives them its staunch approval, and for this reason their poverty and color saves them from the grossest human failings, pride, greed, hypocrisy. The Beatitudes strikingly bring this out, especially with Luke, who describes the Lord's view of humanity as directly opposite to the view of technological society. One is 'happy' or 'blessed' for being poor, for being hungry, for having to weep now, for being hated. Obviously poverty, hunger, anguish and being the object of hatred are essentially connected with the human condition. And one can claim humanity only when one can claim them, or claim them on behalf of others. So it was with the Lord, who was most human in the criminality and despair of his death. Only then could the favor of his Father rest most fully upon him. And in effect, he then became MAN.

Christian justice therefore demands, not confidence in the powers that be, but confidence in the power of people, or power where it ought to be. Since, moreover, power does not largely reside with those whose human rights require it, divine power intercedes to offer a timeless justice. But God has chosen what the world regards as foolish to shame the wise, and what the world regards as weak, God has chosen to shame the strong, and what the world regards as low, contemptible, mere nothing, God has chosen to bring to naught the things that are; so that no human being might boast in his sight'

(1 Cor. 1 : 26–29).

Violence is the last refuge of the incompetent! (Isaac Asimov).

Peace is the mark of a civilized man, war the mark of a barbarian! (Gandhi).

The US must further Western control of 'much needed rice, rubber and tin' . . . Perhaps even more important would be the psychological effect of the fall of Indochina. It would be taken by many as a sign that the force of communism is irreversible and would lead to an attitude of defeatism. [Therefore] Communist forces must be decisively conquered down to the last pocket of resistance.[1]

Most Americans (even more Administration spokesmen and industrialists) emphatically endorse the above without discomfiture or reservation. Very simply, their view is that the first two are self-evident but not yet real, and that the third provides a course to make them real. Civilization equals peace, they say, but civilization becomes unthinkable unless it is built American style. Which means allowing us to do the business of others, and from that business, our own civilization and peace filters down like manna and twice as filling. Look at Western Germany, they say,

[1] State Department release, 1951.

Japan, Thailand, Venezuela, the Union of South Africa. They learned and look at them now—civilized, peaceful and free world allies.

Before such manipulation of reality is taken seriously, the rationale behind American foreign policy deserves to be stated, since it may impel humanity into World War III. Just as clearly, it deserves to be stated that neither National nor foreign policy have been radically different in our history. In a word, both economic and political isolationism are myths as dangerous as racial equality or adherence to fundamental Christian values.

As a people, we have never been reluctant about doing the world's business (or attempting it), and both the attempt and very near achievement are now cause for world showdown, precisely because the East, with most of the developing world in slow accord, now resolves to contain our expansionism. Indeed, the Vietnamese people stand as symbol of non-white rejection of our imperialist ambitions. And it should now be clear to all but our propagandists and militarists that a majority of Vietnamese would rather die than consent to them.

Hopefully, Americans will come to realize before it is useless to do so, that their society has always been expansionist, and that their passionate support of free enterprise could hardly allow it to be other. Calvinism has been our dominant creed and acquisitiveness our main public occupation. We fought the Revolutionary War because we refused to tolerate British interference with American business. We exploded into the continent, land-hungry and vicious, decimating the Indians and slowly driving out Europeans, sometimes by war, sometimes by tokens of purchase. At this point in history, the East has become our West, a juncture following logically upon the Open Door Policy of John Hay, its development up to and through the Truman Doctrine, which in substance is very nearly an act of war, which in diplomacy is the universalization of the Monroe Doctrine. Updating the Monroe Doctrine, or making the Truman Doctrine stick is precisely what Walt Whitman Rostow talks about when he articulates what critics have called his 'rollback' synthesis.

In a word, America has always followed the road to empire, and with its power at present high peak, it ruthlessly pursues national profit at the expense of the world. We have habitually 'colonized' in the poorer areas abroad, not in a conventional sense, but in one far more subtle and insidious—as a world extension of our domestic economy. As our leaders conceive it, what is good for America has to be good for the world.

(One would have to read historians like William Appleman Williams or D F Fleming to gain a clearer view of what has been traditionally a national style.) Free enterprise (or competitive capitalism) means profit motivation; profits demand markets (foreign markets eventually, especially if industry is overproductive as high scale profits cause it to be). Foreign markets mean diplomatic and military machinery to make them secure, *and* credible.

In times of economic recession, our leaders have returned to the fineness of these points often enough to make them thematic. Senator Henry Cabot Lodge spoke of them in 1895:

> We have a record of conquest, colonization and expansion unequalled by any people in the nineteenth century. We are not to be curbed now. . . . For the sake of our commercial supremacy in the Pacific, we should control the Hawaiian Islands and maintain our influence in Samoa.

Woodrow Wilson spoke of them in 1907:

> Since trade ignores national boundaries and the manufacturer insists on having the world as a market, the flag of his nation must follow him, and the doors of the nations which are closed to him must be battered down.

Franklin Roosevelt spoke of them in 1935:

> Foreign markets must be regained if America's producers are to rebuild a full and enduring domestic economy for our people. There is no other way if we could avoid painful economic dislocation, social readjustment and unemployment.

President Johnson, though largely responsible for the current affluence of a war boom, spoke of them in Baltimore on 27 June 1967:

Although we have only about 6% of the population of the world, we have half its wealth. Bear in mind that the other 94% of the population would like to trade with us. I would like to see them enjoy the blessings that we enjoy. But don't you help them exchange places with us—because I don't want to be where they are.

One evening recently, while involved in some local Congressional hearings on Vietnam, I was challenged by a State Department economist, 'Father, I am surprised that you subscribe to the theory that competitive economics are a root cause of war. That theory has been declared obsolete long ago.' When I recovered from my amazement and asked him why it should be obsolete, he could not answer to the satisfaction of anyone present. His failure might spring from the fact that a country cannot have an economic system like ours while its economists condemn it in the abstract. Obviously, our friend was part of the system, he profited from it, found no need to alter it, and so worked mightily to justify it.

I can feel pity for his problem without becoming part of it. The fact is, however, that a nation as unpopulous as our own cannot control half the world's wealth without being party to injustice which staggers the mind. The analogy of America (and Western Europe) as islands of plenty in a starving world does not go far enough. Closer to the truth is the spectacle of island people threatening to crush any restlessness among the starving, and making constant forays in their midst to bleed them further.

Personal greed is not essentially different from national greed; understandably, both are unpopular subjects with people or nations guilty of them. More unpopular still is any discussion of what we will do to keep our wealth and amass it further. Yet in any radical sense, American economic dominance and hegemony has fatefully kept the cold war at boiling point; has legislated arms sales and military give-away programs of 46·3 billions since 1949; has sponsored mutual defense treaties with 42 nations, and military and economic aid with nearly 100 others; has mounted hot and cold warring costs to over 100 billion this year (¢·75 of every tax dollar and 13% of gross national product); has impelled

Congress to appropriate more money for defense than the Pentagon can spend; has allowed the Pentagon to control almost the exact percentage of Federal property in the world (53% or 183 billions worth) as the US controls of the world's productive capacity; has urged America to reserve for every person on this planet the nuclear equivalent of 7 tons of TNT; with a substantial second-strike backup of bacteriological and chemical weapons; has initiated indeed, military interventions in Vietnam, the Dominican Republic, Thailand, Laos, Guatemala, Peru, Bolivia, Ecuador and Colombia; has rationalized the fetid savagery of such an effort with inversions like 'self-determination guarantees', 'Free World unity', and military 'cost efficiency'.

One need no longer speculate about *1984*. It is upon us. The rationality of our technology, our national purpose, our rising standard of living, our individualism, frontiersmanship and morality has caused an irrationality which has set the world afire, and which enthusiastically fans the blaze. Moreover, the irrationality is so profoundly entrenched, so reinforcing of itself, that few who see its nature imagine that it can be peaceably controlled or changed.

Vietnam has taught us that Presidential powers in wartime are dictatorial, though the war be undeclared. Vietnam is teaching us that those who oppose the war go largely unrepresented in local and national government: that, in effect, they make little difference in stopping a war which is patently immoral and illegal and, therefore, the most colossal political and military debacle in our history. With that said however, not enough is said.

The malaise goes deeper. It goes in fact, to the failure to realize that affluence demands a greater price than the ambiguous effort needed to secure it—atrophy of the mind and heart, fear and anger distinguishing emotional life, proclivities to indifference or despair, qualities of deepening violence in one's life. Under such affluence, the hope of becoming human is very nearly destroyed—one can do little more than harm to oneself and others.

Within such a context, it is not surprising that government is in reality a type of technological fascism whose controls are much more subtle and pervasive than those of an oligarchy. It is not surprising that Christianity prospers not as Gospel community, but as ethical management system under a thick veneer of rubric and ritual. It is not surprising that 'defense' appropriations dwarf public ones, or that military control of national effort now supercedes civilian control. These factors and others mesh to form a style of life accepted uncritically and evangelized with ingenuous good will—a style of life which includes redoubtable productive genius, unimaginable military might, moralistic fervor, and the convinced belief that peace and plenty will be bestowed by us on the world, or it will not come.

Evidence to the contrary is ignored or is contested as unreal: our inability to secure domestic peace by welcoming our blacks and alleviating our poor; our depressing contribution to two world wars and the cold war through commercial expansionism; our usurpation of developing economics (Peru?), and the fact that we have brought these people neither peace nor plenty. Or only plenty to the oligarchies who serve our mercenary interests, and who betray their people for our sound coin. In effect, our style of life is a machinery of catastrophe simply because it says that world peace equals American economic domination.

A Catholic correspondent returned from Rome and the Bishop's Synod tells me of the anxious uncertainty affecting nearly everyone there. Our conversation supported assumptions long suspected as valid: uncertainty embraced not knowing what needed to be said; but even more, not knowing what needed to be done. I asked my friend if the hierarchy and laity represented had no grasp of how the Church could realistically serve man under war, poverty, racism, nationalism, what have you. He answered that such was not exactly so—rather, there was on the one hand confusion that the Church should identify with man in his appalling circumstances, and on the other, whether the Church *could* identify with him. Which makes the dilemma triple-headed: is the Church for itself, is it for man, and how can it be for man?

A few years ago, when authority exiled my Jesuit brother to

Latin America for his peace convictions, another priest expressed outrage at his treatment, 'It is impossible to be a Christian in this Church!' His outburst, however well-intentioned, was not exactly to the point. However maddeningly reactionary the Church might be, to hold it responsible for a climate in which pure Christian witness cannot flourish is as foolhardy (untheological), as expecting it to mass produce Christians of the instant variety. If one can qualify as a Christian (one never does this fully), it is both because and in spite of the Church, which historically has been unremitting in its efforts to share Christ's bed and the world's—to be both a bride and a whore. Like all of us.

Beyond such comments, a great deal more probing becomes necessary. Without it, generalization is indeed dangerous. Somewhat more helpful is a reflection on our immediate past—before World War II, when the Church fulfilled a need for Catholics. Life then was sort of a local struggle, simple and relatively placid. The world had not begun to impinge on religious and national life with its strident demands and complexities. One accepted without question a format of life purified by time, authority and experience. One did the best he could with the format; one failed in responsibility if he questioned it. In those days, so attractively wholesome and uncomplicated, what alternatives were there to parochial education, to job, college or religious life after high school or, when crisis approached, to do the decent and just thing by military service against monsters like Hitler or Tojo? To be a good Catholic was to be a 'good' citizen; both Church and State opted for the same life in different terms. One's response was clearly to 'measure up'.

World War II destroyed that life-style forever; it suggested that both nation state and institutional Church were obsolete and doomed. Neither seemed capable of doing much to avoid or limit the slaughter and ruin of the war years. In fact, theirs was the main responsibility—the nation state by its fixation on national interest, the Church by its curious allegiances to local interests. Under such a heading, Pius XII could offer support to the hierarchies of both Allied and Axis churches, while promulgating his classic condemnations of total war to the world.

In a sense, and sometimes in spite of state and Church, the war freed men for distinct choices, atomic destruction or world family. 'Freed' in such a context may be a loaded word, decidedly simplistic when applied to a majority of men. Yet a vanguard of thought and compassion saw the issue as precisely this—man would allow world tension to gather to a point of fury, he or would control them through new and more humane institutions. Before long however, it appeared to those gambling on a human future that the struggle was becoming despairingly unequal. In a word, all the residues of human fear, greed and national pride from the pre-war era seemed to gather new momentum and force. One war ending became hope for peace, but more than that, excuse to start another one.

The cold war began; nationalism throughout the world received strident life from the hypernationalism of the great powers. Technology settled on a course of arming mankind with conventional and atomic weapons, while the starving and powerless looked to it mostly in vain for hope and alleviation. Power consolidated in the white 'have' world: it grew to fearful proportions as profits multiplied with the arms necessary to defend them. Colored identity and outrage spread in the 'have-not' world from ghetto America to Vietnam to Southwest Africa, taking the form of riots and wars of national liberation, only to be condemned by the white wealthy as Communist inspired and threatening to the 'free' world.

Almost predictably, the Church took the side of power. While Rome spoke with declining authority and/or conviction of the horrors of poverty, nationalism and war, local initiatives were rigidly controlled by institutional need and national advantage. In a very real sense, ecclesiastical confidence lay with wealth and affluent support, likewise with the respect of men whose commitment to privilege coincided with that of the Church. Religious 'renewal' meant the play of immense and trivial energies to upgrade establishment housekeeping, with priorities like birth control, clerical celibacy and married deacons.

In actuality, Church efforts to undergird its establishment by limiting the human choices of its subjects, parallels inhibitions imposed by other bureaucracies. None of them—whether business, government, military, Church—can promote or allow strictly human freedom. Controls differ only slightly, some entice, some pressure—emolument, position, fear, power, security. Logic and dynamics, it seems, are roughly similar, and the lessons of efficiency are exchanged. The only differences in the bureaucracies are their institutional aims under the flag—business to create profits, government to supply economic politics or diplomacy, military to exert muscle, Church to moralize the whole procedure.

The Christian therefore, who takes both Gospel and Church seriously, finds himself on two fronts: he must fight the opaque and arrogant power of both Church and society. And for anyone to be scandalized by this, or made apprehensive, is to admit failure in conviction, observation, experience and homework. All tell one that the integral bureaucracies of a technological society are an alliance which, despite disclaimers, no longer promote a human society.

One takes off the blinders, so to speak, to come to terms with human life in all its diversity—its richness, promise, uncertainty and sometimes brutality. To serve human life today is to unmask it when it is inhuman, to enrich it when it is poor, to claim it justice when it is crushed, to give it peace under conflict. And all of this is to join the human race and to serve the Church, particularly when it sees Christian community as its greatest enemy.

The Church is in the way, someone has said. It is the moral custodian of the status quo, and therefore a power which honors the conventional tools of privilege: wealth, racism, war. It is not for self-determination, either personal or international; it is not the friend of revolution, even when revolution be justifiable and non-violent. It is not for justice and not against injustice, but rather for its own institutional self. Which is to say that it serves life on its own terms, molding man to its own turgid shape, or taking him not at all. Somewhat similar, one might reflect, to our government's effort to make Southeast Asian-Americans of Vietnamese peasants.

The Church rarely speaks of its institutional values, only when one catches it off guard in crisis. Apparently, it spoke of them when we used blood symbolically against draft files in Baltimore. One can be grateful for the honesty employed in labeling our act 'flamboyant', 'bizarre', 'self-defeating', and in the case of myself, compromising to 'the priestly ministry'. But nonetheless, one suspects that the vigorous repugnance and disassociation expressed by the official Church, as compared with its silence over genocide in Vietnam, is far more betraying than the petulant indictments of a Davis or a Kavanaugh. One official remarked with defenseless anxiety that I would have to 'bear the full consequences of the law'. I hardly needed him to tell me that.

Indeed, we are grateful for honesty, for without it one is taken off guard and true positions can hardly be known. If anything, such reaction broadens the scope of one's responsibility, for it speaks unequivocally of values, covenants and alliances which can stand neither the test of history nor human need. In knowing them for what they are, and in confronting them with whatever faith given, one begins to grasp the grandeur of humanity, and Christ's efforts to gather it to himself. And that is gain enough.

The Ecumenical Plateau

EUGENE C BIANCHI, SJ

It is my contention that the Churches are now stranded on an ecumenical plateau in their climb toward Christian unity. This situation might be viewed as normal after a breathtakingly rapid ascent and amelioration in Catholic–Protestant–Orthodox relations in recent years. That we should sit down and take stock of where we were but a brief time ago and of who we really are in relation to one another—all this is to be expected.

But a serious malaise is beginning to drift across the ecumenical landscape. On the grassroots level, separated Christians are getting bored with smiling at one another during formal church services for Unity Week. Intellectuals see many possibilities for new breakthroughs in thought and action, but the leaders seem fearful of pressing on with the journey. Progressive younger churchmen on all sides are becoming disaffected with their guides, and are beginning to strike out on their own. But the road leading up from the plateau to new heights is clouded and uncertain.

Before attempting to search out creative roads to further Christian unity, it seems valuable to assess what we have learned up to this point in the ecumenical quest. Therefore I will view from a Roman Catholic perspective the sizeable gains in Church unity on the American scene. Then I will attempt the more difficult task of pushing beyond the present stalemate in ecumenism to point out possible new ways toward unity. However, before addressing ourselves to the question of the present malaise and where we might go, it is important not to lose sight of the advances that have been made. For new steps in ecumenism should not be gestures of despair, but rather movements launched from a basis of hope and encouragement.

During the last seven years, American Catholics have generally undergone a serious change of attitude toward other Christian communities. Many Catholics are still confused about the ecumenical revolution as it suddenly stormed the barricades erected by their preconciliar, Roman world view. But even amid the fears and confusion about protestantizing Catholicism, there is widespread rejoicing that the long polemic has given way to a new dialogue. For a growing number of Catholics in this country, especially after the Second World War, it was becoming increasingly unsatisfactory to maintain a dual attitude toward separated Christians. As fellow citizens, they could be esteemed colleagues in economic, political and cultural life, but as Protestants they were heretics, who rejected the truth and stood in need of conversion to Rome.

To a considerable extent, the tension between Catholics and Protestants in America had been heightened by the alien and immigrant status of the former in a land long dominated by a Calvinist-American ethos. On the Protestant side, Catholicism was seen as a monolithic authoritarianism, an anti-democratic, religio-political force, and a tyranny over human conscience. From a theological standpoint, Rome was viewed as a corruption of Gospel freedom, which lay prostrate under the despotism of papacy, sacramentalism and devotional superstition. To the contemporary reader this may appear to be an exaggerated description; the fact is that our memories are short. A serious review of Protestant literature across a wide spectrum of denominations would confirm the judgment that these negative opinions of Roman Catholicism, with some modifications, were in the ascendancy right up to the era of John XXIII.

Among Catholics in the pre-ecumenical period, other Christian communities represented erroneous threats to true religion. It was, of course, admitted that sincere, individual Protestants could be

B

saved in spite of their waywardness. Their ecclesial life, however, was considered to be of little value. The less informed but typical Catholic wondered why anyone would want to be a Protestant, unless he simply desired an easy and nominal religious affiliation. To lose one's Catholic faith was regrettable but understandable; to become a Protestant was irrational. They had no pope, no Virgin, no saints, no real sacraments and no rules. Protestantism was seen as individual interpretation of the bible, hymn singing and doing pretty well what one pleased.

Eastern Orthodoxy was even less known or appreciated. In large urban areas, Catholics sometimes encountered these strange dissidents in Greek, Slavic and Russian ghettoes. These people were more objects of curiosity than of fear or rejection. They were known for long, incense-filled liturgies, bearded priests and foreign accents. But as a small minority group of mostly immigrants, the Orthodox presented no threat to the Catholic psyche. They had for all practical purposes slipped out of the Western Christian memory, which remained locked in the struggle with the Reformation.

Among the sources of this Catholic view of non-Catholic doctrine and life was chiefly a well-cultivated ignorance. A number of American Catholic leaders in the nineteenth century, like Bishops Ireland, Gibbons and Keane, had begun to formulate a more open and conciliatory attitude toward non-Catholics. But the Catholic Modernist crisis of the first decade of this century virtually closed off any sympathetic understanding of Protestant Christianity, especially in its then prevalent liberal forms. Catholic schools and seminaries adopted a rigidly defensive apologetic against Protestantism, which was often equated with godless secularism. To protect the faith and allegiance of masses of un-educated immigrants, Catholic leaders hedged their communities about with restrictive laws and pejorative views towards Protes-tants. Contacts were minimized and often sanctioned with severe ecclesiastical penalties. A general attitude of superiority was fostered among Catholics; they had the truth and were not to allow themselves to be contaminated by these lesser Christians. This attitude was nurtured not only by religious considerations, but also for social reasons. It fulfilled a need in the insecure Catholic community to feel superior in some regard to the dominant classes. 'They' had prestige and power, but 'we' had God on our side; they got to the White House, but we got to heaven.

To trace adequately the gradual change in the American Catholic attitude toward Protestantism would require a multifaceted study, especially of the period following World War II. But it is safe to affirm that the real dissolution of perennial prejudices did not begin on any large scale until the advent of Pope John's revolution. It was only then that bitterness, mistrust and stereotypes started to give way to some understanding and a new hope for reconciliation. This development was in part made possible by the advances in Catholic theological appreciation of Protestant thought in the countries of Northern Europe immediately preceding and after World War II. But it was the open-minded and open-hearted attitude of John XXIII, assisted by Cardinal Bea, that began to re-educate and reform the polemical stance of American Catholics. Vatican II itself launched Catholicism into a profound reflection on its own nature and purposes; this renewal in depth shattered many hardened caricatures of Protestant and Orthodox Christianity. The Council also legitimized the peculiarly American Catholic experience of appreciation for separation of Church and state and respect for religious liberty.

The positive gains in Catholic ecumenism during the past seven years are in many ways remarkable. Not only have hostile attitudes receded, but concrete institutions for dialogue and cooperation have been created. The Secretariat for Promoting Christian Unity under Cardinal Bea has established close ties with the World Council of Churches. Catholic membership in this organization has become a subject of increasing discussion from both a practical and theological perspective. Pope Paul's friendliness towards Eastern Orthodox Churches is reflected in America by new contacts with Eastern Christians and a deeper understanding of their tradition. A very significant institutional development in America has been the formation of special episcopal commissions to dialogue with various Protestant and Orthodox Churches, as well as with the Jewish community. Some results from these high-level conversations have been especially promising. New grounds for accord have been found on such controverted subjects as eucharistic doctrine, justification by faith and the meaning of the ordained ministry. Closely related to these doctrinal advances is the new look in Catholic scholarship on the Reformation tradition. American thinkers like Avery Dulles, John P Dolan and Thomas M McDonough have made distinguished contributions to this new body of literature.

The most important accomplishment, it seems to me, in the Catholic reappraisal of the Reformation tradition is echoed in the Decree on Ecumenism's appreciation of Word, sacrament, ministry and witness in Protestant Churches. Fundamental to these insights is the new grasp of the ecclesial dimensions of Protestant communities. Precisely because they are families of faith through the Lord's one baptism, these Churches are in some way incorporated as communities in the one Body of Christ. The Catholic vocabulary of 'true' Church, which tended to cast other Christian communities into a position of being 'false' Churches, is no longer adequate to carry the insights of our age. Within this one Body, the theological relation between the Roman Catholic community (or communities) and other Churches is not clearly defined.

For a number of reasons, the somewhat quantitative criteria for judging this relationship have proven inadequate. The operations of the Holy Spirit in the Churches cannot be easily categorized. In one sense, this is as it should be, for it is a futile and distracting temptation to seek to judge who has a higher place in the kingdom of heaven already begun in the Church. Although theological research into the relationship between the Catholic and other Churches is certainly worthwhile, it seems far more vital for the future of ecumenism not to gaze idly at the heavens, but to shoulder together as one-body-in-service the burdens of humanity.

This mutual cooperation in a common mission in the world has recently been termed 'secular ecumenism'. As will become clearer in the more critical and projective section of this essay, secular ecumenism is presently more of a longed-for event than an accomplished fact. There are, however, a few striking developments in common witness and mission among Catholics and Protestants in America. The East Harlem Protestant Parish has established a supportive relationship with the experimental Catholic community of Emmaus House in the slum area of New York's Spanish-speaking quarter. Parishes based on various forms of ecumenical co-operation exist in a few places such as Columbia, Maryland, Kansas City, Mo., Oakland and San Jose, Calif. The great national dilemmas of peace, poverty and race are challenging the complacency of Churches across denominational lines. This fertile area of mutual mission, if taken seriously by ecclesiastical decision-makers, will prove to be the seedbed for a new rapprochement in theology, worship and polity.

The new friendships being formed among scholars and pastors in the separated Churches is leading toward the fuller realization that divisions within a particular communion are frequently more acute than those between many Catholics and Protestants. These groupings cut across denominational barriers not only on social issues, but also on questions of moral and theological importance. Ethical issues involved in racially-open housing and in the American intervention in Vietnam do not divide Presbyterians from Catholics, but rather these problems separate Christians within each Church. Even topics like the purpose of liturgy, the role of Church authority, and the meaning of faith do not necessarily separate Christians into Catholic and Protestant groups. It is more likely that the division will occur within a given Church on the basis of theological and pastoral presuppositions. Nor is it unusual for closer Christian ties of friendship to develop between a Methodist professor and a Jesuit priest than those which link them to many of their own coreligionists. Some would still view this as a breach of denominational or order loyalty. Yet a wider concept of loyalty to the whole Body of Christ in mission is being fashioned in the new ecumenical experience. If Church leaders feel worried or threatened by this development, perhaps they should be. The lines of demarcation are no longer being drawn according to the old handbooks. It would be well for Church leaders to read the handwriting on the wall; it may keep them from living in an unrealistic world and it should impel them to rethink their own roles in a changing ecumenical pattern.

Another important shift of attitude in the Catholic community is a growing recognition of our own failings against Church unity in the past, combined with a willingness to repent and to forgive others. The examples of Popes John and Paul have done much to promote this change of heart on which true ecumenism must be built. The word 'conversion' itself has taken on deeper meaning as a result of the ecumenical experience of recent years. Not long ago, conversion meant for Catholics the coming over to the Roman persuasion, the true faith, of individuals from other religious affiliations or from no religious attachment. Excluding coercive proselytism, conversion from unbelief or the crossing over from one religious family to another continues to have a legitimate meaning. A more profound sense of conversion, however, is coming to the fore. This understanding would be described as a constant and mutual converting, or turning, of all Christian groups to the spirit of the Gospel. The emphasis here is not on sheep stealing (or saving) from another group, but rather on a reciprocal influence among the Churches to live the Gospel more fully amid the real needs of mankind today. All the Churches must strive for a greater universality (catholicity) of mission in the world; movements of individuals from one Church to another should be respected, but left to the inspiration of the Holy Spirit.

American Catholics have also learned to pray with and for Christians of other Churches. This spiritual ecumenism, joined to a spirit of sacrifice and mutual self-giving among separated Christians, is broadly recognized as vital to genuine Church unity. Yet formalism is already endangering the value of inter-Church prayer services. An annual meeting of separated Christians to recite ritualized prayers and reflect on the past is fast becoming a bore for many. There is a growing desire among the more progressively committed to move into the area of mutual eucharistic liturgies, which are still officially taboo. These Christians believe that common undertakings in the world call for fuller common worship to sustain unity in mission. They feel that Church leaders, who do not concretely experience this friendship in mission across denominational lines, are stifling creative Christianity with outmoded categories.

Among university students today, institutional ecumenism, according to the gradualist timetable set by their elders, is not much more attractive than are the institutional Churches themselves. Earlier in this century, dynamic students movements contributed greatly to the rise of the Protestant ecumenical movement. But today the Churches fail to excite the imagination and interest of the most talented university students. Institutional Church mergers sometimes appear to be motivated by organizational expediency rather than by a renewed sense of service in the world or by a deeper grasp of theology. Merger ecumenism, as it has been seen in the past, looks, to the young, like a desperate attempt to keep alive senile institutions by large economic transfusions. In part, however, this attitude among the young indicates their ignorance of the ecumenical movement in general and of various promising attempts of Church renewal in particular. This situation among youth presents a huge challenge to the Churches to rethink their image in the eyes of tomorrow's leaders. An education for ecumenism will have to consist of listening as well as teaching. A good beginning of such education would occur if ecclesiastical and lay leaders could gather on Catholic and other campuses to hear the candid views of university students on the Church.

Although university students lack interest in the institutional Churches today, there are a few vibrant ecumenical groups on campus, such as the University Christian Movement. But the orientation of these groups is not toward the institutional Churches, but rather toward significant issues of modern life that call for a Christian response. (It should be noted that since Catholic universities generally have a homogeneously Catholic population, student ecumenism can be little more than an academic affair.) Already in student life the seeds of the underground Churches are being laid. A more educated laity and many of the young clergy are disillusioned by the dull formalism and status-quo thinking that reigns in the institutional Church. These younger persons are seeking a more meaningful liturgical-spiritual life and a mission in the world that is worthy of their generosity and commitment. A number of them, often the more creative types, are simply walking away from a Church that appears to them to be a quaint museum piece commemorating the past but with no life for the present.

The development of underground or non-affiliated Christian communities is an ambiguous phenomenon. On the one hand, these small groups can foster a more intimate community of love and service. They can provide the environment for experiments with a more flexible and meaningful liturgy. They can also devote themselves to important issues calling for Christian witness, without the incumbrances of the staid and even reactionary institution. Yet, the same underground movements can, on the other hand, become destructively divisive elements in the Church. They can move in the direction of elitist groups that look down on ordinary church-goers and reject institutional authorities almost on principle. Being relatively small communities, these non-affiliated groups cannot exert the influence in such worthy issues as racial justice and peace that the established institutions can bring to bear. But perhaps the most unfortunate result of the disaffiliation of elite groups is that they cease to be the needed leaven in the institutional dough. The educative and reforming powers of the separatist underground group are not infused into the established Churches.

The dilemma of the underground Churches that are springing up in various parts of the country will not be easily resolved. On the part of the disaffected progressives, it will call for a good measure of patience with chanceries and pastors and religious superiors. The common good and unity of the whole Church, Catholic and Protestant, should not be lost sight of. But the more serious responsibility and burden rests with our bishops and other Church leaders. They will do great injury to the Church and the cause of ecumenism if, in their fearful attachment to the past, they indirectly drive the intellectuals and the progressive activists out of the visible Body. By their failure to listen and to allow more experimentation, the bishops could contribute to the further fragmentation of the Church. It is, of course, true that a bishop must not alienate the more conservative members of the Church by disregarding their viewpoints. But the danger in the American Catholic Church today does not seem to lie in that direction; our leaders seem to be listening to the voices of prestige and power more than to the voices of prophesy and renewal.

The view from the ecumenical plateau elicits mixed reactions. The undeniable accomplishments of recent years are encouraging, but a sense of apathy and stagnation is beginning to be felt. The novelty of ecumenical acquaintances with separated Christians is over; it is now a time to stop marking time and to move forward. The question, then, is where do we go from here? I will try to point out a few possible directions, although it is more important to realize that new openings for ecumenical progress will appear only when we risk moving toward some limited goals. New insights are often born out of experimental ventures.

To do the creative thinking necessary for a dynamic Church unity movement, we will first have to rid ourselves of our fixation on the past. One of the main reasons why we fear to move ahead is that we are constantly looking backward, trying to resolve the sixteenth century issues between Augsburg, Geneva and Rome. This respect for traditional obstacles is understandable and necessary. Our reflexes towards each other have been formed for four hundred years according to the accepted stances on creed, code and cult. We cannot simply delete our history, nor should we. It is important for scholars to explore our mutual history, searching out new avenues of possible rapprochement. Our collective Christian memory since the Reformation is most valuable, both as a deterrent to committing again past mistakes and as the groundwork for new breakthroughs.

The problem, however, is that in our backward gazing at history, we fail to recognize the pressing dimensions of a living tradition that in the present is posing new questions. We are not sufficiently cognizant of what the Holy Spirit is doing now in the Churches. Whether it be the question of the Eucharist or of justifying faith or of the role of bishops, we tend almost instinctively to confront the issue with yesterday's mentality and terminology. We are inclined to ignore what the Spirit is telling us today about Protestant and Catholic understandings of eucharist, faith and episcopate. We can only begin to achieve some concrete ecumenical goals in these areas when we begin to realize that *today* many Christians across denominational barriers hold similar views on Christ's presence in the Eucharist, that *now* there is a much more unified appreciation of the nature of faith, that *at present* the function of episcopacy is viewed in ways that many Catholics and Protestants can accept. In our fixation on the past, we have neglected the prime New Testament conviction of Emmanuel, God with us *now*. Tradition is not primarily a dimension of yesterday; it is rather the continuing, creative presence of the Holy Spirit in the Church today.

Lest we remain fixed in purely ecclesiastical concerns in our ecumenical efforts, the voice of the Spirit must also be heard in the anguished concerns of humanity. For many Christians a new sense of secular ecumenism is transcending many older boundaries of Church division. Intrachurch and even interchurch problems begin to pale in face of the dilemmas that vex the great majority of men today: discrimination, poverty, population, hunger and war. A new Church-world consciousness is growing among many committed Christians. For these persons the older denominational labels and structures retain less meaning than they did for previous generations. One's Christian identity is less consciously cast in terms of being a Methodist, a Baptist or a Catholic. Instead of these more parochial classifications, these laymen and clerics draw a sense of Christian self-consciousness from many sources in Church life and history, and especially from the present interaction between Church and world. There is little that is specifically Presbyterian or Catholic about their concern for racial justice, for a termination of the Vietnamese War or for a less exploitive capitalism.

This approach of secular ecumenism consists of letting the now-present Spirit write the agenda for the Churches through the real human cries for justice, freedom and hope. If these growing communities of Christians were asked to root their strivings in the

Christian heritage, they would probably not cite Luther or Calvin or Aquinas as justification for their commitments. Denominational heroes would take second or third place after theological bases stemming from the Gospel itself. These theological sources for secular ecumenism would consist in such denomination-transcending doctrines as incarnation, redemption, Christian service and mission. Just as these contemporary Christians spend little or no time distinguishing their denominations, so too, they find it unnecessary to distinguish between the reconciling concerns of their secular commitment and their life in the Church.

This does not mean that secular ecumenism describes some kind of mundane reductionism, which would collapse Christianity into secular humanism. The Christian faith-horizon and motivational force elicits and gives power and direction to reconciling activity in the world. Far from falling prey to 'worldliness', true secular ecumenism would point to the need for prophetic distance from the powerful and oppressive groups and movements in the world. Secular ecumenism demands a renewed sense of prayer life and a considerable spirit of self-sacrifice. It is precisely the mentality and structures of the denominations that sometimes seem 'worldly' to these less denominational Christians. They are dismayed by the worldliness of Churches that curry favor with Mammon, that place institutional survival above prophetic witness and that retreat defensively into past formulas instead of facing up to present ecumenical realities. They are disconcerted by the worldliness of Church leaders who exercise their authority in the manner of feudal dominance rather than Gospel service.

A strong sense, therefore, of what the Spirit is saying to and doing in the Churches and in the world now is becoming the new touchstone of ecumenism. On the level of social involvement together, many cherished barriers that give us a feeling of security or superiority will have to come down. Although there has been much talk about a common witness among the Churches, the duplication and divisiveness of our service organizations and church building programs continues. We are talking out of both sides of our mouths when we urge a consolidation of ecclesiastical resources to help the down-trodden and then proceed to build wastefully expensive buildings on four corners of an intersection. In witnessing to our self-centered Western nations on the plight of the world's poor, the Churches could jointly raise some of the billions needed for economic, social and cultural development in the awakening nations.

The whole Church unity movement would be much further advanced today if the various Churches took more seriously the formula of the Lund Conference in 1952. There it was affirmed that the Churches should do together all things that conscience did not forbid. Rather than manifest our agreements, we have maximized our differences. If carried out, we would not only be witnessing together in areas of social action, but we would also teach in unison whenever it was feasible. Common statements of understanding and purpose on subjects of race, peace and hunger could be jointly issued by the Vatican and the World Council of Churches. Such pastoral letters could be the next step toward a fuller Catholic participation in the life of the WCC. The same policy might be followed with gratifying results in ecumenism on national and regional levels. These documents of mutual understanding need not be restricted to matters of Christian ethics; they might also deal with issues of spiritual life and worship, of the function of authority and the role of the ministry in a secularized world. Of course, official statements from Churches have a limited effect, but the educational value for separated Christians could be enormous.

That the sacrament of baptism incorporates a new Christian into the one Body of Christ is a rather generally accepted conviction among Catholics and Protestants today. It is somewhat surprising that little or nothing has been done to proclaim ecumenically in the rite of baptism what we mutually hold in baptismal theory. Could not a section of the official baptismal ritual be rewritten to include the express participation of a Protestant minister or Orthodox priest, provided, of course, that this did not violate their consciences? It might also be possible for close non-Catholic friends of the family to explicitly confess their faith in the sacramental rite of incorporation in the Church. It is even conceivable that the children of a seriously ecumenical (mixed) marriage could be baptized into the Church by the joint action of a Catholic priest and a Protestant minister.

Moreover, there is no intrinsic reason why the same could not be done for an adult baptism, especially if the person to be baptized has decided to affiliate himself to a Christian communion as a partial result of ecumenical friendships. In all these developments, the important principle of reciprocity would have to be maintained, and a strict respect for consciences on all sides would need to be observed. Rather than be an occasion for confusion or scandal, such joint rites could be opportunities for ecumenical education. We already have the sacramental precedent of Protestant and Catholic ministers taking some part in marriage services.

According to the present Catholic guidelines for ecumenical worship, eucharistic intercommunion is not encouraged. For many Christians, however, ecumenical friendships and involvements seem to call for an occasional sharing of the Eucharist. It is not enough to repeat to these persons that abstention from the eucharistic table of the other is a painful sign of their continuing institutional separation. Although this is one acceptable reason for not sharing the Eucharist as a regular event, it does not satisfy the concrete ecumenical experience. For these Christians also know that the Eucharist is food along the still-divided way and a nourishment towards healing the wounds of separation. Those who have participated in a liturgy of another Church up to the point of communion, only to refrain from receiving, know what a shattering human experience it can be. This is especially true if those present at the liturgy know and love one another because of many other mutual Christian involvements.

Sacramental participation, even on a limited basis, is further complicated by different theological understandings of both the sacraments and the ministry. Without minimizing these difficulties, however, it can be held that complete theological agreement is not essential for sacramental sharing. Even within the Catholic Church there have been various theological explanations of sacraments and of ministry. Yet a certain degree of accord on the nature of sacraments and of ministry would be necessary for an honest reciprocity in sacramental life. In recent years, some very gratifying progress has been made among Protestant and Catholic theologians in breaking through seemingly impenetrable doctrinal log jams of the past.

On the question of the Eucharist, for example, Catholics now see more clearly that the mainline Lutheran and Calvinist traditions held a much stronger sense of Christ's presence in the sacrament than was previously thought. Other dimensions of the Eucharist, such as memorial, meal and eschatological pledge, have also been a part of Protestant eucharistic theology. Ecumenical reciprocity would require that Catholics be able occasionally to receive a Protestant Eucharist. If the eucharistic doctrine of a particular Protestant Church be not impossibly at odds with Catholic teaching, such communion would be occasionally helpful. Catholics could receive the Lord in such liturgies in whatever way he allows himself to be present.

On the Catholic side, contemporary developments in sacramental theology have corrected overly physical and mechanical understandings that crept into Catholic practice of the Eucharist over the centuries. Important attempts have been made by Catholic scholars in recent years to speak about the eucharistic mystery in language more meaningful to contemporary man. The whole subject of the nature and functions of the ordained clergy has undergone significant development since Vatican II. A greater appreciation of the role of the Christian community in calling a man forth to serve its religious needs has complemented and modified an overly hierarchical interpretation of ordination. Furthermore, we are coming to realize more adequately that ecclesial offices must take their sense and direction from their function and mission for the larger community. A number of these theological developments are opening up new possibilities for ecumenical rapprochement not only in theory but also in concrete practices.

The present Catholic legislation on mixed marriages, although a favorable advance from previous laws, is still largely inadequate to our ecumenical responsibility. In order to truly reform specific legislation, however, we must first re-examine our basic attitude toward mixed marriages. Until very recently, the Catholic outlook on such unions was almost totally pejorative. It continues to be true that these marriages face special difficulties, because of the differing religious orientations. Yet in the new climate of ecumenism, the partners of a mixed marriage need not be seen as victims of circumstances, but rather as ecumenical pioneers. For serious Christians with different Church backgrounds, marriage maturely entered into can be understood as an initiation into a special way of being a Christian.

With great respect for the religious liberty of both parties, the Church should leave the determination of the number of offspring and their Christian education to the consciences of the parents. This does not impugn the Church's duty to give counsel and to indicate guidelines for responsible Christian wedlock. But the Church's educative function should not encroach on the conscience decisions of either party. The present practice of demanding a solemn promise from the non-Catholic party to educate the children as Catholics does not sufficiently respect the integrity of this party. New steps could also be taken to make the marriage ceremony itself a more truly ecumenical service. This would serve to remind both parties that a still divided Church is at least able to witness to its oneness of purpose in showing its concern for a holy and enduring matrimony.

The present state of the question of a married priesthood in the Catholic Church is ambiguous. On the one hand, a papal letter has reaffirmed the traditional law of celibacy for priests. The American bishops have also voiced their opposition to optional celibacy for priests. But serious surveys show that thousands of priests favor the option to marry and to continue to function as priests. Although these ambiguities exist, it does not take much historical perspicacity to foresee a change in the present Catholic legislation on priestly celibacy when a new generation of bishops is at the Church's helm. This problem has important repercussions for Church unity.

Contacts with Protestant and Orthodox clergy, most of whom will continue to be married, are not as favorable as they might be, because of the celibate status of nearly all Roman priests. This does not mean that a celibate is incapable of understanding married people. But when a whole clergy is constrained to be celibate, various dimensions of rapport with a married clergy cannot be established. It is a question of different mentalities and life styles. Although in some ways a celibate clergy can beneficially complement married life, in other ways, there is almost bound to be a lack of experiential understanding.

Another aspect of the same problem concerns seminarians. One of the reasons, on the part of our Church officials, for fearing increased contacts between Catholic and Protestant seminarians revolves around the question of different orientations in training for a married and an unmarried clergy. This should not be interpreted as an argument for the education of a celibate clergy in monastic isolation; on the contrary, celibate candidates to the priesthood should have contacts with the non-celibate community. The point being made here is that a Catholic clergy, in part married, would offer new modes of friendship and understanding with Protestant and Orthodox Christians.

It should also be added that Protestants could help the cause of Church unity if they would overcome in their own ranks the prejudice against a celibate witness. Single Protestant ministers sometimes complain about the social forces in the congregation that almost demand that they be married. On both the Catholic and the Protestant sides, a greater sensitivity to human rights and to the gifts of the Spirit is called for in the matter of married and celibate clergies.

To direct the ecumenical movement from the present unsatisfactory plateau to new heights of unity in thought and action will require a great educational effort on the part of all separated communities. Small beginnings have been made with the living-room-dialogue programs. It is still rare, however, to hear a parish sermon on the meaning and values of ecumenism. Often enough, this neglect of the pulpit is due to the arrested education of the priests themselves, who fail to read and stay alive to the movements of a changing Church.

The problem is thus thrown back on the seminaries, where a considerable renewal is fortunately under way. One might characterize the change going on in seminaries as the movement from an attitude of having all the answers to an attitude of quest and openness to new solutions. The Graduate Theological Union in Berkeley is a pioneer program in religious study on an interdenominational basis. Similar joint ventures are being organized in other major American educational centers. On the professional seminary level, Bishop Fulton Sheen's Rochester diocese is experimenting with an interchurch effort to educate future clergy. A noteworthy aspect of this new ecumenical education is the widely-felt need to place seminary formation into a university context. More than a question of spatial relocation, the movement toward the university indicates a desire among seminary educators to establish a fuller dialogue between the traditional theological disciplines and the rapidly expanding frontiers of knowledge in other areas. A pluralism of inquiry is the keynote of future ecumenical education.

This need for pluralism raises some important questions for other sectors of Catholic education. How ecumenical is the teaching in Catholic grammar and high schools? Will the next generation know and esteem more fully various religious and humanistic traditions? On the Catholic university level many significant strides have been taken in the last two decades to improve the quality of education. But Catholic colleges must also ask themselves some difficult ecumenical questions. How autonomous are they from outside pressures, lay or ecclesiastical? Are their theology departments places for Catholic indoctrination or centers of religious inquiry worthy of a university? How ecumenical is the faculty in theology and philosophy? Are these schools too Catholic and not Christian enough in the makeup of their student population? If there are many Protestant and Orthodox students on these campuses, are they officially cared for by non-Roman chaplains? Perhaps the future of the Catholic colleges that survive their present financial and quality crises will consist in becoming loci in which the Christian heritage can dialogue fruitfully with other traditions. This would mean that as much as possible Catholics and other Christians find in these universities a forum for interchurch dialogue, but especially for dialogue with Marxists, humanists, capitalists, colonialists and many other persons who hold different or conflicting value systems.

The road up from the ecumenical plateau is uncertain and rocky. The guides on this adventurous journey will have to be both sensitive and daring. They will have to be very careful in their use of ecclesiastical pressure tactics that infringe on the consciences of non-Catholics. Here one thinks of Catholic campaigns to secure government funds or to oppose birth control and other legislation. Of course, Catholics as well as others have a right to profess their beliefs publicly. The delicate issue, however, concerns the methods of pursuing Catholic goals and the relationship between these goals and the broader common good of society.

The ecumenical guides towards new regions of unity will need to be not only sensitive but also daring. On all sides, we secretly worship our barriers. Behind them there is at least a sense of comfort and security in a rapidly changing world. We must be willing to examine again the religious security blankets that keep us warm and isolated on the ecumenical meadow. If the time of the ecumenical smile has run out, the era of strong strides toward Church unity has yet to begin. Are we truly willing to risk a mutual venture into the unknown?

Youth, Schools and Hope

WILLIAM BIRMINGHAM

The story is told of a clinical psychologist who wished to determine the behavioral differences between optimists and pessimists and devised an experiment to that end.

Into a room filled with a galaxy of new toys he led a pessimistic little boy of ten. Into a second room, piled high with horse manure, he led an optimist of the same age. The doors were then shut and the boys left alone in their respective rooms for half an hour.

First the psychologist visited the pessimist in his room full of toys. The boy sat crouched in a corner, weeping piteously. The toys had not been touched.

'What's the matter?' the psychologist asked.

'I'm afraid I'll break them,' the child wailed.

Next the psychologist visited the little optimist, whom he discovered digging busily in the manure while singing a merry song.

'What are you doing?'

The boy smiled and replied, 'I'm looking for the pony!'

In my judgment, so far as the Roman Catholic Church in the United States is concerned, the pony may well be found among the new generation. The operative word is *among*: the new generation is many people and many groups, not all of them signs of hope.

43

If taken with high seriousness, the term new generation is mis-leading. It seems to indicate that young people form a homo-geneous group, which is clearly untrue: more young American Catholics may seek religious relevance and mystical experience today, but those who do are a minority within their own genera-tion, which includes in far greater numbers those who are in-different to any but the tribal aspects of Christian commitment.

Worse, the term reinforces the notion of a 'generation gap', a journalistic device that distracts us from the significance of sociological processes at work among the young since it implies total discontinuity between their experience and that of their elders. (The belief that each generation is born fresh into a world where all things must be named anew is deeply ingrained in the American psyche; the literary aspects of the phenomenon are well described in R W B Lewis' *The American Adam.*) The gap between generations is primarily the psychological rupture be-tween children and parents, as in adolescence the child is called on to forge an identity; the rupture is followed by reconciliation (in a rather theological sense) if the parents possess a mature identity and the child achieves one. The gap is only incidentally sociological and, if the normal events of personal growth are projected uncritically on to the level of social processes, distortion occurs. The term new generation is used, then, for convenience rather than precision.

This is not to say that the young are not new but to state the obvious which is often missed; their experience is simultaneously continuous and discontinuous with the past and, in addition, what is discontinuous with the psychological past or an aspect of the sociological past may at the same time be continuous with other aspects of the sociological past. For example, the young man who practices civil disobedience to the US selective service system may feel that he has broken with Roman Catholicism, Americanism, and his parents, all in one act. On the other hand, the observer may justifiably assert that, while he may have broken with his parents, his action is continuous with the emerging Catholic tradition of responsibility based on freedom of conscience, and with the more lively American tradition of disobedience in the face of unjust laws or unjust actions by the government.

All debts paid to tradition, however, one must admit that the element of novelty plays a great part in the experience of the new generation, especially the experience of young Roman Catholics. For all young Americans their society contains a number of givens that were not present in their parents' childhood: the society is affluent and has the means of continued affluence in its hands; the cybernetic revolution has upset familiar equations of existence—from methods of research to the relationship between work and leisure; the immediacy of communication that obsesses Marshall McLuhan is taken for granted; religion, easily dismissed by many, is in the United States probably becoming more private and certainly in any institutional sense becoming less public, with the result that few young Americans expect institutional religion to structure a significant part of their public lives.

To these givens common to all of the new generation may be added two that affect Roman Catholics: the acculturization of the Church in the United States[1] and the restructuring of the experience of being Catholic that has taken place since the beginning of Vatican II. Though logically separable, the two reinforce one another. They are, I believe, creating a sense of religious possibilities among Roman Catholic youth that remains quite literally unimaginable to most of those whose religious outlook became set before World War II.

Until this generation, most Roman Catholics in the United States grew up in relation to immigrant parents and grandparents and to an immigrant Church. The immigrant Church strove simultaneously for American respectability and the preservation of its own religious identity. Religious leaders tended, as a result, to be men who were externally Americanized in their ability to manipulate the system and their anxious dedication to the flag while internally they rejected such American values as the intro-

[1] The process has been traced by Edward Wakin and Joseph Scheuer in *The De-Romanization of the American Catholic Church* (New York: Macmillan, 1966) and by Andrew Greeley in *The Catholic Experience* (New York: Doubleday, 1967).

duction of democratic processes in all spheres of life and the irenic religious attitudes that follow on acceptance of pluralism. Thus was set a style American in its economics and nationalism but opposed to Americanism in its specifically religious values. (The predominant style admits, of course, of exceptions, which are well treated by Greeley.)

The new generation is not immigrant nor is the predominant style of the Roman Catholic Church that they have experienced. The leaders whose skills seemed limited to financial wizardry and theological obscurantism are dying off. Since the election of Kennedy, jingoism no longer seems a magic key to acceptance as American, though it remains a vice of the unthinking. The young people—third and fourth generation Americans—are less apt to question genuine American values from the standpoint of Roman orthodoxy than they are to question Roman orthodoxy from the standpoint of their American experience. The rebels have become American rebels: the matter is as simple as that.

Vatican II has reinforced the effects of acculturization. Certain decisions of the Council—the acceptance of ecumenism and of religious liberty—give theological foundation to values American Catholics were in the process of accepting fully in the practical order. The notion that the Church must change may be difficult for Catholics to accept, since an unchanging Church provides psychological rest in a fluid society. Nevertheless, the rhetoric of change permeates all other spheres of American life and was bound sooner or later to reach into the Church. All this remains relatively fresh for those over thirty. But the young have 'always' lived in a relatively open Church. They are the first generation of American Catholics for whom there has been relatively little tension between the best values of the American culture and the best official theology of the Church. The most likely result will be the development of a distinctively American Church.

The most distinctive characteristic of the American Catholic Church, however, is a creation of generations past, the Catholic school system. (It is not, really, a system, either in the country as a whole or in many individual dioceses.) It began with the nine-teenth-century ideal of a parochial school near every parish church and reached its zenith during the postwar building boom when the ideal was reversed to read, near every parochial school a Catholic church. Robert T Francoeur captures the reality:

> . . . Let us take a ride out through suburbia. Typically, on a choice corner lot there is a large plant: a very large school, of many classrooms. Somewhere in the middle of the L-shaped, or wing-shaped school, there will be an auditorium. Near the school there will be a large, dormitory-style structure, whose cross identifies it as the convent. On the other side of the school there is a smaller building, partly a home, partly an office, which is the rectory. This plant is identified by a large sign as St Somebody's church.
>
> And yet the passerby on the highway sees no church. We who are among the initiates know that the auditorium doubles as a church.[1]

The church, once it has been built, will be an appendage of the school.

The size of the Catholic school system is extraordinary. In *Catholic Education in a Changing World*,[2] George N Schuster, assistant to the president of the University of Notre Dame, reports that in school year 1966–7 there were 10,427 elementary schools with an enrollment of 4,245,786 and 2,417 secondary schools with an enrollment of 1,107,767. Replacement cost of the parochial school plant has been put at $7 billion. Annual savings to non-Catholic taxpayers are estimated at $2 billion. Yet the elementary schools are able to admit less than 50% of the Catholic student population, while only one Catholic high school student in three attends a Catholic secondary school. To put the matter bluntly: the distinctive enterprise of the Roman Catholic Church in the United States is directed not toward the world or, even, toward the country as a whole; not toward the poor of Asia or Africa or, even, Appalachia and Watts . . . but toward a minority of its own children of school age.

[1] 'The Price We Pay', *Federal Aid and Catholic Schools*, edited by Daniel Callahan (Baltimore: Helicon, 1964), pp. 133–4.
[2] New York: Holt, Rinehart & Winston, 1967.

Higher education presents much the same picture. In 1966 there were 309 Catholic colleges and universities with 413,261 students. More than 920,000 Catholics were enrolled in secular institutions, with estimates running as high as a million. The religious needs of the students on secular campuses have, until recently, been neglected. The nearly 1,100 Newman apostolate programs at secular colleges and universities were served by only 272 full-time chaplains. Actual Newman centers, where Catholic students might meet, take courses, celebrate the liturgy, numbered less than 250. The six largest religious orders—all of them engaged in higher education—devoted less than one percent of their personnel to Newman work.

The financial outlook for Catholic education is bleak. According to Schuster, 'Catholic schools would, of course, have to close their doors tomorrow were it not for low salaries'. (Interestingly, he cites evidence that in elementary schools it is no less expensive to maintain a teaching nun than a teaching layman: the average for both is about $3,500 a year.) These salary scales are under severe pressure. Lay teachers who remain in the parochial school system (many teach in parochial schools only until they qualify for certification in public schools) cannot long tolerate an average salary that is less than that of a beginning secretary. Strikes for higher wages have already been threatened in New York and Philadelphia. In Chicago teachers at one high school struck until the administration recognized the Association of Teachers of Catholic Secondary Schools as a bargaining agent; at Marquette High School in Yakima, Washington, strikers for higher wages were joined by Father Frederick Brenner, superintendent of schools.

Religious orders, too, will have to demand more money for the services of their members. At present, the median education of teaching nuns is a college degree, which is substantially below the public school median. In Los Angeles, for example, no public school teacher can be certified without a BA. Yet in the fall of 1967 about one-fifth of the Immaculate Heart nuns teaching there did not yet have a college degree: the Immaculate Hearts are probably the most progressive teaching order in the nation. Parishes will ultimately have to meet the costs of adequate education for religious teachers, since the number of nuns who believe that the Holy Spirit will compensate for inadequate training is growing fewer day by day.

The financial outlook for colleges and universities is also disheartening for those who feel that Catholic education is a central mission of the American Church. Catholic (and other denominational) graduate schools have long been hampered by their inability to match the salary scales of secular institutions. The growth of public colleges and junior (two year) colleges in recent years has increased salary pressures, since decent salaries are easier to get. Expenses for the training of religious for college-level teaching have grown especially since a growing percentage of religious are working for higher degrees at the better (more expensive) universities. The colleges and universities are under-endowed. By raising tuitions to meet rising costs, the smaller college can continue but, as state-financed college education becomes more readily available, capable students will reject second-rate Catholic colleges in favor of public institutions with nominal tuition.

Meanwhile the better Catholic universities have entered a transitional phase. They

> must of necessity strive to acquire the status of their illustrious secular contemporaries (Schuster says). For these possess the keys to research methodology and success; and unless a Catholic university can find out how to get those keys for itself there is hardly a chance in the world that it can attract students wishing to become full-fledged scholars—unless it pretends to be able to do what it cannot do.

Only Notre Dame and Fordham University have so far made a serious effort at transition. In doing so, both have made staggering investments of money and remain inadequate in many areas of graduate study. The libraries at both universities remain deficient despite improvements. Laboratory facilities are inadequate. Salaries leave much to be desired. For example, two years ago a young associate professor at the City University of New York discovered that his salary already exceeded by $2,000 a year that of his mentor, a distinguished philosopher in his mid-sixties.

The present financial needs of Catholic education are beyond the capacity to pay of the Catholic community. Several options are possible, some of which are being exercised. In some areas Catholic elementary schools have eliminated the first few grades. In others no attempt is being made to have classrooms keep pace with the growing population. (As class size is cut down—classes of fifty to sixty presided over by a nerve wracked disciplinarian nun are no longer the rule—schools fall even further behind.) In Philadelphia, where secondary education had been tuition-free, nominal charges have been introduced, charges that are sure to increase as financial pressure mounts. But these do little more than postpone the day of reckoning. There is now sufficient commitment to excellence in education in the Catholic community for costs to be pushed closer to the level in public schools.

A second option is more radical, to seek methods other than the parochial school for Christian education. The suggestion was made in 1964 by Mary Perkins Ryan, whose *Are Parochial Schools the Answer ?*[1] was widely denounced but little read. (The book sold less than eight thousand copies.) Mrs Ryan's mistake may have been to focus on theology instead of arithmetic. The next year statistics brought Our Lady Queen of All Saints parish in Fraser, Michigan, to her conclusion. The parish already had a two year old, four grade elementary school serving 160 pupils. At the request of the pastor

> the school board . . . surveyed the parish during the summer of 1965. The median age for men was 34, the median age for women 33, and each family had an average of 22·2 children whose median age was five years. . . . The survey showed that there were 720 grade school children in the parish and 190 in public high school. The board estimated that even with the addition of four class-rooms the school could handle only 10% of the grade school students by 1970. To accommodate 50% of the parish school

[1] New York: Holt, Rinehart and Winston, 1964.

children in 1970 would cost $2 million. And additional $180,000 a year would be needed to cover maintenance and operating expenses for the school and convent.[1]

In cooperation with the local public school, Catholic children are given an extended lunch hour two days a week. Buses pick them up at the public school and deliver them to the original building, where they eat lunch in twenty minutes and have fifty minutes of religious instruction. Six teachers now educate all the children of the parish in religion only, have more time for preparation and catechetical study, and have undertaken visits to homes in the parish that were previously impossible.

The one hope of those who reject phasing out Catholic schools is increased state and/or federal aid. Proponents make an argument in simple justice:

> The heart of the matter is . . . freedom—freedom of thought and freedom of conscience. It is a question of the integrity of the individual child, under his parents, in his thoughts and beliefs. It is a question of the freedom of the child to pursue particular secular truths and to associate them freely with his own religious convictions. To deny education-tax funds to a child because he wishes to relate truths to Infinite Truth, is to penalize him for his religious beliefs.[2]

The argument is compelling in isolation. It is difficult to see how the US constitutional prohibition against establishment of a religion obtains against it. (I have, needless to say, oversimplified the constitutional question: the size of the Catholic school enterprise means that in fact aid to parochial schools would primarily be aid to the Roman Catholic religion as it now conceives itself.) The distinguished Protestant journal, *Christianity and Crises*, made the point well in 1963 when it discussed the need for federal aid to education, which was blocked by the demand of Catholics for aid to parochial schools and the refusal of political liberals

---

[1] 'Parish Closes School to Open it Up', DeWitt Henricks, *National Catholic Reporter*, 29 March 1967, p. 1.

[2] Virgil C Blum, 'Freedom and Equality', *Federal Aid and Catholic Schools*, p. 51.

(joined by opponents of all federal aid) to permit such a breach in the wall of separation between Church and state:

> Our society long ago decided to exercise major public responsibility for education through government; thus most formal education has come through government-sponsored schools. The benefits of this policy are so great as to need no argument. But we have made exceptions—notably the G.I. Bill, which subsidized students, letting them take their education in any certified school. Such a plan was surely better than requiring veterans to attend state universities if they wanted financial help. The same logic might endorse a comparable plan for elementary and secondary education.
> ... What we urge is experimentation, openness to new ideas, willingness to reason and discuss.[1]

On the other hand, more and more Catholic intellectuals question whether aid to parochial schools is the direction that experimentation and openness should take. Some of their reasons are not our direct concern here: the greatest injustice in education is injustice to the poor, especially urban blacks, and it is to the poor that money for education must be given now; federal aid to private schools will accelerate the establishment of such schools at the expense of public schooling and its commitment by law to integrated education; the political muscle that must be used if Catholics are to receive substantial, direct aid for their schools is detrimental to ecumenism, to the Catholic position in a pluralist society and, above all, to the Church's Christian mission to the government, which is not selfish but for others, else it is not Christian.[2]

[1] 'Federal Aid to Education', reprinted in *Witness to a Generation*, edited by Wayne H. Cowan (Indianapolis: Bobbs Merrill, 1966), p. 61.

[2] In the fall of 1967, citizens of New York State voted on a new constitution which, among other things, opened the door to aid to parochial schools, which had previously been barred (though often circumvented). Official Roman Catholic pressure for passage of the new constitution was tremendous. In Brooklyn, it is alleged, pastors were told to tap funds of parish organizations, which were to be sent to the Citizens for a New Constitution. A fact sheet cautioned that 'this drive is not to be publicized. ... No announcements— either pulpit or printed—are to be made.' The sheet suggested that a dollar per child registered in the parish school be contributed. Checks were to be drawn 'To Cash'. See 'Charge Secret Plan to Finance School Fight', *National Catholic Reporter*, 1 November 1967, p. 1.

More to our purpose is the question of precisely what the Catholic school accomplishes. One has only to read the novels of James T Farrell to realize that in some cases at least the schools help to drive good men out of the Church. 'New nuns', who are now meeting fellow Catholics on an adult basis, are often taken aback by the resentment directed toward them by mature men and women who for the first time are able to talk back to a major symbol of childhood repression, the good sister. Most important of all, of course, is the fact that the parochial schools focus Christian energy on the Church rather than the world.

This is not to say that the schools are without good effects. These are highlighted in recent sociological studies:[1]

... Students in Catholic elementary and high schools rate superior in potential achievement. Since the schools are largely middle class and tend to reject problem students, their superior rating is hardly surprising.

... There is some relationship between Catholic education and observable religious behavior. Family religious life is a far more important religious influence, however. 'Only those having at least one parent who went to communion every Sunday,' the Greeley–Rossi report says, 'seem to show notable signs of improving their religious behavior as a result of Catholic education.'

... Catholic school students are somewhat less likely to be prejudiced against Negroes than students in public schools, and their relative lack of bias is more likely to have religious motivation. On the other hand, prejudice does not decrease significantly as years of Catholic schooling increase.

... The students do not have a favorable image of Jews. A surprising number seems to have no image at all.

... Girls in an all-girl Catholic high school seem to be most affected by Catholic education. They have a better understanding of their faith than any other group.

... A complete Catholic education from elementary school through college is most apt to affect religious behavior. Attendance

[1] Andrew M Greeley and Peter H Rossi, *The Education of American Catholics* (Chicago: University of Chicago Press, 1966) and *Catholic Schools in Action*, directed and edited by Reginald A Neuwien (Notre Dame: University of Notre Dame Press, 1966). I have conflated their findings.

at a Catholic high school and college affects religious behavior, it seems, only if it follows Catholic elementary schooling.

. . . Parochial schools help to maintain the institutional system of the church. Though they educate only half the children, the elementary schools produce seventy percent of the 'vocations', while Catholic high schools produce sixty percent.

These studies, though useful, are limited by what they attempt to discover. The studies indicate that the schools are fairly successful in implanting the right attitudes toward Negroes, for example. But black Americans have had their fill of the right attitudes. The central question is whether Catholic education creates proportionately more effective action than the public schools, a question not taken up in these attitude audits. There is at least some reason to think that Catholic education fails in this regard. For example, my own children attend public schools which are more than twenty percent black—our town has total integration of its schools. Were they to attend parochial schools, they would have few if any black classmates. They could very well learn to hope for Negro equality without ever having met a Negro peer. And those they did meet would in all likelihood be middle class (like themselves), since the black poor of our community could not afford the parochial elementary school, let alone the quite expensive Catholic high school that serves our area.

Nor do the studies investigate the effect of Catholic education on religious experience. It is one thing to feel pleased that three students in four have gained religious understanding because they answer that the best way to join in the liturgy is 'to follow rites and rituals in approved books' or 'to take an active part in performing the liturgical acts'. (Exactly why anyone who values liturgical experience would be pleased with the former answer is a mystery that only the framers of the Notre Dame study could unravel.) The relevant question, of course, is whether attendance at a Catholic school enhances experience of the liturgy. A friend of mine whose children attend a parochial school in the Morningside Heights area of New York—a school that has a fine reputation—tells me that it is being drilled into his children that it is a mortal sin to miss

Mass on Sunday unless one is sick. The theological dubiousness of the teaching aside, it is difficult to see how, given our present understanding, such a teaching can do anything but distort the simple joy with which these children under other circumstances would join of a Sunday in eucharistic celebration.

To be brief: There is no evidence that Catholic schools are effective in terms of their cost unless one's values are narrowly institutional. That is the sad fact: they are not bad so much as they are not very good.

Saying this, however, is of little use in the short run. Andrew Greeley once remarked that being against the Catholic school enterprise is like being against the Rocky Mountains. I might rather say that it is like being against the pollution of the Hudson River: the idea is easy to come by, but purifying the waters involves massive practical problems. So far, the Church in America has not faced the problem with vigor. Meanwhile enrolment in Catholic schools is declining (by 4,399 in the New York arch-diocese when school opened in 1967) but relatively few are asking what alternatives there are and—if these alternatives are accepted— how the mortgages will be payed off. For that last is one reason that few pastors can imagine a decision to eliminate their schools: what motive would the faithful then have to contribute enough money to liquidate the debt on the educational plant? The process has begun on a professional level, however. In 1964, the National Catholic Educational Association responded to Mary Perkins Ryan's *Are Parochial Schools the Answer?* with total defensiveness, even suggesting that a fund be made available to 'publicize in popular terms the remarkable success story of the American parochial school'. The sum of $40,000 was mentioned. By 1967, the same organization sponsored a symposium at which its executive secretary, Rev. C Albert Koob, said that 'this is a serious time for reappraisal of the general thrust of the educational endeavor of the Catholic Church'. At the same symposium, Dr John J Meng of Fordham University said:

> American Catholic education is in disarray. Whether this disarray is the result of decrepitude and confusion or of exuberant

vitality and rapid growth is not yet entirely clear. What is obvious is that the whole structure, from preschool programs through graduate school, is in flux.

Catholic colleges and universities are responding to the crisis with greater flexibility than the schools. The reasons are several: the administrations and faculties are more aware of what is happening in the Church and the world; since it is only since World War II that the United States as a culture has decided in favor of close to universal college education, and there is a consequent need for more colleges, religious or not, the Catholic college is serving a need that is public rather than churchly; where the Catholic elementary school can hardly escape its Catholic identity, it is relatively easy for the Catholic institution of higher learning formally or informally to become secular; it is also psychologically easier, since those involved in higher education, including the students, are more likely to be acculturated, less likely to look to the school for protection from the American world.

Oddly enough, the firing in 1965 of about two dozen teachers from St John's University in Queens and Brooklyn, New York, may have done more to reform Catholic colleges and universities in the United States than any other single event. The issue, though often blurred, was the question central to Catholic academics: is the Catholic university to be a university in the accepted sense of the term or is it to be a catechetical extension of the parish?[1]

The Vincentians, who control the university, were basically motivated by their desire for St John's to remain a catechetical institution. The key intellectual figures among those fired— notably Thomas Berry, a Passionist historian of Eastern religions, and Dr Rosemary Lauer, a talented philosopher and notable controversialist—wished to have St John's enter the academic mainstream, to accept as its purpose the investigation of ideas rather than the salvation of souls. The secondary issue (which was more widely publicized) had to do with professional conditions of

[1] The phrase is that of Msgr John J Clancy, one of those fired by the university. My own understanding of the event is developed in 'Academic Freedom at St John's University', *Christianity and Crisis*, 7 March 1966, pp. 39–43.

work; the key figure here was the Chicago priest Peter O'Reilly. The result of the firings was a strike —which was technically lost but in fact resulted in reforms at St John's that on paper at least have transformed the university.

More important in the long run, the issue of respect for the academic process was brought before Catholic educators with a clarity that had previously been missing. The Vincentians looked stupid. If conversations I have had with Catholic college and university people are any indication, the fiasco conveyed one message before all others: anyone who follows the older patterns (which continue to be the preference of the Vatican) will look stupid, too. There are few more effective motivations for reform.

At the same time, other Catholic institutions are leading the way in a more positive fashion. Fordham University provides an example. Under the enlightened presidency of Leo McLaughlin, SJ, the university has established a women's college, reformed its theology department (among other things students can take courses for credit at the Protestant Union Theological Seminary, with which teachers are exchanged), the Bea Institute for the investigation of spirituality in the modern world has been opened and, in 1967, there was founded Bensalem College, an experimental college directed by the poet, Elizabeth Sewell.

Among smaller colleges the best known is Webster College in Webster Groves, Missouri. Jacqueline Grennan, its president, has been dispensed from her vows as a Sister of Loreto and the college itself is now a secular institution 'with the power of Christian presence'. As at Fordham, the rigid old rules of daily Mass, early curfew and the like have been done away with. The students by and large govern themselves. Theology is a subject of investigation. On a pragmatic basis, the college, since it is no longer denominational will more easily qualify for state and federal aid.[1]

There is an increasing lay voice in Catholic college education.

[1] Fordham was refused aid by New York State after it had given an Albert Schweitzer chair to Marshall McLuhan in September 1967. If it had been a private but not denominational institution, the state would have provided $100,000 for McLuhan and his staff.

C

The *New York Times* reports that a study indicates that

> more than 45 per cent of the Catholic colleges have lay participation on their boards, and 40 per cent of the others indicated plans during the year to follow suit. . . . Only 15 per cent are not considering lay participation.[1]

In addition

> since 1956 there has been an increase of 190 per cent in lay teachers, while the increase in religious teachers was but 14 per cent.

Equally significant, of course, is the greater confidence of the lay faculty in their dealings with priests and religious: the demystification of 'states in life' brought about professional rather than familial relationships within many, perhaps most, colleges.

It is the students themselves, I suspect, who are doing the most to transform Catholic higher education in the United States. Though there are differences between Catholic students on parochial campuses and those on secular campuses, the resemblances are most marked. We may therefore return to the new generation and look at what is happening.

The majority of young Catholics, not surprisingly, is conformist, middle class in its values, bored by intellectual pursuits, relatively untouched by religious values, secure in the belief that the right practices, as described by the Church, will earn them a place of undefined happiness called heaven. (I make the statement because it is conventional wisdom and, I suppose, right.) For them, presumably, the revolution at a school like Fordham means little more than a few tougher courses compensated for by the right to drink beer at the campus ratskeller. They join the Reserve Officers Training Corps in order to avoid the draft but look on in dismay when what they consider a hippy dares to decry the Vietnam war as immoral. They would be shocked at anyone who questioned the historicity of the Virgin Birth or the infallibility of

---

[1] 12 January 1968, p. 73. The study was prepared by the Institute of Higher Education of Teachers College, Columbia University.

the pope but have in fact given these things no thought at all, living in the faith of ignorance. They avoid mortal sins like the plague but are armed with an elaborate casuistry concerning 'how far you can go' in making out, a casuistry that ignores, of course, the question of personal relationships. (Besides, there is always confession.) They will remain faithful Catholics, but their fidelity will never be allowed to conflict with their prime values, which are grossly material.

But what of the others ? Three assertions might distinguish them most sharply from an earlier generation: they are increasingly indifferent to the hierarchical Church and to what is usually taken to be Roman Catholicism as such; they have less and less interest in what has conventionally been thought of as the supranatural; they value life and experience rather than doctrine and discipline. These differences are expressed in two ways: social activism or the personal religiousness of which the hippie phenomenon is a part.

Indifference to religious institutions should not be confused with angry anti-institutionalism which is more common among those over thirty than it is among those under twenty-five. After three drinks, the middle-aged priest may suddenly reveal his hatred of his bishop, his doubts about the value of the priesthood. It takes less time than that for the housewife of thirty-five to denounce the discipline that forbids contraception. It is chiefly middle-aged Catholics who thrill to the outrageous statements of James Kavanaugh in *A Modern Priest Looks at His Outdated Church* and are seriously troubled by Charles Davis's *A Question of Conscience*.

In a *Commonweal* symposium, 'The Cool Generation and the Church'.[1] Martha Ann Brazier, a college junior, speaks about the pope and birth control in a not untypical way:

> I agree that on birth control Pope Paul has proclaimed what seems to us an obvious lie. On the other hand, we young people have to develop a tolerance of the other person's opinion and have got to learn to see the other side of the questions. On birth control, Pope Paul has to remain silent. Think of the thousands of people who

[1] 6 October 1967, pp. 11–23.

have 10, 11, 12, 13 children, because they lived the Catholic faith as it existed four or five years ago.

This at first seems less threatening to the institutional Church than, say, the statements of Charles Davis. In fact it is far more damaging: the speaker is willing to admit the Church's bind but it is difficult to imagine her troubled by anything the pope might say about contraception, for or against.

Some months ago, I was discussing with a theologian the experimental liturgies that are held on the campus where he teaches. He said that he had been most interested in the response of students who were told by one priest that there would be no liturgical experimentation, since this was forbidden by canon law.

> The students were perfectly polite—perfectly happy to let him do his thing. But they wouldn't go to his Mass. It didn't mean anything to them. And his concern with obeying canon law didn't mean anything to them either.

In the end, the priest in question joined the students and presided at celebrations meaningful to them.

As often as not, this indifference to the discipline of the Church stems from the conviction that the Church is irrelevant. The young people see that if Pope Pius XII could not speak out effectively against Hitler, the Church was in that instance unreal. Another undergraduate participant in the *Commonweal* symposium says:

> I really don't give a damn what the Church has to say. It's speaking to its own line of people, in their own different world. . . . Leave us alone and we'll leave the Church people alone to follow their foolish practices, their superstitions, their Masses. We have a world that has relevance to the way we live.

A final example of this indifference may be found among seminarians. A teacher at a New England seminary recently told me that the rules would be substantially changed in a few months. Many on the faculty were opposed, he said, especially to the idea that the students be allowed to come and go as they please, so long as they are home by midnight. But he predicted that one fact would override the opposition: a good number of students had informed the faculty that, if the rules were not changed, they would leave—perhaps to enroll in another seminary, or else to give up the idea of ordination. A fifty year old priest put it well on another occasion:

> When I was in the seminary, we wanted to become priests. These kids want to become Christians. There's quite a difference.

The supernatural in the conventional theological sense seems to have little meaning for the new generation. They read Harvey Cox, Teilhard de Chardin, Dietrich Bonhoeffer—and more recently Hans Hoekendijk. But the notion of a separate supernatural order—or a particular sacred space—is apt to leave them cold. There is sadness here, since many of them find it impossible to empathize with such men as Henri deLubac, whose thought is in fact congenial with many of their better insights.

The phenomenon is often referred to as a loss of the sense of the sacred, an inability on the part of the young to make contact with religious mystery. This, I believe, is to misunderstand the direction of their experience. It would be more accurate to speak of a diffusion of the sacred, their sense that the holy is not in one place, or to be found in one way, but that it is everywhere, waiting to be discovered. The young will speak seriously of a peace march as eucharist. It is a spirituality not of the Church, but of Emmaus, of the discovery of Christ through listening to the Word of the world.

The experience of the sacred as present not in the tabernacle but in the world, not in the anointed hands of a priest but in the eye of a suffering brother, leads some into social activism. A disproportionate percentage of the New Left is made up of Catholics and former Catholics. After a eucharistic celebration at Emmaus House—an urban centre of reconciliation in Manhattan where experimental liturgies are held openly—a young leftist spoke of his convictions concerning Christ. He was not sure that God existed, he said, though he had faith in God. He had greater faith, though, in Jesus, the man in whom all that he could possibly mean by God seemed to live. He saw Jesus as healing and as suffering—and ultimately dying for being what he had to be, but then going beyond death and living wherever there were men who would heal at any cost and suffer if need be for the sake of others.

It is easy enough to dismiss all this as social gospel—a Catholic repetition of outmoded Protestant experience. I would suggest otherwise, however. Theologically correct or not, the young man conveyed an experience of the sacred, the sacred in others, which no theologian would dare deny as an imaging of God himself. That this experience issues in action that is more secular than churchly is all to the good.

The so-called hippy phenomenon has equal promise. The runaways who flock to the East Village and Haight Ashbury are, many of them, deeply disturbed, though there is at least some good sense in fleeing from an intolerable situation. The psychologists who point out that many of the hippies are incapable of sustained interpersonal relationships are right. Yet there is more to the movement than flight and withdrawal, sustained by drugs and sexual promiscuity.

Among many of the new generation one senses a return to the aesthetic, to the sense of play and leisure, that the Anglo-Saxon West has long repressed. The parent who hopes for his son's success in a meaningful profession may be disconcerted at his rejection of study and, above all, of the analytic approach to life that characterizes our culture. To anyone brought up on Aristotle it is disconcerting to see that among many of the new generation logic is not a key to knowledge but a block to experience. The hippies drop out of competition and striving conspicuously; but there are innumerable others who do so quietly. Ravi Shankar will hold an audience of high school and college youth spellbound as he plays for two hours without interruption. Bob Dylan, Donovan, the Beatles—all are writing significant music to which those young people attend. And they are kind, very kind. In a culture just becoming aware of its addiction to violence, that kindness is refreshing.

These young people seem to relate to the Catholic Church and Christianity in a different way. They have a sense that is almost primitive of fellowship, of being glad to be in a good place with good people. They wear sandals—'Jesus boots'—many of them and talk with considerable silliness and affection of J.C. They will even talk of him while smoking pot. It is surprising how few of them have taken LSD more than once or twice. More important, they find just as much experience in nature, in holding hands (Catholic sexual inhibitions play little part in their decision-making processes) and thinking about God. They have an extraordinary ability to take the good of reality on its own terms, and to experience there what they consider sacred.

All this is distressing to conventional Catholicism, of course. For one thing it cannot be controlled. For another it stresses personal/mystical religious experience and all but ignores accepted ways of prayer and contemplation. The particular scandal here is the tolerance of drugs as a means of evoking religious experience. 'When you read the Gospel concept of Jesus Christ,' one of the participants in the *Commonweal* symposium says, 'he seems to be, pardon the expression, hip, cool, with it. Right? . . . Someone said youth groups resemble the early Church. That's a good observation. We're starting all over again. Christ would have fit right in at a pot party.'

Such young people can be forced to leave the Church. But the significant thing is this: by and large they do not leave unless they feel forced to do so. They blandly assume that they remain Catholics.

The primacy of experience over truth in the value system of the new generation is, in part at least, the product of acculturization. John J McDermott has developed this theme from a philosophic point of view:

It can be said of the Roman Church that, for the most part, her past is on the side of doctrinal unity, reaction as a sociological cast of mind, and a correlative refusal to be led by the press of the wider cultural experience in which she finds herself. The American tradition, by contrast, is characterized by an historical series of compromises and adjustments, called by some a declension in doctrine, be it religious or constitutional, and a general responsiveness to environmental pressures. . . . Put another way,

America tends to understand itself in behavioristic rather than conceptualistic terms.[1]

The new generation tends to define the Church in terms of behavior rather than ideas. It tends to evaluate the liturgy in terms of experience rather than theology. And it is American in doing so.

The ecumenical movement, for example, is irrelevant to most of the thoughtful young. They have no objection to those who devote their talents to institutional union and to the refined differences of dogma between, say, Roman Catholics and Lutherans. But they see little point in the activity: 'Suppose there was complete agreement', one of them said to me, 'on the doctrine of justification. What difference would it make to my being Christian?' A Jesuit seminarian who took part in the *Commonweal* symposium comments: 'Why one teacher I had was hopping up and down with delight because Karl Rahner had "discovered" quasi-formal causality. These people are talking a language that nobody understands and that nobody wants to understand.' When I told a young Catholic woman studying at a Protestant seminary why I found the doctrine of the Trinity meaningful, she was fascinated: she was not worried that she did not 'believe' or (disbelieve') in the doctrine but was deeply concerned to discover meaning that had to do with life and experience. For these people faith is not something one thinks but does; the Church is not a closed circle but a point—a personal point—of departure into the world.

It is within terms of experience that the Roman Mass is judged. After Mass one day, my twelve year old daughter asked, 'Do you really think Jesus fed his friends bread like that?' The young are vividly aware that reserving the chalice to the priest and the placing of the host on the tongue are symbolic actions and, when they interpret the symbolism, are apt to be caustic. The new English canon with its litanies of obscure names (' "Linus, Cletus . . ." that means nothing to me.') is measured by the standards of communication: its words, they feel, are not speech.

Experimental liturgies, on the other hand, are meeting a need

---

[1] 'The American Angle of Vision', part I, *Cross Currents*, Winter 1965, pp. 69–70.

that is deeply felt: to give thanks in community. At one such liturgy in which I took part, the priest was twenty-eight. The liturgy of the Word had been prepared by a boy and girl of sixteen and seventeen. The opening was unfortunate: a Donovan song which could not be understood because the record player was momentarily broken. The readings which followed were taken from Aeschylus' *Prometheus Bound*, Heinrich Hesse's *Demian*, Ezra Pound's 'The Ballad of the Goodly Fere', and the first epistle of John. It closed with the playing of 'Suzanne' sung by Judy Collins. The eucharistic prayer, composed for the occasion, though not by the teenagers, reflected the content of the readings. It was read seriatim by those present. The priest recited the narrative of institution and all together said the words of institution over a loaf of Italian bread and common wine. Following communion the celebration dissolved slowly into conversation among the thirty or so persons who had taken part.

This kind of liturgy is not rare among the new generation. Ones like it can be found on many college campuses. I see the problems involved, of course. But I also see among the best of these young people an insistence on valid religious experience that has for a long time been rare in the Roman Church. And this is a sign of hope, of very great hope indeed.

The Church's Ecumenical Outreach

ROBERT MCAFEE BROWN

Ecumenism is going to move in a new direction in our day, the direction of increasing involvement in the secular order. Unless it does this, it will become increasingly precious and ingrown; if it does this, it can become increasingly creative and forward-looking.

Until recently, discussions of ecumenism have concentrated on the problem of unity, a noble theme in the light of the tragic disunity that has so blunted the witness of the Church as a healing and redemptive force in the lives of men. Quite rightly, the conciliar decree *De Oecumenismo* highlights this concern:

> The 'ecumenical movement' means those activities and enterprises which, according to various needs of the Church and opportune occasions, are started and organized for the fostering of unity among Christians.[1]

Concern for unity has also been a major thrust in Protestant and Orthodox ecumenical activity, particularly through the stream called 'Faith and Order', one of the tributaries leading to the formation of the World Council of Churches. Here also the goal was the restoration of the unity of the Body of Christ throughout the whole of the *oikoumene*, or 'inhabited world'.

But there is another meaning attached to the various words derived from *oikoumene*, so that when we speak of 'ecumenism' today we ought also to be speaking of mission, of the task of the

[1] Abbott, ed., *Documents of Vatican II*, p. 347.

66

Church to reach out to the entire *oikoumene*. It is not unimportant that the original impetus toward the unity of divided Christians, symbolized by the Edinburgh Missionary Conference of 1910, received its propelling force from the mission field, and from the missionary societies even more than from the denominations. This second meaning of ecumenism, the task of mission to the world, is one on which increasing attention should be focussed. Very early in its History, the World Council of Churches discovered that concern for unity seemed to be absorbing much of the attention that likewise needed to be directed toward concern for mission. The minutes of the Central Committee in 1951 point to the need for retaining an emphasis on both concerns:

> We would especially draw attention to the recent confusion in the use of the word 'ecumenical'. It is important to insist that this word, which comes from the Greek word for the whole inhabited earth, is properly used to describe everything that relates to the whole task of the whole Church to bring the Gospel to the whole world. *It therefore covers equally the missionary movement and the movement toward unity*, and must not be used to describe the latter in contradistinction to the former. . . . Every attempt to separate these two tasks violates the wholeness of Christ's ministry to the world.[1]

If I concentrate on this second aspect of ecumenism, it is not to violate this injunction of the World Council, but simply because I believe we can presuppose widespread concern about ecumenism as unity, and need to highlight concern about *ecumenism as mission*. To those of you who are wary even of a temporary disjunction, I would point out that not only do these two understandings of ecumenism need each other if we are to do full justice to ecumenical concern, but that either one, carried through in any kind of significant way, sooner or later embraces the other.

This point is important enough to illustrate by an interesting example out of ecumenical history. After the 1910 Edinburgh Missionary Conference, two subsequent conferences were held on the theme of 'Life and Work', i.e. the ways in which Christians

[1] Cited in Vischer, ed., *A Documentary History of the Faith and Order Movement, 1927–1963* (St Louis: Bethany, 1963) pp. 177–9, italics added.

could register the impact of the Gospel in their daily activities both individual and corporate. These conferences (at Stockholm in 1925 and Oxford in 1937) pursued themes dealing with the economic order, political responsibility of the Churches, education, the state, and so on. At the beginning of Life and Work, doctrinal concerns were rigorously eschewed, for, as the slogan went, 'Doctrine divides, service unites.' But it soon became apparent that the slogan was a half truth at best, and that theological considerations inevitably intruded; to raise a question about the nature of the Church's responsibility in the political order, for example, was to raise the previous question about the nature of the Church itself, and to be led into the theological arena of questions about unity, ministry and sacraments.

During the same period, and also growing out of the Edinburgh Missionary Conference, two further conferences were held, focussing precisely on the theological issues of the Church, unity, ministry and sacraments. These conferences on 'Faith and Order', held at Lausanne in 1925, and Edinburgh in 1937, dealt with ecumenism in terms of the search for unity. But those in Faith and Order made the obverse discovery of those in Life and Work; they discovered that they could not do their theological task properly if they were not also concerned about the outreach and mission of the Church. To raise a question about the nature of the Church itself was also, from their perspective, to raise a question about the nature of the Church's responsibility in the political order. Thus Life and Work (concerned with mission) discovered that it needed Faith and Order (concerned with unity), while Faith and Order (concerned with unity) discovered that it needed Life and Work (concerned with mission). Each presupposed the other; neither could adequately define itself without the other. And it was the marriage of these two partners, each unfulfilled without the other, that produced the World Council of Churches.

Subsequent assemblies of the World Council of Churches have therefore addressed themselves to the themes of both unity and mission. Amsterdam (1948) dealt not only with 'The Universal Church in God's Design' but also with 'The Church and the

International Disorder'; Evanston (1954) dealt not only with 'Our Oneness in Christ and Our Disunity as Churches' but also with 'The Responsible Society in a World Perspective' and 'The Church Amid Racial and Ethnic Tensions'; New Delhi (1961) dealt not only with 'Unity' but also with 'Service'.

It is my own belief that this theme of concern for the secular order is the direction in which the next ecumenical steps are going to be most creatively taken, and as evidence for this prediction I offer two pieces of evidence:

a. The report of the Geneva Conference of 1966 on the theme, 'Christians in the Social and Technical Revolutions of our Time', which concentrated its attention almost exclusively in this direction, dealing with 'Economic Development in a World Perspective', 'The Nature and Function of the State in a Revolutionary Age', 'Structures of International Cooperation—Living Together in Peace in a Pluralistic World Society', and 'Man and Community in Changing Societies'.

b. The forthcoming fourth world assembly of the World Council of Churches, to be held in July 1968 at Upsala, will pick up on a number of these items, for in addition to dealing with themes related to unity, it will also discuss the mission of the Church to the world, the Church in economic and social change, international affairs, worship in a secular age, and the nature of a Christian 'style of life'. If the assembly ever begins to take seriously its overall theme, 'Behold, I Make All Things New', it could be a turning point in ecumenical history.

It is important to realize another aspect of the ecumenical development here. At the Geneva conference just mentioned, Roman Catholic theologians were not only present, but participated actively in the discussions, and two of the major papers were given by Roman Catholics, Canon Charles Moeller and Lady Jackson (Barbara Ward). It is also important to realize that at Upsala fifteen Catholic observers will be present, not merely to observe, but to have the privilege of the floor, if not yet the privilege of the ballot.

Let us briefly examine what has been happening from the Roman

Catholic side in this area of ecumenism. One need only recall the earlier 'social encyclicals' from Leo XIII on, to realize that concern for the secular order has been a part of Catholic teaching to Catholics for many decades. *Rerum Novarum* and *Quadragesimo Anno* are landmarks on this road, as is the more recent *Mater et Magistra*, which consciously attempts to stand in their succession. But with the ecumenically-minded Pope John, something new emerged. *Pacem in Terris*, while still a papal encyclical, was addressed not only to Catholics but also to 'all men of goodwill', indicating that a decision had been made to deal ecumenically with the most pressing problem of the *saeculum*, world peace.[1]

This tradition was continued at Vatican II. Consider the famous 'schema seventeen' of session two, which became 'schema thirteen' of session three and finally *Gaudium et Spes* in its promulgated version, the pastoral constitution on *The Church and the World Today*, the longest conciliar document and the one dealing specifically with the issues of the life of contemporary man in areas such as marriage, economics, politics, war and world peace. This was one of the two Council documents likewise addressed not only to Roman Catholics and other Christians but to the whole of humanity. In like fashion, the encyclical of Pope Paul, *Populorum Progressio*, dealing once again with matters of concern to all men, particularly in the economic order, was addressed not only to Catholics but likewise to all men of good will.

What this brief history suggests is that from both sides, our concerns about the *world* have led us closer to *one another*, and we have discovered in the process that we cannot properly concern ourselves about the secular order save ecumenically, save in close concert, working together. When talking about such issues, pope and council no longer address a Catholic constituency exclusively; they address all their fellow Christians and, indeed, all men.

[1] The only earlier encyclical I recall that was similarly directed to non-Catholics as well as Catholics was Pius XI's *Mit brennender Sorge* (1937), addressed to the German nation and dealing, albeit cautiously, with the issue of Nazism. In this case, even the customary Latin form was foregone. Unfortunately, the message did not get through to non-Catholics (cf Albert Camus' critique in *Resistance, Rebellion and Death*).

Similarly, Protestants and Orthodox in the World Council of Churches do not only consult among themselves when dealing with such issues; they reach out to an ever-deepening Roman Catholic involvement in their own concerns. Ecumenism as mission has gained a substantial foothold.

To concentrate on ecumenism as mission, as an outreach to, and concern for, and involvement in, the secular order—to do this is not to eschew the importance of ecumenism as a quest for unity. I believe, indeed, that it may be only through the concern for ecumenism as mission that we will break some of the theological binds that constrict us in our present concern for ecumenism as unity, and that a pursuit today of what were, in an earlier day, the concerns of 'Life and Work', will help us see more incisively the ongoing concerns of 'Faith and Order'.

I. *The diaspora situation—and some consequences*

There is a quotation from Fr Avery Dulles, SJ, that I have found increasingly challenging, and that, though it may seem to imply a greater division between these two types of ecumenism than I would want to make, sets the context for where we must go from here:

> Ecumenism has become too exclusively taken up with religious questions—with matters of doctrine and worship. . . . From many quarters therefore one hears the call for a new ecumenism— one less committed to historical theological controversies and more in touch with contemporary secular man; one less turned in upon itself, more open to the world and its concerns. The greatest decisions affecting man's future are being made in the sphere of the secular, and Christianity does not seem to be there.[1]

This is both a description and an indictment, and I have an increasing feeling that unless we are truly found in the *saeculum*, the things we do elsewhere are going to amount to no more than trivial irrelevancies. I therefore accept *both* the description and the indictment. We have not sufficiently concerned ourselves with this arena of the secular in the past, and we must do so in the future. We no longer confront a 'Catholic' problem or a 'Protestant

[1] Cited in *Convergence*, The Gustave Weigel Society, Vol. I, No. 1, pp. 4-5.

problem', we confront a 'human problem'. Men are in desperate need. Time is running out. How shall we respond?

The most seductive response, and the most fatal, is the one to which we almost instinctively turn: let us shore up the crumbling walls of the Church, regroup our scattered forces, and assault the enemy as we have done in the past; let us, in other words, recapture our lost territory, let us restore Christendom.

Now I shall not take long to respond to this (as I regard it) highly mistaken plea. There can be no simple return to the past; we cannot restore Christendom, whether of the thirteenth century variety (as some of you might like) or the sixteenth century varieties (as in some moments I might like, provided I could locate the center in Geneva rather than Wittenburg). The Church is not going to dominate our society, and even if it could, to attempt to do so would be to misconceive its role. After centuries of both Catholic and Protestant triumphalism, we have begun to see that the proper stance for the Church is not as Lord but as servant, since its own Lord was a servant. It would be hard to overstress the importance of the fact that the servant imagery was prominent in Vatican II, even if a lot of the old triumphalist language still lingers on. The Church's task is not to assume power from the state, but to offer itself so that the state can use its own power more responsibly. In our time the Church will represent at best a tiny minority that might, by the grace of God, become what Toynbee describes as a 'creative minority'.

The biblical image for this stance is, of course, an image that Karl Rahner, Stephen Neill, Thomas Merton, Richard Schall, Hans Reudi-Weber and others have recently been expounding— the image of diaspora. The Church is scattered, dispersed, to the ends of the earth. It no longer has terrestrial power nor should it seek it once again. It is that band of people, here and there, united along the conduits of power mysteriously supplied by the Holy Spirit, who, wherever they are, offer themselves and the resources of their institution in the service of all men, and not just in the service of those who happen to belong to the institution. Richard Schall describes the situation:

Christendom is rapidly dissolving around us ... without our going into exile, the non-Christian world has engulfed us as modern means of communication create one world in which we are a small minority, and as the population explosion indicates that each year the percentage of Christians decreases. We are thus in a situation similar to that of the Jews of the diaspora, scattered among people whose culture, mores and thought patterns are not like ours nor will they become so; our cathedrals and temples are no longer in the center of life nor do they bring the whole community together under God. If we hope to reach modern man, it will not be so much in terms of gathering him into the church as of going to him in the midst of our dispersion.[1]

In such a situation Rahner reminds us not to yearn wistfully for an earlier era but to accept the present era joyfully. The diaspora situation is no cause for despair. It is the situation in which God has placed us today, and we must live the diaspora-life affirmatively, rather than seeking to restore the Christendom-life frantically. The Church need not, as Thomas Merton and Hans Küng have pointed out, speak in the language of victory *communiqués* (cf Merton, *Seeds of Destruction*, p. 186).

I am not sure how much any of us have really understood what a radically new set of outlooks and postures would be required if we took this description seriously. And I am not sure how many of us, if we did come to such a realization, would be willing to cope with it. For such a discovery would be very threatening and very risky, even at the level of our accustomed ways of doing things and our ordinary day to day structures. The geographically isolated seminary, for example, seems to me a structure reflecting the old Christendom mentality. Earlier prescription: isolate your shock troops for sufficient years to insulate them thoroughly against contamination from the world, and then set them loose to regain all that lost territory for the Queen of Heaven. The new prescription would read: educate your shock troops right along with the enlisted men (for which read 'in the context of an urban university') so that they are completely at home in secular culture and can

---

[1] Cited in Marty and Peerman, eds., *New Theology No. 2* (New York: Macmillan, 1965) p. 271.

share in its best while offering a fresh alternative to replace its worst.

But this, of course, is only a small symbol. Let us not flatter ourselves that seminary education is the key to secular man's redemption. We are going to find that many of the other things we have taken most for granted, most associated with the 'fulness' of the faith, are going to have to be put up for grabs. The religious orders furnish a further example. Is it right, in the diaspora situation, that whole communities should live together in isolation, even on a university campus? Should not members of such communities be dispersed through the dormitories, through the surrounding area, in the apartments and the slums, sharing fully in what it means to be a modern man, rather than being protected from the political, social and economic problems that beset ordinary mortals?

The plight of many Protestant ministers extends the problem. Selective service exempts from military duty the physically unfit, the mentally incompetent and the clergy. Why should ministers have exemption? Why should they not be full men, either fighting if they so choose, or declaring their conscientious objection if they so choose, like other men. Why, to press another point, should they be professional holy men, exempted from the task their parishoners face of earning a living day by day? Why not, after the manner of Paul, earn their living at a 'secular job', and thereby be freed from being beholden to those who ante up the salary check? If the criterion is *diakonia*, service, involvement in the affairs of men in today's world, is the structure of a 'kept clergy' really defensible any more?

What about the very physical structures in which we worship? Are they not also a reflection of the Christendom mentality. The medieval cathedral *dominated* the town. The New England meeting house *dominated* the village green. We like our church spires to be higher than surrounding structures—though the fate of St Patrick's Cathedral, dwarfed for decades by Radio City, symbolizes the fate of such ecclesiastical *hubris*. The rank and file still insist that a church must 'look like a church', by which they mean, I discover, what John Betjeman calls the 'ghastly good taste' of nineteenth-century Christians who decided that pseudo-gothic was ordained by God at the moment of creation in an irreformable *ex cathedra* decree. Does not all this still create the impression that God is somewhere else than where people normally are, and that if we want to find him we must go apart to find him, withdrawing from the *saeculum* into the holy?

I am always baffled by the high degree of initial resistance to having the Mass elsewhere than in a Church, since on historical grounds alone the precedent of having Mass on the second floor of somebody's house would seem most scripturally fitting. I suggest that if we take the diaspora situation seriously, we are going to be far less concerned about Church buildings in the future (save for concern that we probably have too many of them) and will find that in our scattered existence, wherever we happen to find ourselves may be the ideal spot in which to worship the Lord of all creation, since it will be precisely in the midst of his creation. Jesus did not choose a very religious spot on which to be crucified —in fact, it was chosen for him by the secular authorities and it turned out to be the city dump heap. Perhaps a sanitation project would be a more appropriate place to celebrate Good Friday than before a high altar.

But we must not linger overmuch with such matters, which are merely illustrations of the fact that if we take seriously our new situation in the *saeculum*, as the scattered and dispersed people of God, many things are going to be up for grabs, and everything will have to be rethought in the light of our new situation. The posture in that new situation must be one of *diakonia*, and it must not be *self*-regarding, i.e. for the sake of the Church, but *other*-regarding, i.e. for the sake of the neighbor in need, whether in the Church or not.

II. *Involvement in power structures*

Now such a possibility, unfortunately, can become hopelessly romantic and unrealistic. If we really want to minister to the neighbor in need, it will not be enough to do so merely on a personal, individualistic scale, important or rewarding as such an action may be to all concerned. Nine Jesuits, let us say, moving to the slums of St Louis and living among the people, sharing their hardships, being there as humane individuals, can engage in genuine ministries of healing and compassion, but they are still likely to remain what I call 'Band-Aid ministries', i.e. effective only in repairing damage that has already been done. But nine Jesuits, in concert with some ministers and rabbis and informed lay people, moving in on City Hall to demand new Rent Control Commissions, or helping people organize to fight corrupt landlords, or setting up precinct caucus groups to force politicians to do something about ambulance service or price gouging—such groups could begin to have an impact on the whole structure of the city, and on the basic structure of human lives. Apart from such action, both structures will remain pretty much the same, for there is a clear axiom of modern life (which the doctrine of original sin corroborates), that those with power do not voluntarily surrender it. What I am saying is that the Christian, living in diaspora, who does want to serve his fellow men must, whatever else he may do, act politically. He must gather others together, form groups that can exercise power, and work from some kind of power base, with all of the temptations and abuses to which he thereby becomes liable.

There are those who become very nervous in the face of such suggestions, and who feel that overnight the Church will reduce itself merely to the level of another secular social service agency. I concede that we would be in difficulty if the Church in fact were nothing but a kind of equivalent of the AFL-CIO sprinkled with holy water, or if the Church became no more than one pressure group among the other pressure groups. But I passionately insist that this is not our problem, that it is not likely to be our problem for at least half a century, and that in the interval we can count on the inertia of good Christian folk to keep us from rushing pell-mell into the secular arena leaving everything else behind us. Surely the thing we need to fear is not over-involvement in the world of contemporary politics; if there is to be an indictment of the Church today it will not come from our over-involvement but because we are so pathetically under-involved. The terrible thing, as Martin Luther King has said, is not the evil actions of the bad people but the appalling silence of the good people.

What have we been doing, we church people, for the last few decades, that the painfully obvious conditions in our cities, with their inevitable (I repeat, inevitable) outbreak into riots and violence, simply were not acknowledged by us until too late? What have we been doing, that our nation can become involved in the wrong war at the wrong time in the wrong place, and we church people engage in only pitifully feeble protests of a foreign policy that is killing thousands of Americans and hundreds of thousands of Asians in an exercise of demonic futility? Do not let anyone say that civil rights and Vietnam are political rather than theological issues—they are both, but they are fundamentally human issues, which means that they are also fundamentally theological issues, for any issue that involves the life and death of the children of God is a theological issue, whether the proper theological formulations are pronounced or not.

III. *A sampling of problems*

What I am saying is that if modern ecumenical history demonstrates that Christians are now beginning to attack contemporary problems together, modern world history demonstrates that the kinds of problems we must now attack together are problems like civil rights and Vietnam. (Perhaps the problem of poverty is the overall problem that encompasses them both.) This raises baffling predicaments for many churchmen. Let me cite four of them, and indicate how it seems to me we must begin to face them. Without turning this essay into an essay on Vietnam, let me use Vietnam as a way to illustrate these issues—and I remind you in advance that I use Vietnam for illustrative purposes, so that even if you disagree with my analysis there, you will not use that pretext to evade the overall point I wish to make.

The period of recent Church history by which I am most instructed in facing the task of the Church in the late '60s in America is the period of the early '30s in Germany. The German Church, Catholic and Protestant, faced the rise of a monstrous evil, Naziism, and was unable to speak an effective word against it, or do an effective deed to counter it. Either because it felt that politics was not its business (part of the legacy of a Lutheran 'two-realms' doctrine of Church and state) or because it kept waiting for the 'right' moment to speak and act (part of the legacy of a Catholic heritage that over-emphasized the virtue of prudence), the time passed when the Church could speak and act. There was left to it nothing but the individual voice from the prison cell. The voice from the prison cell counts—perhaps it speaks to us across three decades more powerfully than it did contemporaneously—but it comes too late to affect the immediate situation, which in this case was the build-up of Hitler's demonic power, the systematic slaughter of six million Jews, and the death in warfare of many more millions.

And my great fear today is that those looking back at the Churches in the late sixties will pronounce upon them the same indictment pronounced upon the Church in the early thirties— 'too little and too late'. Let me therefore single out four kinds of problems that usually inhibit us from acting ecumenically in the secular arena and attempt to speak to them.

1. There are those who say that the issues are too complex for the Church to be able to speak. Some issues are morally clearcut, we are told, but other issues, such as Vietnam, are perplexing and ambiguous, demanding a degree of political, historical and military expertise the Church cannot claim to have.

But recognizing the complexity and ambiguity of a problem will simply not get us off the hook. Every social issue is complex, full of implications we may not have grasped. To favor a minimum wage for migrant farm workers may be a matter of simple justice, but it does indeed jeopardize the profits of the owners of the farms on which the migrants work. To vote for any candidate for public office is to support policies of the candidate of which one does not approve, as well as supporting the policies of which one does approve.

But there is nevertheless a point to the complaint, and the point is that churchmen must never let piety go bail for expertise. In this much advertised 'age of the laity', we must call upon our laity who are experts in Southeast Asia, or Sino-Russian relations, or international diplomacy, and learn from them. We must not presume to a political or military expertise we do not possess. But even a decent humility in the face of the immensity of the problem does not permit uninvolvement—silence is merely complicity with existing policy. The Church need not say everything, but it can say some things, and say them well. One example: a little over a year ago our government was loudly proclaiming that we would not bomb the civilian areas of Hanoi; whatever civilian targets we hit were 'regrettable mistakes'. But now we appear to be hitting such targets openly, without apology, as a matter of 'military necessity'. Hanoi aside, we bomb, strafe, napalm and bulldoze whole towns and villages, utterly destroying them, also as a matter of 'military necessity'. Can such things go unchallenged by the Church? Father John Sheerin has pointed out that our daily military actions are almost perfectly described in the Vatican Council document on *The Church and the World Today*:

> Any act of war aimed indiscriminately at the destruction of entire cities or of extensive areas along with their populations is a crime against God and man himself. It merits unequivocal and unhesitating condemnation (article 80).

Splendid. But where is the 'unequivocal and unhesitating condemnation' that should be on the lips of every churchman today? If, in solemn Council, we are willing to speak strongly, but then not apply such speech to particular situations, it would be better not to have spoken at all.

As far as the danger of making wrong judgments is concerned, we can be sure in this secular day and age that if churchmen make mistakes they will be so informed by their fellow-men. I speak from the vantage point of considerable personal experience that the day when clerical statements had sanctuary from critical dissection has passed. What is called for, in this situation, is not reserve and timidity, but a certain daring and even brashness. A statement by Karl Barth in the last volume of his *Church Dogmatics* might well be the charter for such a day: 'Better something doubtful or over-bold, and therefore in need of correction and forgiveness, than nothing at all.'[1] Let us get past thinking that our political pro-nouncements have to be infallible truths. Such a criterion is an almost certain guarantee of silence—the papacy, after all, has exercised this privilege only once in ninety-seven years, but has been quite willing to risk opinions on a variety of other issues, including statements about Vietnam that are far ahead of all the American bishops with the possible exception, *mirabile dictu*, of Fulton Sheen. So let us do our homework, on Vietnam or whatever, and not let complexity become a device for avoiding involvement at risk.

2. A second problem involves the degree of specificity we should give to our statements or actions. Can we advocate specific programs, specific actions, specific candidates? Doing so involves many risks, not all of them wise. The great danger is creating the impression that a given policy or candidate is the 'Christian' one, and that others are by the rules of logic anti-Christian, or at least sub-Christian. There is a great danger in claiming too much for our insights, illustrated by the remark of the great Missouri theologian, Harry S Truman, that American foreign policy during his administration was based squarely on the Sermon on the Mount. What I am pleading for is considerably to the right of such a claim, but it is also considerably to the left of those who would permit us only to utter platitudes. Our danger is more from platitudes than from particularities.

Let me illustrate once again in terms of Vietnam. I write as one who has had his knuckles rapped a number of times by his fellow Christians. I have felt for many months that we cannot discharge the prophetic duty simply by saying earnestly that we are for peace in Vietnam, or that the love commandment should be implemented

[1] *Church Dogmatics*, IV/3, part 2, p. 780.

in Southeast Asia. I have advocated that the Churches, as Churches, must *at least* back such proposals as U Thant's Three Points—cessation of the bombing of the North, de-escalation elsewhere, recognition of the Vietcong at the negotiation table. In a book recently published in conjunction with a Catholic lay theologian and a Jewish rabbi (by which format we were trying to demonstrate the need for secular involvement in *ecumenical terms*) I repeated these and other suggestions, such as greater use of international agencies to initiate negotiations, and made some less than cordial remarks about Mr Johnson, Mr Rusk and Mr Humphrey. My good friend, Msgr George Higgins, who knows more about the Church and social action than I ever will, faulted my portion of the book, however, on the grounds that I was too specific. While sharing many of my concerns about the war, he did not feel the Chruches should so unqualifiedly back certain political actions designed to bring the struggle to a conclusion. Similarly, in sharing a platform with Father John S Cronin in Washington, I discovered that he agreed that the Churches should urge our country to find ways of ending the war, but disagreed that we had any right to recommend a bombing pause as a way to achieve this end.

Now it may be that to stop bombing the North (and to do so unconditionally, as I would further argue) is not the way to persuade Hanoi that we wish to negotiate. But it might be; certainly our two years of gradually escalated bombing have not achieved such an objective. To propose a specific alternative is at least to call upon the policy-makers to justify their contention that the opposite course will bring about what we all desire, an end to the war. Nothing in the public debate thus far, I must insist, has persuaded me that the government's response to the suggestion is adequate. In such a situation, I would further insist that rather than being silent, the Churches should become more vocal than ever, forcing the *experts* to constant scrutiny of our policy. And when we discover, as we have, that the experts themselves do not agree, and that most Asian experts, as a matter of fact, feel the bombing policy is wrong, we have an even greater responsibility to keep such issues alive and on the conscience of our nation.

3. A third problem is a tactical as well as a theological one. To what degree do we make common cause, in the public arena, with those whose presuppositions we do not accept? The old fear was always that to espouse anything to the left meant being manipulated by the Communists. (In California at least there is a new fear that if you espouse anything at all you will be manipulated by the Birchers.) But let us not surrender too quickly. We need not be embarrassed if some of the convictions of Christian faith are shared by Marxists. To be for social justice is not wrong just because people with beards are also its champions. Opposition to Vietnam is not evil because others couple their oppositions with disenchantment over the procedures and traditions of Western democratic culture.

Let me illustrate concretely. I was asked (by the editor of *Ramparts*, if truth be told) to speak at the April 1967 Mobilization Against the War in Vietnam. It was clear that the planning for the mobilization was in the hands of what would be called the far left, that anybody could appear under whatever presuppositions appealed to him, provided he was against the war, that Vietcong flags would be flying, and that almost all of the Church groups had officially foresworn support. I was engaged at the time in a pretty intensive tour of speaking and writing on Vietnam, aimed at the middle class, which is where I figured the votes and the power were. So I declined the invitation, fearing that I would become 'tainted' by such an appearance, and would be written off by those I most wanted to reach, as a tool or pawn of the left. But the more I reflected, the more it seemed to me that this was a very superior, condescending and even snotty attitude to take, so a couple of weeks before Mobilization I changed my mind and did appear on the program. And while there were a couple of speeches that made me cringe, by and large the affair (regardless of what the mass media did to it) was an amazing display of concern, outrage and moral protest, 62,000 strong—in which the Churches were virtually unrepresented. The absence that day of the religious community was a very conspicuous absence since all other segments of the community—doctors, union officials, public entertainers, professors, whatever—were present. But we church-men had been afraid to sully ourselves by contact with those outside our ranks. We insisted on a privilege one doesn't get—the privilege of fighting on a battleground solely of our own choosing.

I hope the religious bodies of San Francisco learned a lesson from that day. I think I did. It is that we must not be so concerned about our own purity that we forget about human need. If Pope Paul and the Vatican Council address their concerns to 'all men of good will', we had better be willing to associate with such people and make common cause with them.

So I am not very much afraid of the Church getting contaminated by too great a degree of involvement with those who work for social justice from presuppositions different from its own. I am much more afraid of the Church trying to stay so pure that it becomes irrelevant.

4. The final complaint against Church involvement in the secular arena that I shall mention goes: 'But if we take a stand, we'll divide our membership.' The statement is true. We will. But the question is whether this is such a bad thing. I am persuaded that people are going to leave the Church in droves in the next decade or two, and that they are going to do so for one of two reasons: either (a) because the Church takes too clear a stand on social issues and they disagree with that stand, or (b) because the Church doesn't take a stand on anything and they figure it's not worth bothering with. I'd much prefer to be caught on the initial horn of that dilemma. The question is not, 'Can we avoid offending people?' but rather, 'Can we relate the offense of the Gospel to the contemporary scene?'

It seems to me inconceivable that in the name of the Christian Gospel our Churches could condone a public policy stating that we must achieve a military victory in Vietnam at any cost, even if it means risking the involvement of China and thus triggering World War III, the direction in which our present policy seems irretrievably to be taking us. And if we cannot condone such a policy, then we must oppose it, however unhappy that fact makes some churchmen.

And if there is going to be too much institutional lethargy for us to move as far as Pope Paul or the Geneva Conference would like us to move in opposition to Vietnam, and if the kind of corporate voice and action we need are simply not, sociologically or tactically, going to be available to us, then at the very least the Church must give massive support to those within its ranks who are constrained to move beyond the present ecclesiastical consensus. There is a witness of conscience that many individuals within our fellowship feel constrained to make about civil rights or Vietnam, based on the attitude of that old ex-Augustinian monk who said, 'Here I stand, I can do no other, God help me.' The witness is not only for the sake of conscience, but also for the sake of the Church, offered in an effort to move it from timidity to venturesomeness. There are some who feel about this war, in the words of Fr Régamey,

> The setting in motion of certain causes inevitably begetting others sometimes leads so clearly to such excesses that modern man must prepare himself at some point to make this stand, just as the martyrs of the early centuries had to be prepared for martyrdom. There must be downright refusals, no more talk. One has to oppose evil, even if one cannot prevent it; *the time will come when one will have to choose to be a victim rather than an accomplice.*[1]

That time always comes sooner for individuals within the Church than for the Church itself, and yet it seems to me quite conceivable that Vietnam is forcing such a choice even upon the institution. And we always run a danger of being institutionally insensitive to those prophetic spirits within our midst who summon us to higher degrees of commitment and risk than we might otherwise be prepared collectively to take.

IV. *Conclusion: the need for risk*

What I plead for, therefore, in conclusion, is the willingness of the Church in our day to take immense risks in the arena of involvement in the secular order. Let us be prepared to fail a few

[1] *Non-Violence and the Christian Conscience*, (New York: Herder and Herder, 1966), cf. pp. 434-6.

times, if only that we may learn by those failures how not to fail the next time, if only that we may persuade the suffering race of men that we desire to stand at their side, sharing their burdens, working on their behalf, bearing their cross.

If the Church is to err in our day, let it err on the side of over-involvement rather than under-involvement. Let it be specific rather than general, making mistakes of commission rather than of omission. Let it be too far to the left rather than too far to the right, or (as is its usual posture) comfortably and complacently in the middle. Let it be too radical rather than too conservative. Let it spend itself now for a bleeding and bent world, rather than conserving itself for a future it may never have. Let it, finally, trust not in its own wisdom, much as it must employ its own wisdom, but let it trust rather in the resource of the divine wisdom that can overrule human folly, even ecclesiastical folly, for its own ends. Let it trust not in its own power, but in the grace of God, who can turn our weakness into his strength, and out of our faltering footsteps erect a clearer highway for the pilgrims who follow us.

The Church and the Black Man

DENNIS CLARK

Within the mass society that we inhabit there are profound streams of discontent that, though virulent, remain mostly sub-terranean. In a delicately balanced technical culture these currents of social disaffection represent a mordant threat to all our pre-tensions of order and ethics. Like dormant diseases they lie beneath life's surface, full of deadly epidemic potential. One of the most dreadful of these streams, one that forms vast reservoirs of rage and confused bitterness, is the racism that bathes the root structure of American life.

In recent years this deep confluence of tradition, tragedy and contradiction has burst forth to cause urban disorder and political tremors. This has only been the latest in a long sequence of erup-tions that have been occasioned in our nation's life by the heritage of racism.

It is difficult for Americans to comprehend the horror that these eruptions inspire among those who cannot comprehend the twisted background out of which they emerge. In a broad sense, the continuation of racial cleavage in American society negates the ideals on which that society is founded. This is a truism. But, if we view the future as well as the past, the implications are even more harrowing. Not only has our own democratic tradition been com-promised, but because of the demographic proportions of our society and the dynamics of exploitation within it, no reasonable observer can look forward to the dissolution of racial antagonism among Americans in this century.

Negroes, being only a tenth of the population, do not have the political leverage to lift the burden from their backs. Indeed, ideologically, the younger Negro leadership recognizes this and is campaigning for a segregated black power sub-system. The persistence of the racial iniquity among us may be even more fateful than we dream, for the turbulent emerging societies of three continents are overwhelmingly composed of peoples of color, and the antagonism bred by American racism could portend a racial alienation of the United States that would threaten the desperately needed international peace that is such a precious talisman in the shivering nuclear age.

It would be simplistic to infer that the social enigma of racism could be dissipated by moral leadership alone. The problem is too complex to sustain such a view. Yet, the quotient of moral leadership in American life does have something to do with the way in which racism is regarded and how we have responded to it.

It would similarly be a delusion to believe that moral leadership can be equated with organized religion. It can be safely asserted, however, that religion has had an historic connection with the course of American racism. For those interested both in the history of the moral tragedy of racism and the evolution of American religion this connection bears careful study. The United States has been a nation in which our institutions, our aspirations and our social reform movements have been strongly influenced by religious factors. My concern, here, is with the Roman Catholic tradition and its response to race relations.

Racism in America was, at least in part, a reaction of white European Christians to the trials and difficulties of conquering the New World. Because of the levels of the colonial cultures of the white man and the colored races with which he was interacting in the vast task of exploration and settlement, the white man was unable to coalesce with Negroes and Indians. The alternative that he developed was a policy of alienation and oppression. There were, of course, heroic stands for justice such as those of

Bartolomeo de las Casas and the seventeenth century Jesuits, but these were insufficient to alter or overcome the broader social policies of segregation, exploitation and antagonism fostered by the colonial societies. Organized religion, and especially Catholicism, became part of the drama of white domination and non-white subserviance that has characterized American life in both the Anglo-Saxon and Hispanic countries. To understand the relationship of Catholicism to this drama as it was enacted in the United States, it is necessary to look at the phases of the racial problem that the Church confronted at different times.

During the period when slavery was a strong and growing institution, Catholicism in North America was relatively weak. Only in Louisiana was there a Catholic system of enough significance to represent a cultural tradition. Here the Catholics acceded to the slavery practiced in the area. The slaves of Catholic masters were baptized and became an accepted part of the creole culture of Louisiana. The sprinkling of Catholic landholding families in Maryland and other states of the old South similarly accepted slavery as part of the culture of the new nation, but their evangelization of the slaves was more irregular. Thus, in the earliest period, Catholicism did not contradict slavery, but accommodated to it.

As the movement for abolition grew, it gathered ardent adherents among Protestant worthies, many of them children of the stern New England Protestant religious tradition. The Catholic Church of mid-nineteenth century America was beset by a plethora of problems that constrained it from joining the great crusade against the slavocracy. The prejudice, social disorganization and ethnic competition among the huge waves of Catholic immigrants left scant room for Catholic involvement with Protestant leadership, whose enthusiasm for manumission of black men was not matched by any parallel benevolence toward Catholics. Although some lay Catholics asserted abolitionist views, the mass of Catholics held opposite opinions.

In the period following the Civil War emancipation, while a substitute system of exploitation of non-whites was developed in the rural South where most Negroes lived, Catholics grew into the new urban centers that were the mainsprings of national vitality. Since most Negroes lived in the rural South, and most Catholics in the urban North, most Catholics were never directly confronted by them. A time of deepening segregation was ignored by Catholics who were emerging from their own immigrant ghettoes. Catholics did launch a network of missionary enterprises among Negroes and Indians, but these were conducted almost exclusively with intimidated respect for segregation practices. They did not challenge the institutionalized exploitation of American racism. They simply tried to ameliorate the damage where they could.

The latest phase of the American racial experience has seen a dual social development decompose the previous system of rural segregation. This has occurred through the great migration of Negroes to urban areas outside of the South, and the reawakening of the national conscience due to Negro pressure and white humanist educational and legal campaigns. The influx of millions of Negroes into urban areas that has been underway since World War I has at last placed the black man in a position of strategic leverage. Abetted by the opinion of leaders in law, social science and the press, segregation and exploitation have been challenged on a national basis.

The response of Catholicism to this latter phase has been a mixture of pronouncements echoing the secular progress, some token leadership and a general incapacity in the face of the surge of change. Since Negroes did not form a substantial component of the Catholic population itself, the expression of their distress was not a major motive force for Catholic officials. Since the attitude toward social science within Catholicism was skeptical at best, the pioneering studies exposing the gravity of the damage of the segregation system were not accorded early attention. The legal evolution leading to the historic Supreme Court school decision of 1954 was a redefinition of civil rights that caught Catholics, as it did most of the nation, unaware.

Two basic conditions pertaining to American Catholicism help to explain the record of compliance with the native racist tradition. First, the American Catholic Church was a projection and a

D

byproduct of a European Catholicism. The European ecclesiastical structure was antique, legalistic to the point of obscurantism, and chastened into a posture of caution and retrogressive delay. This slow moving ecclesiastical system was reflected in the United States. The approach to a major problem was most often 'when in doubt, refer it to Rome and don't move without an answer'. The contrast between ecclesiastical lethargy and the rapid pace of American development rendered the system intolerable long before the time of John XXIII. Second, the American Catholics had been effectively exiled from public decision-making by the separation of Church and state. Without a tradition of public responsibility such as Protestantism had experienced, the Catholic group found it difficult to criticize public policies. Still unsure of their own position in the social structure, the Catholics hung back from assailing widely accepted institutions. There was no Christian Democratic party or vehicle for them to utilize. On most issues of moment they remained mute. What Daniel Callahan has termed 'religious narcissism' prevailed.

There were, of course, efforts to move Catholics into a creative relationship with non-whites despite segregation. They ranged from the Victorian benevolence of the wealthy Mother Katherine Drexel in founding and endowing a missionary system for Negroes and Indians, to the work of Father John La Farge, SJ, in the promotion of Interracial Councils. The work of Father La Farge at least aimed toward a desegregated society. The missionary endeavors of a variety of religious orders were more frequently patronizing, content with the status quo of Negro inequality and willing to emphasize works of mercy over the need for fundamental conditions of social justice. Such efforts, however, were not able to move even the Catholic population to an active partisanship in behalf of Negro aspirations.

This is all now history. The militance of Negro leaders has at last stripped away the sophistries and excuses. Negro disgust with social and economic exploitation has forced the issue of civil rights and social development into constant prominence since the early 1960's. The animadversions of American Catholicism since

Vatican II have provided the opportunity for some fairly honest self-criticism among Catholics and occasioned some actions that have deviated from the time honored habits of conformity. As early as 1960 a group of Catholics had organized the National Catholic Conference for Interracial Justice to attempt to shake the Catholic structure out of its passive composure. These efforts were mildly successful and at least provided a national network free of the episcopal control that insisted upon dealing with the country-wide issues of racial change on the basis of diocesan balkanization. Catholics were indicted and challenged, however, not by a moral awakening from within, but by the Negro upheaval from without.

The writings of James Baldwin signalled the new era. This gifted, passionate critic with his acid cynicism and bitter contempt for religious pomposity poured scathing invective on the white man's system in his book *The Fire Next Time*. Most Catholics, steeped in pietism and propriety, did not read the book. If they had, they would have sensed the upheaval that was in the offing. The burst of Negro idealism and energy first emerged among Negro students in the South who challenged segregated public facilities and transportation. Paradoxically, despite the disillusionment with religion among Negro activists, Rev. Martin Luther King arose as a remarkable leader of the Southern Negro protest. His religious leadership was possible because the Church structure among Negroes in the South retained a folk quality and a wide adherence, and because of his personal courage. The dramatic march and confrontation at Selma, Alabama, largely under King's leadership, put the South and the nation on notice that the system of coercion and exploitation of black men was under the hammer of a new Negro vitality.

The religious response to the challenge to white power at Selma was one of the most unpredictable and poetic events of recent years. Even the Catholics, for all of their circumspection and the tight control of the movement of their clergy and religious, were caught up by it. Young priests and nuns, older social action priests who remembered the labor struggles of the thirties, and lay people, got on planes and flew to Selma to join that testimony for justice. It was a watershed event. Catholics had defied the prevailing opinion of their group, their superiors and the bishop of a diocese in Alabama to join the Negro protest.

Following this event a new mood gained currency. Dioceses, under the prodding of Catholics in the interracial movement, began looking for opportunities to in some way redeem themselves from their long quiescence in race relations. Bishops spoke out increasingly. Since the major issues of employment, education and housing came to a focus most acutely in the huge ghetto areas of the industrial cities, it was the urban Catholic populations that had to face the racial problem most squarely. The War on Poverty provided a means by which numerous dioceses and Catholic organizations could match their manpower and facilities with public funds to perform needed tasks of education and social service in the ghetto. In some places the intransigence of authority and the incomprehension of Catholic officials contradicted the efforts to place Catholicism in a position of substantial leverage with respect to the future of Negro life. Cardinal McIntyre of Los Angeles became the symbol of the old line clergyman, at a loss to understand the uproar.

The urban Catholics were to be shaken repeatedly in the years after Selma. To the extent that they were prepared to cope with Negro resentment and outbursts at all, the margin of well-disposed people within the Catholic community were prepared to respond within the context of a civil and polite dialog. The work of Catholic schools, charities and opinion leadership was conceived to be constructive and accessible if only Negroes would avail themselves of the Catholic system. Well-disposed Catholics were not prepared to cope with 'Black Power' militancy or violence, and the bulk of the Catholic population was only too ready to use these manifestations as further argument for alienation·and segregation. The outbreak of riots, wild disorder and looting in the Los Angeles area of Watts, in Philadelphia, Cleveland, Rochester, New York, Boston, New Haven and other areas in successive summers prompted fear and foreboding among the Catholics, so predominantly conservative and undemonstrative.

There were various levels of response to Negro militancy and inner city violence among Catholics. In the older, all-white working class areas, often sprinkled with the remnants of ethnic communities, the reaction was both frightened and bitter. These were the nearest neighbors of the ghetto and the prospect of Negro insurgency was terrifying. In the more well-to-do areas, where the majority of Catholics resided as part of the middle class population that stretched out far into the suburbs of the cities, the response ranged from uneasiness or cynicism among liberals to rhetorical wrath and anger among conservatives. Church leaders, to the extent that they commented publicly, urged peace and further pursuit of welfare and poverty programs, improved education and job opportunities. The contention of the Negro militants that the urban power system was corrupt and structurally antithetical to Negroes was not grasped. Catholics were a major element, sometimes the dominant element, in that power system and structure, and they remained unheeding of the scope and intensity of the bitterness against it.

Why were Catholics largely immune or indifferent to the Negro sense of outrage? Why were they indifferent to the need for social reforms that would go beyond the palliatives of the politically hobbled poverty program and the welfare system? The answer appears to be twofold. Vested interest and social distance prevented a significant alliance of Catholic and Negro opinion. The estrangement between Negro and Catholic that had been fostered by slavery, geography and ethnic history could not be bridged, for Catholics were too much a part of the oppressive web of property and practice that stifled the aspirations of the Negro underdogs. In politics the Catholics had long since developed an urban synthesis. The Irish Catholics particularly had conducted themselves with virtuosity in the electoral and legislative arenas. Having attained power, the Irish and Italian Catholic leaders were pragmatic enough to accord patronage and subordinate roles to Negro politicians, but they were not about to give away the entire circus. Thus, Mayor Edward Daley in Chicago and Mayor James Tate in Philadelphia found it immensely useful to have strong Negro components as part of their organizations, but Negro predominance in such cities was not to be conceded until the last push of population and votes dictated it. The Negro population, being segregated residentially and also in terms of social mobility, was not privy to the circles of wealth and power with which the Catholic politicians were allied.

Illustrative of this political problem are two major urban institutions, the police and the public school systems. Both have been prime targets of Negro resentment. The police, long the preserve of strong Irish Catholic influence, have been assailed by both riots and diatribes in the ghettos. To Negroes, the police are easily identifiable symbols of the white domination that has cursed them. The Catholics, politically and often vocationally, still have a deep vested interest in the urban police forces. The public school system similarly represents a vested interest for the Catholics, even where they do not attend it but go to their own parochial schools. The spiralling cost of public education squeezes the dominant Catholic politician. Neither he nor the white urban taxpayers he represents are prepared to make the fiscal investment needed to reconstitute the ghetto schools into the educational power houses they must be to promote Negro social mobility. For decades the public schools have absorbed Negro children, thus diverting the great proportion of them from any approach toward parochial schools. This has permitted a modus vivendi for many Catholics who remain in the inner city areas. They have a stake in preserving the existing de facto school segregation that exists.

The Catholic communities in the urban areas are still functioning on those ideals and attitudes developed prior to the Vatican Council. The Catholic sub-culture is in marked contrast to that of the Negro ghetto. For generations American Catholics were schooled in a rigorous family discipline that imparted to the Catholic family an almost Victorian propriety. This family discipline was added to immigrant family patterns that had been part of strong European peasant traditions. As Daniel Patrick Moynihan among others has pointed out, the Negro family does not share in this tradition of family regulation. The legalism of the

Church and the careful code of Catholic families striving for middle class status has set up a code of family behavior that differs from the crisis arrangements and struggling liaisons that exist in a good portion of the Negro community. The significance of this contrast between buttoned up Catholic family life and the matriarchal and irregular forms of many Negro families should not be under-emphasized. In the areas of child rearing and residential social life, the contrast represents a definite cultural gap. The Catholics recoil from what they perceive as domestic disorder, libertinism and irresponsibility in Negro households. The Negro views the Mass-going, stiff-lipped propriety of Catholic families as smuggery and holier-than-thou posturing.

Thus, the response to the Negro militancy and its attendant disorders has not been courageous communication or a driving parallel initiative on the part of Catholics. It has been, rather, a cowering fear and a recitation of platitudes. This is especially true where the Negro militants have made common cause with the opponents of the Vietnam war. The Negro's perception of the Asian war as an imperialist adventure dragooning disproportionate numbers of black youths to battle an anti-colonial revolution complements the pacifist and other anti-war sentiment. For most Catholics, raised in the tradition of patriot piety represented by Cardinal Spellman of New York, the Negro defection from the holy war ethic is further proof of his social iniquity.

There have been some exceptions to this contemporary picture of institutional impotence and moral embarrassment. They are small enough by comparison, but not without significance in a Church that frequently demonstrates its propensity for ex post facto adulation of good men who have lost the battle to win the war. In the staid city of Milwaukee with its strong German bourgeois Catholic tradition, Father James Groppi has allied himself with Negro militancy in a one man campaign of recompense, example and leadership. Father Groppi has been reviled and calumniated for his troubles, but he has not relented. His insight has lead him to identify wonderfully with the protest psychology of his youthful Negro entourage. Standing against the mayor of his city and the majority of his Catholic confreres, he has made the splendid psychological leap that enables him to identify with the Nation's distraught, racial minority. His unflinching conviction points the way to the kind of partisanship of suffering and passion for justice that is required to compel human understanding in a world where God is hidden.

In Chicago, that city of raw power and immense segregated crudity, there has grown up since the 1930's an active cadre of laymen distinguished by their independence, ability and social action. One of this phalanx is John Andrew McDermott, former Director of the Catholic Interracial Council. Experienced, stubborn and keenly perceptive of social needs, McDermott has weathered many campaigns of opposition and intimidation. He and others have had to withstand intense pressure from highly placed figures in Catholic officialdom to ease their efforts for Negro advancement. These pressures have not been especially secret.

The knowledge of temporizing, vacillating chancery office maneuverings has convinced a collection of Catholics in Chicago and beyond that the only appropriate response is to aim for a true democratization of the Church. The immense resources and power now immobilized by ecclesiastical inertia must simply be taken away from the present possessors and redistributed in more relevant forms. This implies no little bit of institutional wrecking, but what may become known as the 'Chicago formula' is patent. Christian social action requires resources and power now sequestered in an antique structure by a clerical cartel; the resources and power must be obtained for modern and extraordinary measures to meet modern and extraordinary problems; lay people must take the means to fulfill their Christian responsibilities. The prizes in the contest, which is no simple lay-clergy squabble, are leadership, funds, schools and media of communication. The contest has hardly begun, but it is coming. The social problems thrust into prominence by Negro violence and dissent are hastening the contenders toward a confrontation within Catholic circles. The old system of unified fiscal and opinion support for pastoral policies despite their irrelevance will be challenged.

These exceptions to the general Catholic lack of commitment in race relations, however, do not begin to alter the basic condition. The Catholic Church in the US has a weak tradition of social action. As an institution, the movements of the Church are usually far outpaced by the increased tempo of modern events. If the urban Catholics were unable to respond to the need for social reform in strength in the years since World War II, their Negro fellow citizens have displayed a broadening intention to use 'Black Power'. The Catholics are seen as adept at writing long statements in elevated language. When it comes to marshalling funds, talent and serious programs on a significant scale, their efforts become marginal at best.

It is amazing that a Church numbering its adherents in the vicinity of forty million could produce so little resolve, initiative and activity in the vital field of social development in which the future of the Negro and other minorities is at stake. One is at a loss to explain the quietism, submergence and lassitude. Even considering Negro–white immigrant antagonism, the habits of conformity, the tradition of evolutionary reserve and the official restraints, some large scale inventive departure could have been expected. The Catholics were certainly not a notably tractable and uninspired group in the last century in American life. Perhaps this American Church now functions mostly as a defensive refuge, a sanctuary for individualist reaction to the pressures of mass society. By a curious conjunction, the Catholic system seems to operate as a vehicle for the service of those formally enrolled in it on the basis of a Gospel that is essentially evangelical and revolutionary. The paradox, were it not so much a staple of American religion in our time, would be preposterous. To our discredit, we live with it.

The aspirations for reform of Catholicism stemming from Vatican Council II have had several results in the United States. One has been the beginning of controlled changes in worship and administration. These have led to an even greater indulgence in self-serving debates and preoccupations with internal matters. Another has been a gentle sampling of ecumenical discourse.

These developments have been accompanied by a whole series of authoritarian escapades against bold spirits among the clergy who have engaged themselves in social action efforts and various experiments. Priests and nuns intent upon securing justice for Negroes and migrant laborers, others in the peace movement and education, have been officially rebuked and stifled. In 1967 only a stormy solidarity among students and faculty at the Catholic University of America prevented the cavalier dismissal of a mildly controversial priest theologian. These events and the questioning set in motion by the Council have created an extensive loss of equilibrium among Catholics. The old pietism and authority patterns are on the wane, but no comprehensible program of religious endeavor is as yet available. Unless one is forthcoming, the vacuum will be disastrous. Clergy defections are increasing. Antisocial fads are always available to form pernicious substitutes for a strong Catholic program. Pronouncements from Rome will avail little. American Catholics need a program that is tangible, of challenging proportions and related to the realities of American life.

What prospects are there that American Catholics can find the leadership and make the contributions that will stave off further terrorism and social destruction between the races ? The prospects are not good. Granting that the changes induced by Vatican II will bring about flexibility and a more animated Catholic response to social issues, the Catholics would still be poorly disposed to direct massive blows at racial polarization. First, as a largely white group, they are not likely to experience any fervor over a problem that has persisted as part of the nation's life for generations. For the most part, they do not suffer from the problem in a sensible and immediate way. Second, the race issue is a national one, and the Catholics are unused, and perhaps unequal, to acting on a national basis. The new episcopal conference mechanism may develop programs of national scope, but they are more likely to relate to Catholic vested interests such as parochial schools, Catholic higher education or training for the priesthood than they are to the racial cleavage.

For the Catholic Church to impel some departure in social affairs significant enough to have meaning for American Negroes, the Church has to revolutionize its own tradition. What is required is the projection of a social program that can be popularized among Catholics and others. Catholics have sufficiently worn away their distinctiveness in American life by now, so that it is questionable whether they could be won to any notable program representing radical or simply creative departures. To mean anything to Negroes, such a program would have to argue for a whole new set of conditions for family life, that is, family allowances, fully subsidized housing, a whole new scale of family services on an efficient basis. The amortization of the debt owed the nation's poor and its non-white families would have to be broadly financed. To be of significance to the future of Negroes, a creative social program would have to deal with those problems of employment and urban citizenship that are part of the technological system. Vocational development and employment services on a consistent and highly effective basis must be afforded the economic under-class that is victimized by second rate schools, unemployment and the ascendency of technology over the human need for gainful work. The urban worker must be provided with an environment, too, that makes the metropolis not only humanely habitable, but surrounds it with an atmosphere of pride, social concern and opportunity for personal fulfillment.

The Catholic population, despite its flagging morale and lack of a strong popular social action tradition, could conceivably be rallied around such a program. The spirit, the resources, the popular adherence could be developed—with leadership.

Then, the depressing internal squabbles about turning altars around and picketing bishops could be upstaged. Then, a huge potential for national betterment could be mobilized and the flame of sacrifice rekindled. Then American Catholics, presently lacking some grand design and social purpose that touches them deeply, could move into a period of venturesome action.

Catholic Reaction and the Social Conscience

A V KREBS, JR

Racism, nationalism and militarism have been called by Pope Paul VI the three greatest evils in the world today. A significant number of American Catholics, however, have chosen to ignore the Pope's words. Either through rationalization, ignorance, fear of change, or apathy many Catholics simply regard racism, nationalism and militarism as effective means to fight their own home-grown, self-fashioned 'greatest evil'—'the atheistic Communist conspiracy'.

What is taking place in the Church in the United States, therefore, is that a very vocal, in some areas financially powerful, minority is preventing the American Church from seriously accepting the spirit of Vatican II and becoming a prophetic voice in a nation largely going over to affluence and neo-conservatism.

This minority, no more than two to three percent of the Catholic population, has successfully managed in many areas of the nation to mitigate and compromise the Church's social teachings in the midst of racial turmoil and international violence.

In so doing it has succeeded in creating unnecessary reactionism within the institutional Church. Among the laity this reactionism has begun to show itself in a distinct anti-clericalism—a type which declares that the clergy is pushing the Church too far and too fast.

These reactionary Catholics have rallied behind different causes in various parts of the country. Whether it's shouting Latin and disrupting a Mass in Detroit, Michigan; throwing bricks and screeching obscenities at open housing marchers in Chicago, Illinois; passing about anonymous and libelous Church-oriented smear sheets in Oklahoma City, Oklahoma; white laity picketing the consecration of a Negro bishop in New Orleans, Louisiana; a Dallas, Texas bishop giving an *imprimatur* to a book which states that President John F Kennedy 'has here collaborated with and allowed propagation of Communism . . .'; or the late Cardinal Francis Spellman of New York proclaiming 'my country, right or wrong',—it is all being done in the name of 'anti-communism'.

A number of historical, educational, theological and sociological factors are to blame for this abnormal growth within the American Church. The fact that some of these factors have been recognized in recent years for what they are—impediments to the spirit of Catholicism—is a source of some optimism.

Catholics in America have until very recently been regarded by their fellow countrymen as second-class citizens. The mass immigration of Catholics from Europe in the nineteenth century produced large ethnic ghettoes in many major US cities. In employment, education and housing these Catholic ethnic groups found much of the same type of discrimination being experienced by today's racial minorities. National Churches were established, parochial schools were built, and in their genuine desire to serve their communities they became overly identified with the neighborhood in which they resided.

Meanwhile the momentum of the modern industrial revolution swept many of these Catholics into a newly-found middle class status. Post World War II America accelerated this social mobility and Catholics quickly found themselves accepted as a permanent part of the social scene. With this recognition, however, came a good number of lingering fears.

Parochial classroom and pulpit education, often in seeking to make beleaguered Catholics 'defenders of the faith' against the onslaughts and temptations of the 'secular world', created a ghetto mentality. Morality was something to do with the sixth and ninth commandment, obedience was portrayed as the primary virtue, love of neighbor became simply an intellectual exercise, charity was institutionalized, knowledge for its own sake was to be regarded as sinful, while the institutional Church—in history, art, and everyday affairs—was described in triumphalistic terms.

During the brick-and-mortar pre-Vatican II days, no one area of Catholic education was so sadly neglected as the study and application of the Church's social teachings. It is ironic that while many American Catholics put great emphasis on the teaching *authority* of the Church they remain ignorant concerning what the Church teaches or in what *manner* it teaches. In the age of super-nationalism, economic-colonialism and Communism recent popes have sought, through the social encyclicals, to give Catholics and all men of good will counsel and guidance in dealing with these major problems. Yet, despite their pleas the first thing that happens to most encyclicals, in the words of Robert Hoyt, editor of *The National Catholic Reporter*, 'is that they get hailed. Next they are interpreted. Then they drop out of sight. . . .'

Catholics who have never been taught the significance of the popes' encyclicals become shocked and dismayed when they learn that the 'mind of the Church' changes occasionally. Some, in ignorance, make no effort to hide their resentment. *National Review* editor William Buckley's famous 'Mater, Si! Magistra, No!' reflects this hostility to an evolutionary Church.

Not all Catholics, of course, who have been victimized by social and educational factors are today outspoken reactionaries. Many have overcome their dogmatized religious training and gone on to enrich their own lives and the life of the Church. Others have rejected the faith of their youth and buried their dead God.

If one's training, however, has been directed exclusively toward the avoidance of sin, and one can see good only in carefully described ways, and has received no moral criteria for determining what is just and unjust, then that person will seek to solve complex problems with simplistic answers. For these Catholics the institutional Church has been for 1900 years the unerrant bastion in all matters secular as well as religious. In the areas of the modern world where man has taken the painful and difficult responsibility for directing his own destiny, Catholics unsure of their own role have reacted negatively. The Roman Catholic Church in America throughout its history has tended to encourage this type of behavior with repeated references in the Catholic press and from the pulpit to 'secular influences' in public education, the mass communications media, the entertainment industry, art, etc. By fostering this ghetto mentality the Church becomes easy prey for those who seek to discredit social institutions on political grounds.

While many Catholics have managed to ignore this facility, their reactionary brothers, seeing what they consider evil, conspiratorial forces at work within contemporary society, seek some means to solve their frustration. By boasting of their 'orthodoxy', 'patriotism', and 'anti-communism' these people reenforce their own concepts of piety and love of country.

It is true, in respect to their anti-communism, that many Catholics, particularly the ethnic classes in the large city ghettoes, have a valid emotional resentment of Communism. But before a person can fully justify the sometimes bizarre, occasionally violent means employed by these American Catholics in the name of 'anti-communism', one should reflect on the words of Rev. Louis J Twomey, SJ, to a Christian Family Movement national convention in 1961:

> How explain why the greatest inroads Communism has made in the Western world are in countries with Catholic backgrounds and traditions? I believe I have an explanation. The Church in those countries has been allowed to take on the image of a Church of the upper classes only. And when radical economic and social reforms, as demanded in the modern social encyclicals, were critically needed, these reforms were most often blocked by the well-circumstanced laity who, in Frank Sheed's words, feared that in the new arrangement their own share would be less.

The phenomenon which began to make it respectable for many American Catholics to be militantly anti-communist came at the same time as they found themselves being swept into the American mainstream in the immediate years after World War II. The phenomenon was a junior Republican US Senator from Wisconsin —Joseph R McCarthy.

McCarthy, a Catholic, came on the American scene just as the nation, emerged victorious as the world's mightiest military power, was beginning to feel the first deep flush of an intense nationalism. Americans soon learned that the scientific and technological age spawned during the war was not to belong exclusively to the United States. Many people were unwilling to accept this challenge and with the occasional rebuff at the cold war conference table they began to grow suspicious and search for simple answers to the complex problems faced by the post-war world community.

Capitalizing on these uncertainties McCarthy rallied a significant segment of Americans behind him; utilizing a 'get-tough policy with subversives', he rapidly became for many 'the champion of Americanism'. His methods and vague charges gave the green light to a band of patriotic organizations to form their own investigating committees and join the Senator's anti-communist crusade.

Catholics in the US quickly seized this opportunity to display their own 'Americanism'. In 1954 just before McCarthy's demise, a Gallup Poll revealed that 58% of American Catholics held a favorable opinion of him and his methods, 23% had an unfavorable opinion, and 19% expressed no opinion. The 58% favorable opinion was 8% above the national average. In an address before the 1964 Catholic Historical Association, Vincent P De Santis, chairman of the Department of History at the University of Notre Dame, pointed out that:

> An examination of a variety of Catholic newspapers and periodicals and letters to the editors for the years 1950 to 1954 reveals a preponderance of Catholic opinion in support of Senator McCarthy and his anti-communist program.

Professor De Santis notes one of Father James Gillis' remarks, whose column in *The Boston Pilot*, official publication of the Archdiocese of Boston, Mass., also appeared in many other diocesan newspapers:

> The significant fact for the Catholic moralist is that McCarthy's view is equivalently that of Christian ethics.

Father Gillis' declaration should not be taken lightly, for many non-Catholics erroneously believed that the cause of McCarthy, so ardently supported by Catholics, was indeed the cause of Catholicism and that the Church sanctioned his methods. Some commentators have noted that McCarthy's Irish Catholicism had symbolic significance for Irish Catholics in America and other ethnic groups who felt a deep resentment toward a 'power elite' dominated by an American Anglo-Saxon mentality.

It should be remembered that throughout McCarthy's political career a latent anti-communism was abroad in the land, and by no means confined to Catholics. McCarthy recognized and effectively utilized this anti-communism as a political vehicle during his public career. Even after his censure by his senatorial colleagues, anti-communism remained an attitude deeply rooted in post-war America.

It was in 1958 that the John Birch Society first began under the directorship of its founder, Robert Welch of Belmont, Mass. Catholics were immediately attracted to the character of the new organization—anti-communist, authoritarian and, like their own Church, basically suspect of democratic institutions. In some areas of the nation, Catholics were encouraged to join the John Birch Society by their pastors and other clergy.

Rev. Edward J Cleary, pastor of St Paul's Catholic Church in Whitehaven, Tenn. (the largest in the Diocese of Nashville), recommended to his parishioners that the John Birch Society was 'a good, pro-American, anti-communist outfit'. The birthplace of the JBS in the midwest was Glenview, Illinois, a suburb north of Chicago, where Rev. John J Dussman, pastor of Our Lady of Perpetual Help, encouraged the formation of the Society in his parish hall. In nearly every issue of his weekly parish bulletin, *The Clarion*, were endorsements for the JBS and other 'Americanist' groups. Parishioners were frequently urged to join community anti-communist 'schools'. In *The Tidings*, official publication of the Archdiocese of Los Angeles, Calif., the Birch Society was warmly praised for its stand against 'communism'.

Much confusion still exists among Catholics as to whether Cardinal Richard Cushing of Boston has or has not endorsed the Birch Society. The confusion stems mainly because of Cushing himself. His on-again, off-again endorsements of Welch and the JBS have been widely publicized in the press. In late 1965, however, Cushing wrote to Welch stating:

> I have yet to find a member of the Society whom I would trust as a result of the way its leaders have used a letter I sent years ago to someone in California in which I paid you a high personal tribute. What a fool I was to put in writing my one time admiration and affection for you.

To the best of anyone's knowledge these were the Cardinal's last words on the subject. It is estimated today that nearly 40% of the membership of the John Birch Society are Roman Catholics.

With the advent of the JBS many other anti-communist organizations began to appear on the American landscape. One such group was Dr Fred C Schwarz's Christian Anti-Communism Crusade. Schwarz traveled acrosss the country giving anti-communism 'seminars' and 'schools'. Besides showing such films as 'Communism on the Map' (a film strip which showed how all the countries of the world were 'red' and that the US was 'pink'), and 'Operation Abolition' (a doctored 'documentary' on the 1960 student demonstrations against the House Un-American Activities Committee hearings in San Francisco), former undercover agents for the Federal Bureau of Investigation and a select group of individuals who had fled Communist countries appeared frequently on the program as 'teachers'. Schwarz, an Australian physican, managed to avoid much of the controversy that surrounded the Birch Society's Welch after Welch called President Dwight D Eisenhower a 'dedicated conscious agent of the Communist conspiracy' and members of the Eisenhower family and administration 'outright Communists'.

The Christian Anti-Communism Crusade was well received by many Catholics throughout the United States. In some areas, such as Los Angeles, Catholic school children were let out of classes so they could attend a nearby crusade 'school'. After one such school in St Louis, Missouri, in 1958 a number of Catholics who attended approached Schwarz about forming 'a joint Protestant-Catholic anti-communism organization'.

Schwarz explained to the group that his 'crusade' was Christian fundamentalist in character. He later wrote that he had urged them to establish their own organization. It was on this advice, purportedly, that the Cardinal Mindszenty Foundation was founded in July 1958, and incorporated the following year. Boasting of membership throughout the United States, the Cardinal Mindszenty Foundation classifies itself as 'an educational organization', its purpose to 'combat Communism with knowledge and facts'.

Through a Foundation-recommended do-it-yourself technique, by reading prescribed homework, and by tailoring the study outline to the needs of one's particular study group, the Mindszenty Foundation claims the 'well informed or poorly informed' layman will be able to answer the question: 'What can I do to safeguard our Church and country against Communism?'

'Homework' for the CMF centers around the testimony of witnesses before House un-American Affairs Committee and the US Senate Internal Security Subcommittee, plus a 1958 American Bar Association report. The Mindszenty Foundation also distributes *Inside the Communist Conspiracy*, an annotated bibliography. Among those books which

> Americans must read . . . and make available to the many high schools and college students who have been victims of the 'paper curtain' are . . . *McCarthyism: The Fight for America*, by Senator Joseph R McCarthy . . . Read for yourself the names of the Communist agents McCarthy discovered . . . *Nine Men Against America*, by Rosalie M Gordon . . . The story of the Warren Court and of the special privileges it has given to pro-Communists . . . *The Case of General Edwin A. Walker*, by Kent and Phoebe Courtney . . . How the firing of a patriot was part of an organized smear campaign . . . .

The founder of the Cardinal Mindszenty Foundation was

Rev. Stephen C Dunker, CM. Father Dunker explained that the name of the organization was chosen because 'it sounds Catholic and it sounds anti-communist'. In July 1961, apparently acting on the advice of ecclesiastical superiors, Father Dunker withdrew as director of the organization to devote his energies to the foreign missions.

One of the Mindszenty Foundation's leading supporters is Patrick J Frawley, head of Schick Safety Razor Company and Technicolor, Inc. Also a financial contributor to Schwarz's Christian Anti-Communism Crusade, Frawley gave at least $10,000 to the Mindszenty Foundation in 1962. The middle-age business executive is probably the number one angel of the Catholic far right movement in the United States.

During the 1964 election campaign Frawley sent forty thousand copies of Phyllis Schlafly's book *A Choice Not an Echo* (a book advocating the election of Senator Barry Goldwater to the presidency of the US) to Catholic priests throughout the nation. In a covering letter he wrote,

> I am convinced that how we Catholics vote on November 3 will decide not only the future of America but also the future of 500 million Catholics and of the whole free world . . . .

The Wall Street Journal has quoted Frawley as saying he gives away his annual income of 'several hundred thousand dollars' to numerous right-wing organizations in the United States. Schick Safety Razor Co. also advertises in a variety of conservative, right-wing publications, particularly in the Catholic press. In additions to Buckley's *National Review*, Schick advertises in *The Wanderer*, a lay Catholic weekly published in St Paul, Minn., which is unparalleled in the Catholic press for its conservative, reactionary approach to world events and life within the Church. Schick and Technicolor also are the principal advertisers in *Triumph*, a new national Catholic monthly, which describes itself as

> the magazine which does not hesitate to assert the measure of a manly Catholicism, as a willingness to be counted as a defender of the venerable traditions of the Church, to champion un-

apologetically the truth she uniquely opposes to the secularist onslaughts of the age.

The two companies also advertise regularly in *The Brooklyn Tablet*, official publication of the Diocese of Brooklyn, NY, and *The Tidings*. These two publications, which reach over 250,000 Catholic families a week, have been described as 'organs of the radical right'.

Schick recently announced that it will invest over $500,000 to finance *Twin Circle—National Catholic Press*, the recently inaugurated weekly. Spokesmen for the paper have stated that *Twin Circle* will help fight 'the rebirth of the era of modernism in certain Catholic circles'.

A key figure in this new publishing venture is Rev. Daniel J Lyons, SJ, prominent in a number of American religious and political ultra-conservative groups. Father Lyons has also written extensively in the Catholic press on American involvement in Vietnam. ('I oppose any kind of negotiations with the Vietcong. Any war should end up with negotiations, but the negotiations must be based on the fact that the other side is willing to admit defeat.')

While organizations like the John Birch Society, the Christian Anti-Communism Crusade, and the Cardinal Mindszenty Foundation appeal to the Catholic *nouveau riche* or those socially-mobile Catholics who have become solid middle-class American citizens, Catholics on the local level also have initiated activities to combat communism in their communities and Churches.

It is here where small reactionary groups have made significant impressions on the institutional Church, and in many instances impeded the post-Vatican II spirit. Through small front organizations, publications, and control of parish and diocesan groups these Catholics have helped to create deep division within their communities. Sometimes they are organized around a specific issue or personality and their longevity is usually measured by how much controversy they can cause and sustain. Often those that join these groups will soon leave and later form another group. Always, no matter how short their existence, these groups manage to leave a social scar.

Another far right Catholic-led organization is *Paul Revere Associated Yeomen, Inc.* (PRAY, Inc.). Founded by a sixty year old semi-retired New Orleans businessman, H S Riecke, Jr, PRAY, Inc. is essentially a one man operation even though it claimed in 1965 to have members in thirty-nine states and three foreign countries. Riecke, a Catholic, draws support mainly from fellow Catholics in the deep South and far West. In a 1964 series of newsletters (mailed in envelopes printed with quotes from Herbert Hoover, Lord Beaverbrook, Benjamin Franklin and Thomas Jefferson), PRAY, Inc. worked hard to get Barry Goldwater elected President. Immediately after Goldwater's nomination a PRAY newsletter declared:

GOLDWATER *MUST* WIN IN NOVEMBER! IT IS IMPERATIVE! He is 'The Man of Destiny'; born on New Years Day for a New Era; actually nominated by Los Angeles— 'The City of the Angels', to battle the Synagogue of Satan—the Hordes of Hell! This, truly, is the BATTLE OF ARMA-GEDDON—predicted in the Bible—wherein God and Christ will watch to see WHO is for good, and WHO is for evil; to separate the wheat from the chaff. The 'chaff', He said, 'will burn in the Fire!'

PRAY, Inc. has never completely spelled out exactly what its philosophy is except 'to wake up Americans' and to 'remain—as ever—for patriotism, Nationalism and "Constitutional Government" '. Riecke claims he mails out between eight and ten thousand pieces of 'anti-red' literature every week.

Predictably after incumbent Lyndon B Johnson's landslide defeat of Goldwater, PRAY, Inc. not only explained the Arizona Republican's defeat but enumerated to members what 1965's main tasks were. Riecke said of Goldwater's defeat:

LBJ won because he received the SYMPATHETIC-EMOTIONAL-BACKLASH vote. He won the election the day Pres. Kennedy was assassinated by a MARXIST-ZIONIST-

KHAZAR *COMMUNIST*! Americans were 'grateful' that LBJ was there to take over the reins of government during chaos. But now OUR greatest asset will be the reckless, arrogant enactment of 'America-Be-Damned' SOCIALISTIC legislation. This will SHOCK 20 million disillusioned Americans to their senses! It will do OUR job for us!

He urged PRAY, Inc. members immediately and actively to support a plan for the fifty states to legally take over the federal government; join the National Rifle Association; purchase shot guns, large supplies of buckshot, high powered rifles, and pistols; not to surrender their arms to anyone; join the 'Minutemen' (a paramilitary right wing organization) and the White Citizens Councils while learning the location and headquarters of the nearest Klu Klux Klan unit. In 1965 Riecke joined others, including the South Louisiana Citizens' Council and the Greater New Orleans Citizens' Council, to create a furor over the appearance of Walter Reuther, President of the United Auto Workers (AFL-CIO), as a graduation commencement speaker at St Mary's Dominican College in the city.

(Father Twomey, director of Loyola University's Institute of Human Relations in New Orleans, has observed that if all the Catholics were to withdraw from the White Citizens' Councils in that area, the organization would collapse.)

Reuther spoke at the woman's college without incident principally because of the determination of Sister Mary Louise, OP, president of the college, not to be intimidated by harassing phone calls and letters. Riecke, whose daughter had attended the college, stated in one of his letters to the school:

The 'CRUCIFIED' man on the RIGHT side of Christ was promised Paradise; but what happened to the one on His extreme LEFT, who chided Him?! WALTER REUTHER is an extreme leftist—a self-acknowledged ATHEIST—another such unbeliever in Christ or God!

From its initial venture into the public spotlight *Catholic Freedoms Foundation* appeared destined to become *the* Catholic anti-communist organization in the United States. A statement mailed from the Foundation's Grand Central Station, New York post office box headquarters was circulated in 1965 throughout the nation for written endorsements by Catholic clergy, laymen and others. The statement read:

> We, the undersigned, are firmly convinced that the Kremlin's triumphing strategy (now in advanced stages of development) for our nation's defeat is:
> 'Encirclement + Infiltration + Subversion + Demoralization = Capture!'
> We are convinced that if domestic Communists (so powerfully assisted by American fellow travelers, pseudo-liberals, opportunists and dupes) continue as little exposed and opposed as heretofore, THE UNITED STATES OF AMERICA will inevitably fall into the hands of the USSR—without a bomb dropped!

As of 30 September 1965, 111 Catholic bishops, 37 abbots, 91 Congressmen, 12 Senators, 313 retired Generals and Admirals, and 300 other 'outstanding citizens' had become signatories to this statement.

The National Catholic Reporter, attempting to verify the endorsements of the bishops, reported in December 1965 that four of the five bishops they had interviewed had denied signing the statement and the other 'doubted' if he had. After this story appeared James W Crockett, executive director of the Catholic Freedom Foundation, produced photostatic copies of the statement bearing the apparent signatures of those listed in the *NCR* story.

Among some of the people who signed the petition were: Everett M Dirksen, US Senate Minority Leader; Father Dussman; Bishop Thomas K Gorman of Dallas, Texas; ex-senator Goldwater; Rev. Billy James Hargis, leader of the fundamentalist, anti-communist Christian Crusade; Salt Lake City, Utah Mayor J Bracken Lee; Rev. Carl McIntire, fundamentalist preacher from New Jersey, who until recently considered the nation's number one enemy as being the Roman Catholic Church (who plans to 'sell her secret confessional system for political power'); California Governor Ronald Reagan; Major Gen. Edwin A Walker, and Robert Welch.

A lack of solid financial support, however, made it impossible for the Catholic Freedom Foundation to follow up on their petition 'coup'. The Foundation has listed itself on its letterhead as

> a national organization to sound the alert to the deadliness of the International Communist conspiracy, and to promote a crusade of prayer, penance, reparation, and apostolic, patriotic and anti-subversive action for the preservation of the United States of America—in the natural order, the hope of Western Civilization and of the Church Militant.

The organization's patroness was Our Lady of Victory.

Bishop Blaise S Kurz, OFM, a missionary expelled from China, who had Father Gommar DePauw, founder of the Catholic Traditionalist Movement, as his *peritus* during Vatican II, was listed initially as the Foundation's spiritual advisor. Kurz later became Bishop-Moderator of DePauw's Traditionalist movement. The Foundation also listed a thirty-three man executive board included among others: Rev. Francis E Fenton of Bridgeport, Conn., the only priest on the John Birch Society's national governing board; Father Dunker; Matt Cvetic, a former FBI undercover agent in the Communist Party; and two Monsignors, both former chief of chaplains US Navy and US Army.

In addition to running their widely circulated statement as advertisements in newspapers from coast to coast the only other major activity the Foundation attempted was to ask Catholic artists to prepare posters dramatizing the evils of Communism. They suggested as suitable themes:

> Red soldiers lined up (some with tunics removed), leering at a group of attractive young women being held for their choice (a nun among them) . . . and possibly a screaming woman being dragged by a bestial soldier into an empty room.

Warren King, evidently moved by this suggestion, drew a poster which the Foundation later circulated throughout the country as a promotional piece showing a number of people, hands tied behind their back, being shot by a laughing soldier with a Russian flag in his other hand. As vultures circle overhead, a priest and a nun yet to be shot have their eyes closed in prayer. The words 'It Can Happen Here' appears in the upper left-hand corner of the poster.

Founded in Pasadena, California, in 1960, the *Christian Resistance Movement* is a non-profit corporation open to all faiths

> devoted to forming resistance to Atheistic Communism mainly through the formation and correlation of discussion groups spontaneously evolved from a 'grass roots' experiment.

An early project of the Resistance was a four page printed attack on *Communism: Threat to Freedom*, an eighty page book by Rev. John Cronin, SS, published by the National Catholic Welfare Conference. In his book Father Cronin asserts that the 'basic threat' of communism to the US is external and not internal.

Christian Resistance disagreed with this conclusion in their attack and accused Father Cronin of compounding confusion on the Communist issue and using half-truths and 'downright errors'. In 1962 *The Tidings*, in repeating Christian Resistance's arguments, published a black-bordered front page box stating that Father Cronin's book was *not* the mind of the Church and did not represent *The Tidings* viewpoint.

The Movement placed key emphasis on being 'informed, instructed and organized'. To enable the 'inexperienced person to lead autonomous discussion groups', it published a *Discussion Group Leaders Manual*. Advising Resistance discussion leaders 'under no circumstances' to accept as members persons who wished to debate the subject of Communism, the *Manual* suggested a few proper names for each discussion group:

> Better not to have a name like 'Mrs Jones Group;' instead, the name of your sponsor, as 'St Andrew's Group' or, if none, select such a meaningful name as 'George Washington Group', or 'Bishop Ford Group', 'Katyn Forest Group', 'Cuba, Si—Communist, No Group'.

Publications commended for regular reading were *The Wanderer*; *The Brooklyn Tablet*; *National Review*; *American Opinion*, a monthly magazine published by the John Birch Society, and the literature of a number of lesser, well-known 'patriotic' groups.

Following the lead of the Cardinal Mindszenty Foundation and other Catholic right-wing organizations, the *only* papal encyclical usually recommended by Christian Resistance is Pius XI's *Divini Redemptoris* (*On Atheistic Communism*).

'The most valuable single periodical,' the *Manual* continues, 'and one of the best sources of anti-communist news and opinion in the United States, is *The Tidings.* . . .' Opinion pieces, ads, and meeting notices of many Los Angeles 'anti-communist' groups appear regularly in *The Tidings.*

> A panel discussion on 'Battle Techniques for the Church Militant' will be presented by the Fullerton Affiliate of the Cardinal Mindszenty Foundation at the Jolly Roger Inn. . . .
>   The Truth Shall Make You Free! READ! GIVE! *THE RED FLOOD* 56 Concise Fact Filled Pages—50¢. 'Did you know that Marx and Engels wrote political commentary for the *N.Y. Tribune* for 19 years?' . . . Write Christian Resistance.

Following Dr Schwarz's most financially successful Crusade seminar in 1961 in Los Angeles ($311,263), *The Tidings* published a four page tabloid supplement, three pages of it being an essay 'Our Moral Obligation to Oppose Communism' by Rev. Cletus J Healy, SJ. Father Healy is the moderator of the Political Science Club at Marquette University High School in Milwaukee, Wisconsin, which publishes the monthly *The Truth About Communism* ('To publicize THE TRUTH that frees . . . to expose THE ERROR that enslaves.')

With *The Tidings* masthead, the Los Angeles' paper's supplement was sponsored by the Durand Door Supply Inc. and Metro Hardware Co. and was published as a 'public service'. Gilbert Durand, owner of the two hardware companies and the major contributor to the Christian Resistance Movement, is well-known in Southern California for his support of 'all those promoting patriotism, the free enterprise system, and all those fighting Communism'. The back page of the supplement urged readers to join the 'excellent and economical program' offered by

Christian Resistance. 'Pro-American' and 'anti-communist' book stores which have flourished in the Los Angeles area in the 1960's, among others the Pro-Blue Book Store, The Betsy Ross Book Shop, and the Minuteman, were also listed. In addition, an 'important' method of fighting Communism recommended by the supplement was to join the Network of Patriotic Letter Writers. Suggested by Robert Welch in his *Blue Book*, this group circulated for a number of years petitions calling for the impeachment of US Supreme Court Chief Justice Earl Warren. The Network also seeks to 'alert various congregations to the danger of infiltration by the Red-fronting National Council of Churches'.

Through frequent publicity in the diocesan press and other Catholic publications the above and several hundred other often ephemeral groups carry a degree of influence wholly disproportionate to their size. No one element in the institutional Church is more responsible for the growth of these organizations and the promulgation of their bizarre ideas than the diocesan press.

Some examples of the things Catholics often see in their diocesan press in this regard are: two letters to the editor in *The Catholic Northwest Progress* defending the Klu Klux Klan; an editorial cartoon in *The Brooklyn Tablet* showing President Ngo dinh Diem of South Vietnam and Cuba's Premier Fidel Castro with the former saying, 'I lost my job through *The New York Times*' and the latter saying, 'I got my job through *The New York Times*'; a headline in *The Monitor* of San Francisco reading, 'Cardinal Urges "Kindness" in Dealing With Commies'; a front page picture of Dean Rusk in New York's *The Catholic News* after Diem's death with the photo caption asking, 'What is Secretary of State Rusk walking away from? The murder of an ally?'; a paid election advertisement for a governatorial candidate in *The Mississippi Register* which states in heavy black type, 'As a fifth generation Mississippian whose grandfather rode with Gen. Forest in the Civil War, I was born and raised a segregationist. I have always defended that position. I defend it now'; and three headlines which appeared on three different pages in the same issue of the Little Rock, Arkansas *The Guardian*, accompanying a long letter from the local bishop, 'Bishop's Lenten Pastoral Reassures "Confused" Catholics', (p. 1), 'Some "New Scholars" Rebuked' (p. 2), and 'Faith, Good Works—Not Knowledge—Bring Salvation' (p. 3).

It is not unusual for pastors to forbid such Catholic magazines as *Commonweal, America, Ave Maria, The Catholic World, US Catholic, WAY/Catholic Viewpoints, The Catholic Worker* or publications like *The National Catholic Reporter* from their churches while at the same time using their own parish bulletins to promote 'anticommunist' literature. For example, these thoughts from pastor Rev. Conrad A Altenbach greeted parishioners one Sunday morning at St Mary's Church in South Milwaukee, Wis.,

> I PLEDGE ALLEGIANCE TO THE FLAG (not the President) OF THE UNITED STATES OF AMERICA (not the United Nations) AND TO THE REPUBLIC (not Democracy) FOR WHICH IT STANDS (not Liberalism) ONE NATION (not world government) UNDER GOD (not atheistic conspirators) INDIVISIBLE (not co-existence) WITH LIBERTY (not unconstitutional control) AND JUSTICE (not dishonesty) FOR ALL (not just for the mighty).

Today in America the Church faces a serious challenge. It is a challenge that bishops, pastors, priests, religious, and laity must face together, as the people of God. Pope John XXIII in one of his earlier, and not so famous, encyclicals, *Princeps Pastorum,* said:

> No Christian community anywhere will ever achieve unity with the Universal Church from which emanates the supernatural life of Jesus Christ, if the local clergy and population succumb to the influence of a particularist spirit, if they arouse enmity in other nations and if they are misled and perturbed by an ultranationalism which can destroy the spirit of universal charity— that charity upon which the Church of God is built and is called 'Catholic'.

It is this particularist spirit which is today spreading throughout the Catholic community in America. We are engaged in a fight between Catholicism and particularism. Victor Ferkiss, associate professor of government at Georgetown University, has said:

The danger is that unless the political religion of right-wing Catholicism is soon exposed, isolated and drastically reduced in influence we will increasingly be faced with the existence—in spirit if not also in the flesh—of two Catholic communities, each with its own press, its own clerical heroes and villains, its own organizations and attitudes toward individual parishes and schools. Political extremism—a force which threatens to destroy the health and unity of American society—could also destroy the health and unity of the Catholic community within that society.

Herein lies the challenge. As I noted at the outset, Catholics in the main have been deprived of developing their social conscience through inadequate education and their own apathy. The challenge, therefore, that the American Church (particularly its bishops, pastors and educators) must accept today is to painstakingly and patiently develop *and* mobilize that social conscience.

The social teachings of the Church cannot be absent from the traditional teachings regarding man's life. Those teachings must be diffused throughout our society. As a priest friend has said,

... the formation of the Christian social conscience is not something that develops in an isolated manner; rather it involves a new vision of the theology of the world as a place in which man seeks out his eternal welfare.

It will only be when American Catholics are willing to abandon their social and political isolationism and totally accept a 'new vision of the theology of the world', which is theirs as followers of Christ, that the Church will rid itself of the particularism which nurtures racism, nationalism and militarism.

Sisters, Celibacy and Community

MARYELLEN MUCKENHIRN, CSC

No longer do we serve in the old way of a written law, but in the new way of the Spirit. (Romans 7:6)

Sheer human reality is rearing its wonderful head in every area of Roman Catholic thought and life style. Nowhere does it emerge in a more heavily fortified bastion than in the religious communities of women.

Suddenly the fact of being a human being seems wildly liberating. Prospects of a vitally Christian and contemporary life shimmer in the distance like an oasis on a hot day in the desert. And perhaps the desert symbolism points to the ambiguity and agony of the present situation for American women religious. The desert, the place of withdrawal from ordinary life, can be chosen for an on-going purpose. Then it becomes a place of conversion and conviction. It can create a new vision and desire to return to the city with a stronger message and a warmer love. Or it can be a depressing and silent wilderness entered by mishap and dwelt in as a refuge from the city.

The freedom that sisters seek is not a freedom from discipline and the past. Rather, it is a freedom for love and growth, for involvement and realistic service of human needs. Religious women know that a negative spirituality and a life form of non-involvement make truly Christian and free life impossible today. Their struggle is for personal openness to the Spirit who alone makes men free. It is also a struggle for involvement in the world where the liberated man must love and suffer.

The complexity of the Roman Catholic Church in any one country, if approached at the level of life experience, is so vast as to defy systematization and sweeping generalization. But there are patterns of historical and cultural development which are discernible. This is particularly true of highly specialized groups within the Church like priests and religious. Their numbers are small by comparison with total Church membership. But more to the point, the ecclesiastical forces which molded the persons now living in these life situations were so externalized and so uniform that it seems possible to offer only a personal perspective on the present state of affairs. The Roman collar and the sister's habit have been socio-cultural signs of Roman Catholic presence in this country for many decades. To this very day, anything done by priests and sisters that seems at variance with the traditional stereotype is not only Catholic but national news. Here I will attempt only one thing: to offer a personal assessment of the present thrust among American sisters dedicated to meaningful adaptation of religious life.

Such an attempt, by so many, presumes a richly diversified factual background. To mention only a few factors: there are approximately 180,000 sisters in traditional types of congregations. Such orders number more than three hundred. They are almost infinitely diverse in secondary details (e.g. habits, customs in daily life pattern, actual local history). Until the last decade, the various congregations had, practically speaking, no contact with each other across organizational lines. Individual orders might number from thirty members to several thousand. Many groups are governed as part of an international organization with headquarters outside the United States and with significantly large foreign-born membership. Others are American in foundation, membership and apostolic involvement. Some orders, even with several thousand members, are localized in one city, while others of less membership are spread all over the country. Some are directly under the local bishop, others directly under the Congregation of Religious in Rome.

Obviously, an assessment of such diversified realities must simply announce a point of view and try to stick to it. My personal option is rather simple. The newly released and openly admitted tensions within Roman Catholicism are part of the worldwide tension between personal and institutional values. Since institutional values outweighed personal values in the post-Trent Church, it is not surprising that we are now in a period of overstressing the personal at the expense of institutional values. Sisters, anthropologists tell us, have played the role of tribal totems, visible reminders of the values and stability of the tribe. The institutional overstress permeated religious life with devastating success. The orders of religious women felt its chilling effects with added impact for all sorts of reasons. Thus the release of personal and human values in the Church since Vatican II is having a drastic effect on women religious. Their turmoil also affects the tribe, since religious women must either personally pull out of the fray, or do their corporate renewal in the public eye.

My option is to try to focus the sisters' present struggles and hopes around a personal pole, celibacy, and a corporate pole, community. To succeed even minimally, some historical and sociological comments must precede these two areas of major focus.

I. *Some historical and sociological background*

Each religious congregation, as a corporate person, has its own unique history. Who founded it, for what purpose, with what beginning membership and precisely in what location? These are unique and essential facts. However, there are two conditions which profoundly mark all American congregations of traditional style of life: they have existed in this country in patterns of European nineteenth century religious customs; they have been almost totally isolated within the Catholic institutional world until the present ferment. Most religious congregations arrived in this country from Europe, either with groups of immigrants or at the request of already established national communities. They came to serve the Catholics of the country, not to influence Americans who

E

were not yet Roman Catholics. This is an important point, for it explains much of the myth and unreality in the general American attitude toward sisters. For over a century sisters lived and worked in Catholic schools and hospitals, *mostly out of touch with the local civic community*. They were largely isolated even from lay Catholics through living in separated convent patterns.

However, to keep the picture somewhat balanced, it must be pointed out that during the first decades of most congregations' growth in the United States, women in general were isolated from civic life, and most religiously and/or nationality structured groups tended to keep within their own cultural confines. But as the role of women changed profoundly during two world wars and on into the present sexual revolution, sisters did not move into the world. Rather, they worked harder and with better professional training within their schools and hospitals. Many of the needed changes among religious women are merely cultural adaptations to the present changed role of women in general in American culture.

It seems important to mention here the Sister Formation Movement of the 1950's, for in many ways it prepared the personnel for the present transformation of religious life in the United States. This movement publicized on a national scale the urgent need for better education of sisters if they were to carry out their tasks in education and hospital service. Both of these fields were swiftly increasing not only in the size of their institutions, but also in the demand for highly trained competence for the various roles to be filled. Most communities took up this challenge with varying degrees of success. By the early 1960's, a core of professionally well-educated sisters existed in most orders. Many had shared with other men and women the rigors of graduate study. They were usually in the younger age group, less attached to the old ways. Most of all, they were open to contemporary life and to the needs of persons in society today. When Vatican II happened, such sisters felt in conscience a call to respond to it by trying with their sisters to discover new forms of religious life, a development urged by the Church's highest authorities.

Thus, every congregation today finds itself polarized between two types of women. One type has sincerely lived the pre-Vatican II style of religious life. The other type believes that the past style must gradually give way to new patterns of dedication which genuinely express the values of modern American Christian women who feel called to a life of communal celibacy. There is nothing at all startling about such a polarity. Its seeming suddenness is due to the previous external immobility which masked existing personal differences in religious congregations. They were like persons on a rubber raft in the swimming pool of a large ocean liner. All can seem secure until one discovers that the entire ship is headed for a typhoon.

In a sense the size of the United States has not really had a perceptible impact one way or the other on the present crisis in religious life. The previous isolation was more profoundly psychological. For example in one large city, there are over one hundred different Roman Catholic congregations of sisters represented. Only in the last three years has there been some intermingling at meetings and city projects. Even so, many of the congregations still do not take part. Some sisters come to the meetings, but stay with and talk only to those of their own group. This is a small thing, but it shows how far the old religious life style has been able to eradicate a typically American quality, the sort of superficial friendliness and talking which mystifies many foreign visitors. In any case, segregated existence has heavily marked American religious life for women. It lies deep at the heart of much resistance to change. It is also at the heart of the fear of moving out of our own institutions and into the institutions of the civic community itself.

At the present moment, sociologists provide some essential insights for coming to grips with the structural problems involved in the sisters' struggle for freedom. Religious congregations fall under all the laws of social change, and are de-mythologizing many aspects of their situation. Discussion techniques, group dynamics, better managerial planning, proper role definitions and competence are just as needed for religious functioning as for other organizational action. Perhaps the areas in which sociologists are most helpful at the moment are those dealing with proper methods of ascertaining personnel assets and weaknesses, and in the restructuring of governing patterns using democratic techniques which involve all the members in different ways.

One of the most swiftly evolving areas of sociological insight is that of the changed relationship between institutions owned and staffed by religious and the on-going needs of contemporary American society. In the past it was taken for granted that religious would work in schools and hospitals. Grade schools and high schools are not usually owned by the religious teaching in them, but by the diocese itself. However, colleges and hospitals were usually owned, governed, and staffed by the religious community. But in the 1960's, many circumstances have changed. More and more lay staff must be hired, costs and needed facilities soar, religious orders are diminishing in size. Many of the religious themselves want to do more directly personal work with the under-privileged. Works of mercy for the poor and needy have developed into secular institutions serving the general public. As this is recognized, religious communities are setting up properly constituted governing boards of trustees, so that a specific college, university or hospital will be owned and administered as any other such civic entity. In other words, religious are divesting themselves of corporate properties. What had often amounted to absentee government by religious superiors is perceived today as inadequate for the complicated type of decisions demanded by large modern institutions.

I have attempted to sketch out some of the major historical and sociological factors in the present struggle for freedom which is at work in the American religious orders of women. Each aspect demands major study. Hopefully such study is proceeding with increasing competence and swiftness. What are the attitudes toward renewal among religious women which are most creative, most hopeful, most surely on the way to future presence and meaning in this mysterious and often frightening, yet magnificent modern world?

At the level of personal opinion I would suggest three attitudes as generally accepted and in practice among sisters who are personally committed to serious structural adaptation of religious life forms.

1. Everything about the past form of religious life can and must be examined in the light of Christ and his message, the history of the Church, and the realities of human life today. In other words, *the myth of the divineness of past forms is broken.*

2. Vatican II is seen as a breakthrough out of post-Trent attitudes and into twentieth century awareness, e.g. the primacy of the human person, the reality of historical development, the secular as the locus of God's saving action for man, the place of tested love and healing. *The Holy Spirit is to be found not only in the Word of God in scripture and in the worshipping assembly, but also in the cries of the human heart* and the kind of human action that makes life more livable for others.

3. Diversity has come into its own. The monolith is dead for many reasons. The glory of the living God shines out in the uniqueness of the human person. Thus religious seek to express shared desires, oneness in Christ, but freedom in the modes of such expression. *Not only is religious life assuming diversity of styles, but diverse styles are sought within one governmentally unified group.* Only in this way can the consciences of all those who are now religious be respected. No one style can be imposed. Thus, each group must be free to devise its own style, with all the inner discipline of love and intelligence such a task will demand.

The remainder of this chapter will deal with the implications of these three new awarenesses as they affect the two poles of human existence as they are lived out today in the United States in a Roman Catholic religious community of women. Rosemary Haughton, in her brilliant study of conversion and community, *The Transformation of Man,* has advanced our understanding of the inter-relation of personal and communal factors in human existence. Her chapter on encounter, which analyzes sexual love as a demand for the enduring ritual of marriage, is pivotal for an understanding of religious life as a ritual for voluntary celibacy. Work for renewal of religious life seems to have moved beyond the merely romantic phase of a search for personal fulfillment. It has come to include the necessity for some corporate expression of personal life commitment. However, although the personal and the corporate may be experienced simultaneously, they must be discussed separately. What does a religious woman face as a unique person? What sort of corporate existence will support and make available for others, the inner consecration of life in Christ?

II. *Celibacy for the Kingdom*

> *Others do not marry because of the kingdom of heaven. Let him who can do it accept this teaching* (Matthew 19:12).

For centuries, sisters thought of themselves as having taken the three vows of poverty, chastity and obedience, and living them out in a religious congregation highly organized according to a Rule of life and under a specific hierarchy of religious superiors. Such a notion of religious life is the result of a long cultural evolution, influenced profoundly by the medieval structures of monastic life and by a moral theology which tended to be overly spiritualistic and extremely negative in regard to sex. This meant that a form of life which began in the earliest ages as freely chosen virginity lived in some sort of communal pattern developed into an authority-obedience structure, in which the fact of not marrying was simply part of the system, accepted for obvious reasons. In other words, religious women tended to think of themselves as joining the convent, or entering religious life. The psychological focus was not primarily on the fact of freely chosen celibate existence. As a cultural phenomenon this is understandable. But our twentieth century is in the midst of a genuine evolution of human consciousness, post-Freudian, but also deeply personalist. This fact has moved the question of voluntary celibacy into the very center of each sister's consciousness of herself and of her meaning in today's world.

Two events have accelerated this awareness on the part of sisters. One was Vatican II which called religious women to live as modern women, loving and serving in today's world. This stress conflicts with forms of life left from Victorian and even earlier periods which viewed women as frail creatures to be protected, and ignored sexuality as something never to be mentioned. The other event is the style of defense taken up by the official Church in regard to priestly celibacy.

Because of the continuing refusal to enter into dialogue about meaningful and therefore voluntary celibacy, religious women find themselves searching for their own reasons for being celibate. They do not accept for themselves the reasons offered for priestly celibacy. Such reasons seem to stress more efficient service of the system, or a negative notion of sex and marriage. Whether the case for priestly celibacy is sound is not our question here. The point is that the way it is actually being treated publicly has also called into question the freely chosen celibacy of religious men and women.

Since this topic of the woman, freely celibate for the kingdom, is at the front edge of current thought and discussion, it seems best to indicate some of the areas of questioning, and then some of the searching for new forms which such questions initiate.

1. Today an American religious woman wants to be free to be a woman, an American, an adult person who chooses Christ and her celibate dedication to him as her style of life. She can no longer think of herself as merely a member of an ecclesiastical staffing group. Because she is a person, she cannot allow herself to be depersonalized into an interchangeable part for school or hospital tasks. This does not all mean that she may not freely choose to serve Christ in education or health services. But it does mean that she cannot be defined as 'sister', the faceless nurse or teacher, shifted here and there, valuable mainly because she costs less.

This is not at all meant to sound harsh. No one, least of all sisters, questioned the faceless service version of religious life until very recently. The point is that once such questioning emerges, it cannot be pushed back into a psychic bottle and the lid screwed on. Every modern person and even more so, every Christian must become uniquely what he or she is called to be. Then the celibate must be defined through relation to Christ and fellow men in meaningful human relationships, never through task definition. The whole agony of de-personalization and bureaucratic role-playing which afflicts our society comes down with a crash on women who suddenly see themselves as caught in a de-personalized system in which there is no rhythm between job and personal life, no alternation, for example, between place of work and place of private existence.

2. The modern awareness of the value and uniqueness of every person not only makes identification of person with job a moral evil. It also raises for sisters already professed the very real question of how to become an adult in a situation which so severely limits normal contacts that it makes needed variety of human relationships almost impossible. A modern woman who for whatever reason is not married and not seeking marriage, develops a full life by deepening and increasing the variety and unselfishness of inter-personal relationships possible in her life situation. But, until new forms for religious life are generally accepted, sisters are theoretically limited to contact with other sisters, mainly those with whom they live. Even here, old traces of suspicion of deep human friendship can poison the atmosphere. In centuries past, withdrawing into a local convent may have been the best possible arrangement for living out a life of consecrated celibacy. This is simply impossible in the face of modern knowledge and experience. *Sisters will simply leave such a form of life for it is inhuman in our time.* It is wasteful of human potential for growth and service. Statistics definitely show this to be true, although there are many varieties of specific personal reasons for the final decision to leave.

3. An increasingly urgent area of questioning deals with facing up to the fact that modern adults live in a society in which men and women work together, one in which marriage is by no means the only possible or valuable man-woman relationship. Past religious life customs tended to be subtly Jansenistic, i.e., they had as their real justification fear of contact with men. The eruption of awareness of the need to be adult American women precisely in order to be effectively Christian has blown wide open the question

of types of relationships between sisters and men, often priests and brothers, but also laymen. It is unreal not to face the fact that this is a brand new type of problem for the voluntarily celibate religious women. It raises questions and puts sisters into situations which simply never came up at all before.

Where this topic and its psychic solutions will head is as yet very unclear. Perhaps many who are already sisters will decide that their real vocation is marriage. But this leaves untouched the question of life style for those who genuinely feel called to celibacy, and yet know that adult life today means many relationships, including those with men. Such relationships when they are stable will have somehow assimilated into their very uniqueness the value and meaning of celibacy. But at present many religious women have not yet really lived out their own celibate situation as a choice. Rather, they experienced celibacy as a younger acceptance of non-marriage as part of the package deal of traditional religious life. Thus this area of thought and discussion is in great ferment at the present.

4. There is another problem area related to (3) but rather hard to verbalize. Culturally, in this country, sisters have been living for a century a sort of museum existence in which archaic clothes and customs were matched interiorly by an archaic spirituality, sincerely accepted. Since the latter had been eliminated at the level of theology by Vatican II, those sisters who had already eliminated it from their own lives are willing to experiment with new forms and styles to express their new awareness as Christian persons. But many sisters are still sincerely living by the old archaic spirituality, good in its day, or at least understandable. Such sisters cannot honestly shed old clothes styles or culture patterns.

In terms of celibacy, sisters of the older spirituality still experience themselves as 'daughters' of the Church, of the paternal authority figures in the Church. They are 'loving daughters' even of their own higher superiors who, significantly enough, are not yet dropping their title 'mother', with the exception of a few top superiors who already personally experience Christian life as one of real brothers and sisters in the Lord. Grown women who think of themselves as daughters tend then to treat those they deal with professionally in the only model they have, i.e., as children. They find it appalling to face life as a 'sister' to all men and women. *This would mean establishing and building not dependent, but peer relationships in work, friendship and community authority patterns.*

There is a linguistic key to this paradox. It lies in the fact that religious women are traditionally called 'sister', but they have superiors (i.e., they are inferiors). Such superiors are usually called 'mother' (i.e., they are daughters). The only canonical name for a sister who is not a superior is 'subject'. However, one perceptive sister, studying personalist psychology, has pointed out that we might have a hope for giving 'subject' its new meaning as carrier of personal awareness. Then the old negative 'subject' would more honestly be 'object'. At any rate, there are real semantic problems in trying to discuss religious women's renewal today. They make clear the depth of the personal problem sisters find·in experiencing themselves within the system as adult women related as peers to all those with whom they come into contact.

5. Celibacy raises another important area of discussion not only in terms of one to one relationships with men, but in the larger question of shared Christian life between married persons and celibates. This is crucial because neither style really is self-explanatory. Each style needs the other for stress on different human and Christian values. Each style proclaims differently the mystery of the human person, and the necessity of freedom for choice in the basic decision about one's own sexuality. Perhaps more contact and sharing between celibate and married persons will help to de-mythologize both styles of life. It should also help to discover the radical unity of Christian life and witness, a unity which is not primarily a question of whether a person is married or celibate. In Christ there is neither male nor female. Obviously, there are men and women, but it is precisely in Christ that the human person is revealed as transcending, not sexuality, but the notion that such differences are the last word about the meaning of the human person and his destiny.

6. There is a final area of thought and discussion among sisters

which is not of top priority, and yet is of increasing importance. It is the question of possible ordination of women to the diaconate or priesthood. Ministry today is understood in the New Testament sense as belonging to the entire body of Christians and expressed in a great variety of ways. There seems no intrinsic reason why a woman could not be called to ordination for a function within the Christian community. For women who have chosen voluntary celibacy such ordination, if desired, would give a more stable role in the community and bring into the permanent ministry the influence of women. The present closure on discussion of two life styles of priesthood for men, namely, married and voluntarily celibate, severely limits on-going dialogue on the question of the ordination of women, whether married or celibate. However, the question once raised, brings into high relief the importance of new and fresh approaches to the life of celibacy if it is to have personal meaning and community relevance in an increasingly adult world society. It is small wonder that many persons in the official Church structures are already frightened at the fact that religious women have taken Vatican II seriously and are evaluating their life form and searching for free and adult ways of living out their consecration.

The move beyond discussion and into experimentation with new ways of living is developing among sisters in the United States in significant, yet numerically limited ways. Here we can merely point to some of these tentative beginnings. The awareness of the developmental process of the human person and its thrust toward adult freedom has perhaps affected the early 'formation' years of religious life more than any other. The trend is toward later acceptance age, when the young woman will have had enough experience to make a truly adult decision. Coinciding with this stress is the move away from isolated years of 'formation', and toward training centers in the cities from which young religious will go to ordinary colleges and remain in contact with varieties of persons and apostolic involvements.

There is also developing a major shift of focus in regard to task assignments for sisters. Today, an educated and professionally competent religious woman must have a life work which can demand all her dedication, both in its on-going style of contact with many persons, and its deepening experience of unique personal contribution to some area of human need. In other words, a mere job cannot be sufficient for a celibate person. For the thrust of the gift of self to Christ in and for others must be expressed in a personally meaningful service. The old system of yearly assignments appearing out of the blue and implicitly substituting good will and the Holy Spirit for actual training is fast disappearing. As mentioned already, *the faceless sister, the interchangeable part, will soon be as outmoded as the dodo.* Only those who view sisters as institutional staff will mourn the dodo.

These remarks in no way imply that sisters may not choose to spend their lives in institutions of education, social service and health care. It simply means that they will have chosen such involvement and that they will be professionally trained for their task. The person, not the assignment, will be primary. Thus many sisters at this moment might choose to do precisely what they are doing. But others might move into work and involvement which would much better express their way of loving Christ in others. The celibate religious woman is a person, a unique expression of what it means to be human. Meaningless and particularly external uniformity will disappear with increasing rapidity. This is already obvious in the United States in terms of the religious habit. As soon as experimentation begins with contemporary style clothes, it becomes evident that such clothes should be different for each person for many occasions. If a common dress is wanted for certain community occasions, this is easily worked out. Uniformity of garb is impossible once the unique build, features, and hair style of a sister are in evidence in any really noticeable way. The traditional habits made everyone look alike because the quantity of clothing hid to a large extent the normal appearance of bodily differences.

One of the deepest and most difficult areas of search for new forms for celibate women religious is in the question of prayer and worship. As Christian women, sisters want and need both of these as fundamental realities of their lives. Yet the old form of religious life was at no point more tragically stunting than in the endless routine vocal prayers, the time of muteness spent in sardine-packed chapels 'meditating', and attending Mass in parishes or convents whose liturgy was totally in the control of the local priest. The liturgical renewal in the entire Church opens up new vistas for religious. But its realization through creative experimentation is made possible only through the availability of creative priests. (Might this be an opening for ordained religious women?) Some experimentation is going on with small and authentic house liturgies, ceremonies of penance and bible services which offer forms of spontaneous prayer which is much more genuine than the endless reciting of the monastic office. Time for personal contemplative prayer is an absolute necessity for the celibate, supported by biblical studies, individual counselling and times for periodic withdrawal from work involvement.

The on-going dialogue about the meaning of celibacy is moving then into many new areas of experimentation. But one last topic deserves more space and forms the concluding section of this chapter. It is the question of community for religious women. It is equally true that authentic celibacy is utterly personal and that it cannot be lived in psychic isolation. How can women who forego marriage and family life live communally, joyfully and as contributing members of the common human enterprise?

III. *Communal Existence*

> *The kingdom of heaven is like yeast. A woman takes it and mixes it with a bushel of flour, until the whole batch of dough rises* (Matthew 13:33).

It seems important to recall at this point that American sisters struggling for new forms of Christian and free existence experience simultaneously the questioning about celibacy today, and the questioning about valid community existence. The former topic may be verbalized less. But it lies at the heart of the most urgent and honest discussions of community. *For a real community will be precisely a group of persons trying to grow in love and understanding, trying to support each other in the ups and downs of life.* Within the inherited congregation structures of the past (now not called with any accuracy 'communities') religious women find themselves face to face with their personal destiny and the organizational shape of their religious tradition. A sister may decide that she no longer chooses celibate life with others. But if she does choose it, she is faced with the corporate planning and re-structuring of her congregation, so that it may evolve from a bureaucratic to a communal pattern. Her personal life and her corporate life are experienced together. The only way to avoid this tension is to withdraw from the institute. Many, for good reasons, are deciding to do this. However, in the remainder of my remarks, I have in mind religious women who feel simultaneously called to personal celibacy and to the expression of it in some sort of new communal forms.

There are four questions being raised along these lines:

1. How can religious communities move into multiple life styles so that every sister can make an authentic and yet communally valuable contribution to Christ's kingdom? The era of the simple society in which persons lived and worked, recreated and worshipped in a limited geographical area, often even with the same persons, is obviously over. Today the urban adult is part of many groups. His life unity is in his own personal and developing self-awareness, which unifies and gives direction to his life, as he moves into and out of an increasing variety of relationships and human contacts. As someone has said, the modern man does not live where he lives. The question is more than that of merely geographical mobility, though that is taken for granted. It is a case of psychic mobility, the opportunity and ability to make new relationships, to grow in unity and diversity at the same time. The closed-in convent, based on rural life, is a form of psychic isolation. It is no longer morally defensible, except for those religious who need it to support a personality structure tied to such a pattern. The future of religious life will involve, and already increasingly does involve, participation of sisters in many societies and groups.

We are sociologically at the end of the old one-group total structure inherited from the age of medieval monasticism.

2. Flowing from this awareness is the most obvious question of all, yet it is highly threatening to the existing, even if dying, older religious life structure. Why should sisters live where they work? For example, even if a small group of sisters are going to teach in a parish school, why can they not live like adult women at some distance from the school, creating a normal rhythm of life and contacting a rich variety of persons? Experiments along this line are becoming fairly common.

3. How can the question of authority and government be brought into some sort of proportion with the need for genuine communal existence for religious women? Or as one wag has said, how much ruling does a group of poor virgins need? The question of authoritarianism within the small local convent has probably caused more agony and more breakdowns than any other facet of the entire system, especially in those post-Vatican II years. The local convent should be one's home, a place of psychic support, love and acceptance. But it has been and still is, in large part, as organized in structure as General Motors. There is the superior, the authority figure over the entire group. Roles are clearly de-lineated, jobs are assigned, minute daily schedules are to be adhered to. The atmosphere has tended to be very silent, very neat and very depressing. Convents have been as formally structured as if they were large monastic establishments whose reason for existence was keeping a Rule, an imposed pattern of life, regarded as productive of holiness.

In the old system, the convent, not the school or hospital, was the testing ground of one's religiousness. Such conflict for profes-sional sisters has become almost unendurable. To live in two complex patterns (which tend more and more to overlap as to authority figures and schedule) means that one has no private life, no time to relax, no relationships that are simply loving and open and purposeless. *Convents will not be the dwelling places of new type religious because they need real, if simple, homes in which to live.* Surely obedience is crucial to dedicated Christian life, and authority has its place in the human existence. But obedience is the openness of a person to the will of Christ here and now in the needs of the times, the truth of one's professional competence, the corporate consensus arrived at in dialogue. Religious will develop new forms for group unity, for needed leadership roles, for purified ways of hearing the Spirit through those in special positions of responsibility. But the old primacy of Rule, governing, superiors and rigid convent living is over for good. The values these things carried in a different culture will be incarnated in ways genuinely helpful for modern Christian women.

4. There is one question being discussed about communal existence for religious women which lies deeper than any of the ones already mentioned. Throughout the history of the United States, Roman Catholic religious forms have run parallel to the forms of our society. Whatever the necessity of this in the past, it is being seriously questioned, for example, in the discussion about the viability of a set of schools for general education parallel to the national set. But such parallelism looms largest in the present discussion of religious life forms for women. In the past the sisters' life style was one of organized absence from the society of the United States in every possible way. Sisters even avoided going to Mass in the parish church if there could be Mass in the convent. Sisters still go to movies offered as special showings for religious. Thousands of sisters converge on what is usually a 'religious' film or a totally innocuous musical comedy. Noticing this over the years, it is understandable that the public was appalled to see a few brave sisters on picket lines or in peace marches or interracial demonstrations.

The point is that society is already highly complex and increasingly meets needs only through large organizations. *Should the religious women now searching for more authentic existence be separate communities or should they join the human race as leaven within the dough of Christ's coming kingdom?* Many sisters feel that they should work within the real structures of the world and devise a simple way of living together which is supportive of their human need for love and understanding, and which sends them back refreshed for their mission to others.

The serious questions being discussed about communal existence have already begun to bear some fruit in tentative approaches to new communal forms. These are still scattered and new, so it seems possible only to indicate some of the areas in which there is at least a beginning of experimentation. In obedience to Vatican II directives, most religious communities are having general chapters, meetings of elected delegates to re-evaluate their entire pattern of life and apostolic works. The difficulty here is that such internal renewal of life form is necessarily slow, impeded by the great range of attitudes toward the necessity and degree of change to be sought for in religious life. It is also impeded by the centuries old tendency of congregations to view their own problems in too introspective a way. The documents of Vatican II and the traditional Rules seem to be read more assiduously than the signs of the times, the call of the Spirit present in the history and events of our revolutionary century. Official internal renewal is on the move. But for many sisters it seems too late and too slow. Much more creative experimentation with the type of life forms mentioned above must be encouraged and used to measure change for the whole order.

Some religious congregations have either moved quickly or into quite new areas of involvement and have suffered severe criticism and even rejection by the larger system. They have in different ways been forced to seek life styles by withdrawing from the category of officially approved religious institutes. At this point it is not clear how far the traditional Roman Catholic Church structures in the United States will accept truly new and creative religious life forms for sisters. Many in the tribe still think they need their unchanging totems.

In addition to varieties of tentative approaches by traditional communities, there are several experimental communities in the United States which are made up of groups of sisters who left an existing order as a group and set up a new community. Whether this becomes more common seems too early to judge. On the level of the national image of sisters, it is again perhaps too early to generalize. Mass circulation magazines, TV and a few books have made many of the public aware that there are many sisters who are adult, educated and creative. But then there is also a current prime time TV favorite, *The Flying Nun*, which is a sort of 'Sound of Music' show, with Mary Poppins and even Batman undertones. The National Conference of Major Superiors seems to have little impact either on the sisters of the country or on the national awareness of what is happening to sisters. Although the past chairman, Sister Luke, SL, was a creative person, a courageous and hopeful leader, she seems to have been an isolated example, at least on the national scene. The Conference seems to suffer from over-domination by (or over-submission to) the Congregation of Religious in Rome. It is also hampered by the slowness of the elective process in specific communities which can only gradually produce newer and younger major superiors who understand and will lead really significant adaptation to modern needs.

Conclusion

Throughout the world, the struggle for freedom is one of the great hopes and major evolutions of our time. It is no wonder that Roman Catholic sisters find themselves involved in it. However, the struggle for freedom, like the closely related one for justice, can never be only for oneself. The real question mark about the future of religious life as we have known it is not whether it will change. It is changing. Neither is the question whether all sisters now in congregations want genuine change. Many do not. They have been so formed by the traditional style that they must be loved and respected and allowed to serve in the way they can do so authentically. The real question mark hovers near another topic. How many of the sisters working to make possible a more adult and free style of life for themselves, see this as part of the movement in which they are joined with Negroes, Puerto Ricans, developing nations, the utterly tragic Vietnamese people? One does not have to be a voluntary celibate to need freedom. Far from it. Those with family responsibilities have human demands made on them which a curtailed freedom makes additionally agonizing. Rather, celibacy for the kingdom means being so free in Christ that one is free for consistent and undemanding love and service of all those in any kind of need.

The sisters' struggle for freedom will in all probability work out to some extent, and for some persons and groups. For it is not a fight against persons or against a system. Rather it is the interior struggle, the traditional spiritual combat in which with the gift of Christ's grace and his spirit, the human person can open himself to receive the capacity to love unselfishly. This battle, even if imperfectly won, will find its expression in dwelling places where others can find peace and joy, in worship that springs from the experience of Christian community. Most of all, the sisters' struggle for freedom, as it moves into social visibility, may give heart and hope to all those who still suffer in their search for the freedom by which Christ can make every man free.

The Laity and a Moment of Dread

JOHN MULHOLLAND

The short story of Catholic lay people in the United States before
1962 is a pathetic one: no leadership, few causes that invited the
emergence of leaders, and, for its thirty to forty million membership, a calm tranquility with their role as second-class citizens in a
bureaucratic superstructure. Lay people had no voice in determining the least feature of their religious life, and no evident
desire to have one. Dissent (and variety) was absent from the
community to a far greater degree than in Europe, Africa or Latin
America.

Some qualifications of this general picture have to be allowed. A
few lay people attempted leadership in one or other area of
Catholic life, and three men, at least, left a permanent imprint
on the Catholic community. Dissent, if inaudible to the mass of
Catholics, was heard on a few issues: on behalf of more realistic
response to the world problem of over-population, on the side
of honest reporting in Catholic journalism; exception was taken to
the general Catholic ignoring of the plight of the poor, the dis-
enfranchised and the culturally deprived. But there were exceptions
that served more to highlight the general position of laity as sheep
than anything else. That position, in the half century before 1962,
must be recognized for what it was by anyone who wants to assess
the events of the next six years and find a perspective for seeing

what the future holds for the now forty-five million body of American Catholics.[1]

The absence of specifically *lay* leadership from the American Catholic community in the years 1918–62 is a stunning indictment of the one-time vaunted Catholic school system. It is also embarrassing evidence today of the benumbing effects of the religious sub-culture in which Catholics lived during the period. For there were, as the next six years would begin to show, some substantial issues concealed beneath the calm surface of Catholic unanimity. From the forty-odd years there emerges no single lay name that would be recognized by more than a fraction of the Catholic millions, and only a handful that could be cited by careful observers as having played roles of any importance in the Church's life in that time.

But thousands of men and women who were Catholic became effective leaders in the secular community. In politics alone there were hundreds, from the notorious Mayor Hague of Jersey City to John Kennedy. In commerce, industry, education, science and public service, individual Catholics were increasingly prominent, sometimes eminent, though their quality and numbers were admittedly less than their proportionate size in the national community. That, however, is not the point here. Even those Catholics who gave forceful leadership in secular life had no visible impact inside the religious community to which they belonged. If they had influence with the bishops and priests who shaped policy and directed the public activities of the Church it was a covert influence.

Leadership was exclusively clerical and episcopal in all that pertained even remotely to the religious life of Catholics, including the vast educational system and the use of the Church's unquestioned political power in modifying the domestic and foreign policy of the nation. It was not until 1950 that laymen were eligible to become even department heads in most Catholic

[1] This chapter treats three time periods: 1918–62; 1962–8; after 1968. Vatican II was called in 1958, convened in 1960. By 1962 a sizeable slice of American Catholicism knew that the reform was for real.

colleges and universities. (In 1967, of 150 diocesan school systems, only one, the smallest,[1] is being administered by a layman; of thousands of Catholic elementary schools, not one has a lay principal.) At the meetings where decisions were made on the the employment of Catholic political force, sessions were barred to all but consecrated bishops, agenda were never published in advance. Important decisions, such as the long-standing one to oppose federal aid for either public or parochial schools, became evident to the Catholic community only when their mass co-operation was judged necessary.

There was no place for laymen in setting Church policies even in areas where laymen alone had much competence to offer: fund raising, fiscal policy, educational theory and practice, selection of the social service goals of the Church, or the relation of Church to state in a pluralistic society. This lay docility was accepted as the way things should be. So normal did the situation seem to Catholics that save in one or two obscure journals no suggestion appeared that anything else was desirable or possible. Dissent was dead, and there was no dissatisfaction.

There were apparent exceptions. A man like George B Shuster became 'the noted Catholic educator'. But the tag was misleading. Such men achieved renown, as Shuster did, in secular institutions, and their impact on Catholic theory or practice in parallel Catholic institutions was negligible. Leadership was clerical, and the clergy was more often concerned with protecting the bureaucratic institution than with moving things ahead. The thrust of the Church's energy was thus aimed consistently at a bigger, more prosperous and powerful Church, not toward a more just society or a more Christian culture.

A few laymen, like George Hunton in racial justice, made serious attempts at leadership, but they had no followers, which is an essential part of the definition. Others, like the courageous Dorothy Day in social service to the derelict of society, had somewhat more success. Miss Day had followers, few though they were,

---

[1] Diocese referred to is Brownsville, Texas, with less than five thousand students in eighteen Catholic elementary and secondary schools.

and the ideals she stood for were partly vindicated in the sixties. But in retrospect the independent lay man or woman with a cause in the Church must be seen more as a lonely witness whose leadership was rejected by the establishment and by the mass of Catholic faithful as well.

Thus it came about that the considerable Catholic affluence and energies of this period were directed to the narrow goal of more churches, bigger schools and an increase in the size of the clergy. Political power was cautiously exercised to protect the vested interests of the clerical establishment, and, in the late fifties and early sixties, to obtain federal dollars to increase the size of the Catholic plant. In civic and secular life, the goal of the Church naturally became a persistent effort to show that the Catholic structure was more authentically middle-class American than the American middle class itself. Laymen *en masse* had no dissenting view to all this, either because they were unconcerned about the national character of their Church, or because its narrow goals suited well enough their personal desire. The net effect of the absence of lay leaders was a 'churchy' Church, with no other primary goals in the national community than its own increase. Like most other religious bodies in the nation, the Catholic Church had few visions and, for the realization of such as it had, no heart to take risks.

By contrast to the general scene, three laymen made distinctive contributions to the life of the Church in these years. Before 1962 no one of them seemed to be a very effectual leader, but the stamp they put on Catholic life became increasingly clear in the years after. Each of the three had a specifically lay viewpoint, sought to bring about some radical shift in Catholic life, and attracted enough followers to be at least partly successful in realizing their vision. Two of them were journalists: Michael Williams, founder of *Commonweal* and Robert Hoyt, editor of *The National Catholic Reporter*; the third was physician-researcher John Rock, collaborator in development of 'the pill'.

Williams founded and gave the initial guidance to a journal of opinion genuinely independent of Church authority, the only one for a period of more than twenty years free to comment on state and Church without fear of ecclesiastical repression.

Michael Williams fulfills the idea of leader well; he led people from one point to a further one. He and the ideas he stood for over the next thirty years attracted men as able and courageous as himself who made of *Commonweal* a religious journal almost unique on the American scene. Better known today than Williams are those who took up his leadership: Edward Skillin, John Cogley, George Shuster, John Leo and James O'Gara, the present editor. From the time of its initial issue in 1924 these men edited and wrote in the pages of *Commonweal* a sustained, urbane and forceful dissent to the practices of the Church establishment. But Williams was first.

For most of the period from its founding to 1962 *Commonweal* had a readership of less than 25,000. Yet it became a prominent part of the Catholic scene, respected as well outside the Catholic ghetto. It offered a responsible and calm commentary on national affairs touching the Church, and on the developing issues in Catholic life. It criticized, most often in a quietly constructive way, the Church's departure from basic Christian values, and gracefully and sharply questioned the pressure politics of the bureaucracy, the state of Catholic higher education, the Catholic tendency to support right-wing causes, and was almost alone among Catholic journals in decrying the evils of McCarthyism during that sad period of American life. In 1966–7 it was the strongest Catholic voice asking for moderation in Vietnam and exploring the tradition of Catholic pacifism.

Hoyt, a gentle, almost retiring man whose personality showed little of the stereotype of effective leadership, brought about a veritable revolution in Catholic newspaper reporting as editor first of the Kansas City *Catholic Reporter* and later of the *National Catholic Reporter*. Followed at a distance by other laymen working under the handicap of closer episcopal direction, Hoyt reported week by week the 'other' side of Catholic news, covered the stories that were quashed by clerical editors of other Catholic newspapers, and provided a place where the ordinary man's dissent could be registered. If *Commonweal* gave a voice to the Catholic intellectual, *NCR* reported the discomfort of the Catholic masses with bigger fund drives, crowded schools, heavy-handed episcopal repression of new initiatives by priests, nuns and laymen. What Hoyt did at *NCR* began in the late sixties to have its effect generally on Catholic reporting at other journals.

Dr John Rock was a researcher in the field of human fertility. With others he developed the first widely successful oral contraceptive, 'the pill'. For some time he himself seemed to be of the conviction that his dissent from prevailing Church teaching on the morality of contraception placed him outside the Catholic community. Encouraged to change that conviction by a priest friend, Rock became, in the second half of the fifties, a self-appointed propagandist for a radical shift in the Church's apparently unshakeable opposition to the free use of artificial means of birth control. He was never accepted as a leader by the mass of Catholics, who indeed were led to hold him and his arguments in disdain by virulent attacks from establishment spokesmen and the ecclesiastically owned and directed press. But Rock pressed on with his argument at public meetings and in articles and books.

By the time that Rock had taken this position, there were already hundreds of thousands, or millions, of Catholic couples who had found the Catholic position practically untenable in their private lives. Undoubtedly with great reluctance on the part of most of them, they ceded to the common conviction of the rest of the nation that the fathering of new life was something intended by the creator to be regulated not by physiological accident but by human judgment. Thus Rock gave new hope to thousands of tortured souls that a change might indeed be possible. The men and women in whose behalf he spoke did him little honor and offered little encouragement. But through his efforts, first in research and later in propaganda, a ground-swell of public opinion was set in motion that eventually overtook almost the entire camp of Catholic intellectuals and a sizeable number of clergy. Although the issue is still technically in doubt at Rome, there is little question now that the widespread popular rejection of Catholic practice (if not theory) has wrought a major change in the way Catholics respect the authority of their individual conscience.

In all this time if there were no leaders, there was a plethora of Catholic organizations; each of the over 15,000 parishes of the nation had its men's and women's clubs, pious and fraternal societies of every kind, and diocesan, state and national organizations annually filled the stadiums of the country with religious rallies. But there was no cause to enlist lay enthusiasms, no object for lay ambitions, and nothing to accomplish toward the success of American Catholicism except to have more of the same: an increase of schools and churches, and more proof that Catholics were as American as everyone else. The thousands of Catholic societies (over 50,000 by one count in 1950) bore no witness to Christianity that was not initiated by the clergy and approved by the hierarchy. Every lay group by common consent had priest-moderators, appointed in most cases by the local bishop and responsible to him for the obedience of his charges. If there was the least doubt about the 'mind of the Church', the priest-moderator was always prepared to say how the bishop wished it understood. A conservative estimate in 1960 put membership in Catholic organizations at seven million. Never had so many been organized to do so little. Because these organizations had no causes to propose, no goals to challenge their energy and imagination, it was inevitable that competent, ambitious and energetic lay people would shy away from them to find an outlet in the secular challenges of society. In whatever the essence of middle class apathy and resistance to change consists, it was there to be studied in all its nakedness in the Catholic lay organizations of 1945–60. And in this area of Catholic life only minor changes are visible in 1968.

In that period, the great objective held out to lay organizations and Catholics generally was 'the mandate of the bishop'. If it wasn't at a given moment the mandate of the local bishop who was at a loss to manufacture one, it was the mandate of the national body of bishops, expressed in their annual statement each November. When that was too flimsy to offer even a superficial program, the lay groups fell back on carrying out the 'mandate' of the encyclicals, which traditionally were worded with such extreme caution as to say nothing, and when they did, dragged fifty years behind the needs of the time. There were no leaders among the laity because there were no causes to work for.

What passed for causes proposed to the laity are embarrassing now to recall. The overriding goal was to get everyone into an organization of some kind. In individual parishes, the success of the annual bazaar or weinie roast was paramount; 'spiritual societies' promoted the retreat movement or the return of the fallen-aways. City and diocesan-wide societies worked at the annual rally in the local baseball emporium, at city-wide drives to banish 'girlie magazines' from the newstands, and sought local legislation to prevent shopping on Sunday or the public sale of contraceptives. The positive-minded worked for decency in literature, decency in dress, decency in movies, and the Church became the most decent of decent structures in an indecent world. National organizations, save for a few modeled on the European 'Jocist' movement, offered more of the same. There were no causes.

During most of this time the place of the layman in the Church was so low and his voice so unimportant that pastors and bishops did not feel obliged to disclose even the simplest information about the finances of the parish or diocese. In most of the hundred and fifty dioceses there is still no adequate financial statement open to examination of the faithful, and it will be decades before full revelation is made of the enormous and complex picture on a national level. If Catholic contributions began to fall on a per capita basis (as they did), the fact was lost sight of in the population increase of the period. So far was the layman from having even a consultative voice in the disposition of Church resources that he did not have the remotest idea of what these resources were.

It makes dreary reading (and writing) now to recall how absolutely third class the layman of 1920–62 was in his own Church. To question the wisdom of the bishop's mandate or the pastors's whim was universally accepted as disloyalty, even if the bishop was mad as a hatter or the pastor senile, as not a few were.

Whatever was true of the position of Catholic lay people in the era 1920–62 is still generally so. A mass of forty-five million people does not change its status overnight, or have it changed for them, by anything short of revolution. And revolution there is not among lay Catholics in the United States in 1968. Not even a quiet one.

But in the six years from 1962, at the point where the genuinity of the conciliar reform became clear to a sizeable number of people, certain changes took shape on the American Catholic scene. At first the changes were obviously superficial, and many of them continue to be so. But others are serious changes that will bring radical shifts in the Church's policy of management, its openness to dissent, and possibly in its belief-system.

In these six years, for the first time in half a century, public dissent was heard to episcopal statements of policy. The dissent and dissatisfaction came from a small minority of the Catholic population, and had little popular support. But it covered a considerable range of topics, from the values of the parochial school system to the fiscal policy of dioceses and the morality of birth control, divorce and abortion, as well as priestly celibacy.

At this point, in 1968, coherent dissent in the Church is still predominantly clerical, not lay. Or at least the coherent spokesmen for dissent are most frequently priests and nuns. But lay dissent is also clearly there, both progressive and reactionary in political direction, and very occasionally makes itself visible in the form of dissenting *action*. Thus in 1966–7 scores of priests (out of some three thousand) in the Archdiocese of Chicago publicly expressed dissatisfaction with the fund-raising objectives of their Cardinal Archbishop. The disagreeing clergy claimed that they, and their people, had no share in framing the methods by which money would be raised or in determining the purposes for which funds would be spent. They asked for a voice in both. What began as a clerical dissatisfaction was eventually backed by at least a small number of vocal lay men and women, enough to bring about minor changes in the plans of the archdiocese.

In Philadelphia, an archdiocese described by some observers as more reactionary than Los Angeles, a handful of lay dissenters in 1965-6 demonstrated at the chancery office and the episcopal residence for a more enlightened Church policy in the local racial turmoil. The local Cardinal Archbishop, John Krol, long ambivalent on racial issues, made few concessions to those who wanted the weight of the Church's authority thrown into an aggressive fight against racism. The mass of middle class Philadelphia Catholics saw little sense in the dissent, and thus no perceptible result came from the incidents except a hardening of the lines of disagreement. But the important point was that dissent, even of a small minority, could be registered in the public record without open reprisals or excommunications.

In the US Capital, several hundred lay men and women, and a score of priests, known collectively as 'The People', brought some gentle pressures to bear for more rapid liturgical reform and a measure of liturgical freedom in the two years 1966-7. In practice they formed a floating community of only a few hundred out of the more than three hundred thousand Catholics of Washington's metropolitan area, and took pains to remain strictly within the bounds of what current laws and regulations demanded. But they seemed headed in the direction of forming a more stable group that would ignore territorial boundaries set up for every parish (an experiment already well underway with episcopal approval in Oklahoma City and elsewhere). In one of the more glaring examples of ecclesiastical 'overkill', the usually genial Cardinal Archbishop showed his displeasure and fear with a four page letter read in every parish and a publicly delivered admonition to 'The People' to cease and desist. In this incident the spokesmen were lay, and the determination of what 'The People' aspired to seems to have been largely lay-directed.

Across the country a score or so of individual Catholics, many of them priests, mounted other protests against the practice of the Church establishment. For the most part, they were spokesmen for the repressed dissent of a sizeable minority, but the number of visible supporters was always small. The attention they attracted however, in both Catholic and daily press, was great. Their causes were: a greater measure of academic freedom on Catholic campuses, wider liberty to experiment with Church structures at the parish and diocesan level, a more substantial Catholic contribution to the cause of international peace, greater use of Church resources in the fight for racial equality. In almost every case, the prominent spokesman was a cleric: Father Dubay on racial justice in Los Angeles, Father Daniel Berrigan in New York, and his brother, Philip, also a priest, in Baltimore, on the side of pacifism and selective conscientious objectors, Father Charles Curran and a host of outraged priest-professors in the cause of academic freedom at Catholic University in Washington.

Each of these incidents, and a hundred others that go unmentioned here, appears violently at variance with the accustomed, docile calm of Catholic life prior to 1962. To the one in every thousand of American laymen who read *Commonweal* or *The National Catholic Reporter* it may sometimes take on the appearance of a mild revolution. These two publications, joined in more muted tones by a section of the Catholic Press and the secular dailies, gave prominence to items of public protest in the Church. But the extent of protest, of change, and of promised change thus reported has to be measured against the still placid and undisturbed life of most of the seventeen thousand parishes that make up American Catholicism's most enduring structure. In much of its coverage, the *NCR*, as is natural and necessary for a newspaper, has focused on the sensational, the spectacular and the untypical incident. The probable truth is that ninety percent of American Catholics wanted little change except in two or three narrow areas of their life, were wary and a trifle unsettled by what had happened up till now, and were more or less embarrassed by what the episcopacy often referred to as 'the washing of dirty linen in public'.

Amid the public fanfare over lay officials in Church schools, consultative lay bodies to advise the bishops, parish councils of laity, extraterritorial parishes, liturgical reform and the belated acceptance of the vernacular in the Mass, all peripheral reforms, the most portentous element in the American Catholic Church remains the dissonance between Catholic practice and Church teaching in the delicate areas of birth control and divorce. It is critical for three reasons: (1) it is the issue which touches far and away the largest number of individual Catholics; (2) the change that is inevitable here strikes, or seems to strike, at the heart of the Church's authority, the infallible magisterium; (3) it is the issue most unappreciated by the hierarchy and the one on which they are most inclined to be unshakeable. (For some mysterious reason not clear to the writer, but commented on by others, any proposal to modify the Church's teaching on artificial means of birth limitation seems to be a personal attack that destroys the self-identity of bishops as worthy priests.)

Whatever of that, the issue of birth control (and to a lesser degree of divorce) is central enough to future changes to warrant a closer look at the layman's attitude toward it in the years 1962–8. Prior to 1962 the layman's dissent to prevailing doctrine was entirely by private act, not public disagreement. As some put it in 1965 'the issue has already been decided in the bedrooms of America'. The extent to which Church teaching was ignored is still undocumented; reliable estimates vary from twenty-five percent of Catholic couples in the child-bearing ages to as high as seventy-five percent. Such measuring of Catholic practice as has been done was carried out largely by non-Catholic social scientists, and rarely admitted as valid evidence by Church commentators. But the facts are privately admitted and bemoaned even by conservative elements. Beginning in 1962, however, the silent practice of dissent found voice, at first cautiously in attacks upon the practicality and desirability of the 'rhythm method' and later in questions about whether the Church's stand was indeed a part of the infallible deposit of faith. With Paul VI's creation of an international commission to review the situation, the floodgates of repressed dissent parted more perceptibly, and a scattering of priests in almost every diocese began quietly to free the consciences of such of the faithful as were still bringing the problem to the confessional. More and more articles began to appear, first in *Commonweal* and *NCR*, later in other Catholic journals and still later in a few of the diocesan newspapers. Most significant of all, a growing number of ordinary Catholic lay people gained confidence in following the dictates of their private conscience rather than the public teaching of the Church. They expressed their decision among friends, acquaintances and to the clergy. Dissent was once again alive in the American Catholic community.

The reaction of the episcopacy, at first inclined to be heavy-handed or confused, quickly turned to cautious and low-key opposition. Gradually a wait-and-see attitude on the question developed among the bishops, an attitude which was later to guide them in their response to other calls for change. Thus dissent came not only to exist, but to be listened to. The end is not yet, but the outcome is widely predicted, and the most intransigent opponents of change such as the respected moral theologian John Ford, SJ, are no longer to be heard.

The significance for the Church of what has happened among lay people on the birth control controversy does not really depend on what, if anything, Paul VI and his brother bishops shall finally say to heal the situation. In this question, millions of Catholics of high and low estate have been compelled to consult the moral dictates of private conscience for guidance on how they shall act and speak. A surprising percentage of them found their conscience teaching something other than the official voice of the Church. The experience will be transferred, indeed already has been by some, to other areas of controversy. The men and women who thus were forced to discover, many of them for the first time in their lives, that they *had* a private conscience, and that it exercised a pre-eminent role in their moral decisions, will for weal or woe be more inclined to consult that same private conscience in other matters, and will not be so shocked if the findings of conscience are opposed to the official teaching of a pastor or bishop.

It is too early to read the extent of this transfer in the conduct of forty-five million people, and any shift to be observed in the external conduct of such a large group will have many explanations. But there is reason to believe that American Catholics, priests and nuns as well as laymen, are taking different attitudes toward purely Church law than in the past. Church insistence on Sunday Mass, in Europe traditionally honored more in the breach than in observance, was long a point of pride for American Catholics. But attendance at Sunday Mass (which was probably never more than sixty percent in any of the large dioceses) is reported falling. Recently one official of the San Francisco Archdiocese, to whose department the matter is pertinent, told the writer that a survey showed less than thirty percent of adult male Catholics of the archdiocese attending Sunday Mass regularly. Certainly among one's acquaintances the change in attitude to Sunday observance is notable. For the first time in living memory one hears open disagreement with Church laws like Sunday observance from people who have not left the Church and have no intention of doing so. They merely think that much of the Church's authority has been one-sided and overemphatic on the moral obligations of external conduct.

Next to the issue of birth control in its impact on lay people's attitudes toward the Church are the developments in another substantial question: the Catholic parochial school system, and a host of questions that surround it, including the management of Church finances and absence of lay control over school policy. What happened on this question from 1962–8 can help show the direction of the future.

The question was originally opened over ten years ago by the eminent historian Msgr John Tracy Ellis. When he called in to question the benefits and *de facto* results of the school system he did so on the grounds that Catholic graduate schools were not up to the standards of the nation, that the graduates of Catholic colleges were not entering graduate studies or succeeding in them in the same proportion as other Americans. His criticism asked for a greater dedication to excellence in Catholic higher education and left untreated what has since become the real focal point of

F

Catholic debate: the Catholic elementary and high school system, in which one out of every three Catholic children is sometime enrolled, and in which one out of every seven American children is educated. The controversy rightly concerns not only Catholics, but all Americans, since such a large part of the total population is involved.

Ellis' criticism, scholarly and presented with literary polish and grace, was hard for the establishment and the mass of lay people to digest. But after a rash of hasty refutations it was taken to heart. Segments of the school system worked seriously to update the methods and bring the Catholic college within hailing distance of the higher standards on secular campuses. The final acceptance of what Ellis had to say about higher education in the Church may have paved the way for what was to follow on elementary education, but here the reaction was to be somewhat different.

In 1965 a lay woman who had long been a prudent advocate of change in liturgical practice and religious education, Mary Perkins Ryan, helped to sharpen the issue with her widely disputed (but not widely read) book on the parochial schools. Mrs Ryan asked if the schools were achieving even the minimum results that might justify their continuance. She did not think they were doing the very things that the establishment alleged as the *raison d'être* for the immense expenditures necessary to keep them alive. (Such accounting as is available shows that approximately seventy percent of all Church operating funds are devoted directly to the maintenance of the school system. Exact information, if it is available even to Church officials, is a closely guarded secret.)

Civil, tempered and even cautious as the book was (constructive enough in its criticism to gain an introduction written by New Hampshire's Bishop Ernest Primeau), the book aroused a storm of resentment and refutation from the nation's Catholic school superintendents and bishops. This writer was present in one powerful archbishop's office when a 'war fund' was planned to subsidize the writing of a book-length refutation by another well-known lay author. Rebuttals of the book's argument appeared in almost every diocesan newspaper and in many of the periodicals sponsored by religious orders. It would be difficult to maintain that more than a fraction of the laity shared Mrs Ryan's questioning of the school's value. But her book articulated for the first time a resentment that had been growing for decades at overfilled classrooms, underpaid teachers, the inferior training and quality of thousands of religious and lay teachers in the system.

For years a number of Catholic parents had refused to send their children to Catholic schools, even in places where the school system was not overcrowded. A growing minority felt that the religious formation afforded in them was inferior to that offered in the Confraternity of Christian Doctrine and other religious education centers for public school children. However, the largest number of Catholic parents clung tenaciously to the schools, and apparently still do. In the suburbs of great American cities there is at least as much pressure on pastors to build new schools and enlarge existing ones as there is nationally on the bishops to curtail the elementary and high school program. But the school question will more likely be settled over a long number of years and not by sudden executive decision or general revolt of the laity. The decisive factor will be twofold: success of the Church lobby in obtaining more federal dollars, including grants for building and salaries, and the willingness of Catholics of ordinary means to pay for a private school system that their counterparts in the American economy cannot afford. However it may be one day decided, the issue itself, like the debate on birth control, has other effects on the attitudes of laymen.

The years-long discussion of Catholic schools has caused even the most loyal of Catholics to relinquish the myth that Catholic schools, because Catholic, are superior to public schools. The legends holds on in places like Philadelphia where there may once have been substance for it; but across the nation Catholics have been disillusioned. More important, a large number of lay people have discovered in this issue that the first word of the hierarchy is not necessarily anything like their later words. Most adults can remember vividly the Catholic line most vehemently put by

Cardinal Cushing of Boston when he vowed in 1955 to dismember the school system rather than accept federal aid. The inconsistency of the Church's official statements, and the tentative fumbling for a viable position in the last eight years make it clear that in some areas at least the Church, so far from being infallible, is not even smart.

If, as seems quite possible in 1968, the elementary system, containing over 13,000 schools, should have to be drastically cut back because of financial inability, it will become clear to lay people that they have in their pocketbook a much stronger instrument of registering dissent against hierarchical policy than they have ever wished to use in this century. And Churchmen will be more cautious in excluding those who pay the piper from a voice in what the piper plays.

A third issue that proved of substance for lay development in the six year transition period after 1962 was, surprisingly, priestly celibacy. The issue was first made public in a way that attracted widespread attention in the pages of *The National Catholic Reporter*, much to the dismay and anger of the progressive Bishop Helmsing who had subsidized the paper in its struggling infancy. He and other progressive bishops drew the line in public debate of the Church's affairs at any open discussion of this question. The difference of opinion between the bishop and *NCR's* editor and board was one of the chief factors leading to the separation of the paper from any relation to the diocese, and brought about its full and final independence from Church officials.

That the bishops and many of the clergy should have considered the question of priestly celibacy a matter that did not properly concern the lay people or depend in any way on what lay people wanted and thought is hard to understand. Since the priests are, at least in theory, dedicated to the service of the people, lay people did have opinions and wished to state them. Many did, in the 'Letters to the Editor' columns of *NCR* and later of other publications. The attitude of the bishops, whatever its psychological or logical explanation, seemed to most a regression to the high-handed ecclesiastical conduct of pre-conciliar days. Familiar through the secular press with European and Latin American discussion of the issue, the American Church could not be walled off from the debate. The forthright statements of hundreds of priests in favor of optional celibacy and the results of polls by expert observers such as Joseph Fichter, SJ, showed that once again the bishops were faced with a sizeable dissent in which they might have to make eventual concessions.

Lay opinions were divided, for American Catholics, like the Irish Catholics from whom many of them were descended, had made much of the celibacy of their priests. Their corporate pride would be struck another blow by any radical shift in Church policy on the issue. But the debate, which continues undiminished in the face of a papal message and the November 1967 'Statement' of the American bishops ruling out optional celibacy, again taught American Catholics that there are two sides and that there is possibility of change in another item of Catholic teaching that only a few years before would not have been discussed by a loyal Catholic. Not only was dissent alive and heard, but American Catholics were learning by experience that they lived in a pluralistic society, that their Church itself was a pluralistic Church in which there existed opposing tensions of conviction and the constant possibility of development and change.

Most significant, lay people were beginning to see at the end of 1967 that some of the powers of decision in fact lay in their own hands; that they, unused as they were to any measure of control over their religious life, had it in their power to bring about effective change, and perhaps in the long run to be the determining factor in the future directions that they, with their bishops and priests, would take.

The extent of defection from the Church in the US has never been studied seriously, although statistics from other denominations indicate a substantial conversion rate of Catholics to other Churches. The traditional position taken has been 'once a Catholic, always a Catholic', and much past organizational energy went to retrieving the 'fallen-aways'. Certainly the rate of conversion to the

Church has fallen off considerably in the last decade, averaging now only a few hundred converts per diocese annually. It is also apparent that in the last decade a larger number of Catholics have left the practice of their religion as judged by standards of Sunday attendance and reception of the sacraments.

It would be interesting to analyze the reaction that these two factors of defection and lay dissent within the American Church produces among the bishops, clergy and among lay people themselves. The phenomena are clearly present, and the reaction is detectible. It seems to be one of dismay and fright. Before 1962 the Church and its people were an unseamed garment; if occasional minor rents appeared, the damaged fragment was torn off and forgotten, and the whole incident rationalized out of existence. But since 1962 a new phenomenon occurs: people (mostly priests and nuns) not only leave the Church but make public announcement of their reasons. These years have seen many incidents of this kind, and in almost every diocese the abrupt disappearance of priests and nuns has been too frequent to escape comment. Understandably, the defection of clergy is more frightening to bishops and religious superiors than the lapse of lay people or the falling off in vocations. But it is surprising that the general fear and malaise of the orthodox establishment should be publicly acknowledged by a bishop spokesman (Auxiliary Bishop John Dougherty of Newark, NJ) in a press conference at the 1967 November meeting of the episcopacy.

Dismay more than any other mood characterizes the present temper of the laity as well as the clergy of the United States. A large majority of adult Catholics have the uneasy feeling that change and reform has gone too far too fast. Except on the issue of birth control, they would wish it to go at a more sedate pace. Only a small percent feel that reform has dragged, that the most substantial issues before the Church have barely been touched in America, and are impatient for further signs that American Catholics are maturing to their role in the Church.

I think that one can legitimately conclude from the events of Vatican II and after, that the two greatest needs for radical reform in the Church are (1) in Church management policy, and (2) in the belief system of the Church, particularly in the key motives for belief. This second area, the need for development of doctrine, for the recasting of traditional teachings concerning papal infallibility, the authority of the *magisterium*, the manner of Christ's 'real' presence in the Eucharist, and other heretofore unchangeable doctrines, has not yet come to the attention of most American laymen. The moment is a dreaded one, and should be, for the American Catholic is, as a rule, religiously illiterate. He has not been encouraged until recent years to discuss the nature of his own faith or the meaning of the Church's doctrines, and the older among these forty-five million will be unable to. As long as there was no dissent in the Church, no freedom in Catholic journalism, and no necessity to carry out reform, which was the situation until 1962, the vast majority of lay people were undisturbed in their placid living of the traditional faith. They were comfortably unaware of the winds of change that had already blown through other religious bodies in the western world. But now the American layman, like his brothers elsewhere in the Catholic world, is involved in the 'crisis of belief'. If one makes the judgment on the basis of his preparation and religious education, neither he nor his children will fare well in that crisis.

Perhaps the greatest problems of the layman in the future will stem from the present introversion in theology and in the whole mechanics of reform. The attention of theologians and of the Church generally has been given to matters essentially peripheral to the crisis of belief, which is the decisive issue for the Church today. The American Church has been exercised over the language of the Mass, the disloyalty of those who dare experiment with liturgical formats, the future of its school system, the celibacy of its priests, the obedience of its nuns, and the revision of canon law. All of these are household matters—the trivia of reform. The Church has not prepared itself or its people for an encounter in which the very foundation of their faith will be tested, nor is it willing to do so now. The overriding concern of the Catholic establishment in 1967 was to obtain larger amounts of federal and state funds for its school system; little attention and practically no funds were alloted to the purposes of religious education outside the school system, or for research and preparation of teachers in the field of religious education.

Thus it is likely that the American Church does not know that it is in serious trouble, is still unaware that it exists in a world of unbelief, and does not perceive that the fringes of that unbelief have already touched it.

Women: the Church's Third Class Citizens

ARLENE SWIDLER

Being a woman in the post-conciliar Church can be a frustrating struggle. The laity in general is enthusiastic, even exhilarated, with the new moral theology with its emphasis on communal worship, growth in love, self-contribution in the service of the People of God, independent initiative. But it seems that none of these is really intended for what the Catholic liturgy refers to as 'the fragile sex', who now find themselves transferred from second to third class status, quite some distance beneath the now emerging layman. Women are more different than ever.

Neither poets and philosophers nor popular thought have ever agreed on just what the nature of woman is. Is she self-abnegating or is she hopelessly vain? Is she full of imagination and fantasy or is she a stickler for detail? Is she domineering or is she docile? Femme fatale or saint? The world has never really figured out just how woman differs from ordinary people; why then is it necessary for the Church to define woman and her status?

For define her we do. And with every stroke by which we whittle out an image of woman we pare away some of her potentialities for growth and maturity. In being defined, woman is confined.

Even the greatest heroines of the Church, its women saints, are classified into neatly defined little categories, none of which is helpful as an ideal. The Missal's table of contents has laid them out: the virgin martyr, the virgin, the martyr, and the neither-virgin-nor-martyr. None of these is really positive. The virgin is defined in terms of what she does not do, the martyr in terms of what is done to her; the neither-virgin-nor-martyr is an interesting example of a double negative which does not add up to anything positive.

Our masculine categories are much more inspiring. The title 'bishop' or 'abbot' suggests a man who leads and guides the People of God; an abbess is relegated to the virgin category. Most disturbing is the big catch-all. For men it is the confessor. The Mass in the vernacular has made the declaration 'I confess one baptism for the forgiveness of sins' a part of our consciousness once more. To confess again means to witness, to bear Christ to the world, and we recall that St Luke in the Acts of the Apostles uses the word witness and apostle synonymously. The confessor is the lay apostle; the title is close to being a perfect summary of modern moral theology. Yet women are never confessors; instead they are saints-neither-virgins-nor-martyrs. They are passive.

In recent years the entire Church has made the transition in orientation from an individualistic and isolated love of God alone to a love for God who resides in the entire human community. For women, so accustomed by training and long tradition to focus their affections on their immediate circles, the spiritual strength demanded is unusually great. This new responsibility—and freedom, for here, as always, the two are one—demands a model who does not merely accept the events that befall her but responds to them wholeheartedly. And the Church has not provided one.

For a while it seemed that some of the sisters might give us an idea of what a mature dedicated woman could become, of how a woman encounters the world, but the vision has been lost: sister too has been 'defined' by the Church. The proper sister operates within very narrow confines, we are led to believe. She accepts the spiritual director appointed for her, and with it the direction of her growth. Her extramural activities are defined by men, and with them her intellectual growth. Her hours are limited by law, and with them her gift of self. She remembers the rule too conscientiously to forget herself. If sister is not completely invisible, she appears only as a witness to a static virginity; how then can she teach women to respond to the *kairos* with the warmth and spontaneity which alone will make them the credible witness of Christian love?

The defining and confining of woman's activity and concern is so devastating and cruel because it is presented as having ultimate authority, as linked with the entire divine economy. It is one aspect of the traditional functional view of society. Such a perspective is not, of course, found only within Christianity. The rigid Hindu caste system has been explained in functional analogies: the Brahmans, the head, are the thinkers and teachers; the Kshatriyas, the arms, are warriors; the Vaisyas, or thighs, are the merchants; and the Sudras, or feet, are the menials. More familiar to us is the legend of Menenius Agrippa, who subdued the rebellious suppressed plebeians with a similar image: each of the classes of people is necessary for the well-being of the body, for how can the belly feed the body unless it is itself fed by the members? Our own image of the Mystical Body in Paul's letters is derived from this same classical tradition.

This concept has so entwined secular and religious thought that it does not sound strange to us. Orestes Brownson, an American political philosopher of the nineteenth century, wrote that

> The only sense in which we can use the word equality, when applied to the members of the social organism, is that each member has an equal right to be enabled, by the Laws, to perform his appropriate function.[1]

Yet the applications of this theory are largely abandoned. Men may go from one job to another and shift functions as they please; boys are no longer taught to follow in their fathers' trades; being born into a servile state is unthinkable. Only woman still is taught that she has only one 'appropriate function' which will determine her entire life.

So ingrained is this approach in Catholic thought that whole life-styles have been developed on 'spiritual motherhood', and a

[1] Orestes A Brownson, *Works* XV, 372-3.

book which first appeared in English only a few years ago advises, 'In a woman, aim at forming the *mother*. This is the basic principle in the spiritual formation of women.'[1] Gertrud von le Fort, the most profound advocate of the mystique, says, 'for a woman to be a physician, a guardian, teacher, or nurse is therefore not a profession in the masculine sense of the word, but it is a form of spiritual motherhood'.[2] To profess, like to confess, is to act publicly, and thus to be unfeminine.

The contemporary secular world more and more sees woman's function as fluid, like man's—she too may shift from her job of motherhood to a job in a store or office. But the Church still sees these other jobs as peripheral and somehow inessential. Often even married women without children are advised to remain in the home. The rationale seems to be that woman's real function is to be man's helpmate; the family has long been considered an extension into time and space of the father, whose name alone it bears, and woman acts as man's helpmate by providing him with this family life, of which children are only one part (Father Bouyer notes that in Genesis Eve as woman 'appears to be a kind of extension of her companion').[3]

The term for helpmate in the Old Testament, however, is also applied to God when he comes to man's aid; the helpmate is by no means necessarily inferior and may indeed be far superior to the person helped. Thomas Aquinas was aware of this meaning when he wrote that woman was indeed a helpmate to man in bearing children, but denied that she was a helpmate in other works, as man could be more efficiently helped by another man.

Our Catholic view that women are destined to be assistants to men has its basis in the letters of Paul. It is St Paul who is most often quoted in the effort to restrict women from any office in the Church and to confine her to the role of subordinate in the family. And Paul is quite explicit on the basis for his statements:

[1] Very Rev. James Alberione, *Woman, Her Influence and Zeal* (Boston: 1964), p. 249.
[2] Gertrud von le Fort, *The Eternal Woman* (Milwaukee: Bruce, 1954), p. 87.
[3] Louis Bouyer, *The Seat Of Wisdom* (Chicago: Pantheon, 1965), p. 3.

For a man ought not to cover his head, since he is the image and glory of God; but woman is the glory of man. For man was not made from woman, but woman from man. Neither was man created for woman, but woman for man (1 Cor 11:7–9).

I permit no woman to teach or to have authority over men; she is to keep silent. For Adam was formed first, then Eve; and Adam was not deceived, but the woman was deceived and became a transgressor (1 Tim 2:12–14).

It is quite clear that the relationship of woman to man as Paul sees it is based not on the fall but on the story of creation; and woman's inferiority—for this is clearly what Paul is saying—is based not on history but on her very nature.

There are, of course, two separate accounts of the creation of mankind in Genesis. And a second, but older, version, beginning in the second chapter of Genesis, tells us the story of the creation of Eve from man's side and the legend of the fall. The implications of the story of the fall may differ: was Eve not less to blame because she had been tempted by a superior being? Did Mary not overcome the death Eve brought into the world by bearing the Light of the world? But the story itself remains prominent in our Catholic consciousness as a reminder of woman's weakness.

Other tales from the Old Testament are being understood more and more as figurative presentations, but the story of Adam and Eve is regarded as close to official dogma. The reason is ironic. In the middle of the last century racists were attempting to prove that Negroes were members of an inferior race and thus that slavery was not wrong. To combat any pre-Adamite or polygenist theories upon which such arguments could be based, a strong statement affirming the unity of mankind as one family descended from one stock was prepared for the First Vatican Council: 'If any one denies that the entire human race has come from one protoparent, let him be anathema.' The Council disbanded for political reasons before the dogmatic canon could be voted on and approved, but the proposition retains a certain moral force.[1] And so

[1] An account of the discussion of monogenism in the last century can be found in Joseph T Leonard, SSJ, *Theology and Race Relations* (Milwaukee: Bruce, 1963), pp. 53–58.

what the Catholic Church intended as a means of assuring the equality of the Negro—the story of Adam and Eve—is now used to perpetuate the inequality of women.

Throughout the history of the Church woman has been told she must choose between being Eve or Mary. Either she is self-willed and insists on making her own decisions, which leads her and everyone connected with her to downfall, or she is submissive, silent, and saintly. Men may fit anywhere in the entire spectrum of human goodness, but women, supposedly, are always at one end or the other. Cardinal Suenens is typical:

> Woman has the awe-ful choice of being Eve or Mary: she is rarely neutral. Either she ennobles and raises man up by her presence, by creating a climate of beauty and human nobility, or she drags him down with her in her own fall.[1]

Yet such a dichotomy is completely contrary to the experience of anyone living in the world.

The metaphor is weighted with the analogy of the organic society, and women is told that the fate of the human race depends upon her keeping her place. With the threatening example of the rebellious Eve held before her, the average woman, like the oppressed plebeians and the Hindu outcaste, accepts her fate as the inferior or struggles with the irrational fears and guilts that such superstitious worship of the status quo bring forth.

This attitude of course has been fostered by the Marian piety which has been presented to women over the years. To a shocking extent Mary has been presented as the ideal for women and Jesus as the ideal for men. Bernardine Bishop goes so far as to say, 'Christ is the embodiment of the archetypal masculine. . . .'[2] Such attribution has worked in man's favor in more than one way. The attitude of quiet listening, pondering, and docility of Mary toward God is presented as the ideal attitude of woman toward mere man. And where woman is taught to emulate the outward

[1] Cardinal Suenens, *The Nun in the World* (Westminster: Newman Press, 1962), p. 15.
[2] Bernardine Bishop, 'The Future of the Female', in *The Future of Catholic Christianity*, ed. Michael de la Bedoyere (London: Hodder and Stoughton, 1966), p. 55.

manifestations of Mary—to play 'first century Bible-land woman' —man is taught to imitate the *spirit* of Jesus' teachings, as no one is called to be literally crucified. The fact that Jesus was speaking to all Christians when he said 'I am the way, the truth, and the life' is passed over. Women are admonished to live like Mary who, as one pastor supposedly sermonized, 'was not out playing cards or drinking coffee at the neighbor's house when the angel arrived— no, she was home saying her rosary'. Men are not presented with the parallel life of the humble St Joseph who lived an even more hidden life and seems to have been as home- and family-oriented as his spouse.

Mary's relationship to her God and to her divine Son, which should be the prototype of the relationship of all mankind to God, is instead narrowed to include only women and then broadened to include their relationship to their husbands, the clergy, and ultimately mere maleness.

Gertrud von le Fort, who sees woman as the symbol of the beautiful and mysterious hidden life which is so desperately needed in today's world, finds the apostles 'in an attitude of womanly acceptance'[1] at Pentecost. Most spiritual writers on the subject of woman are far from her profundity, however, and suggestions that women remain subject to men—one pastoral writer warns that the priest should address himself more to men than women so that the husband, by instructing the wife in her religion, be enabled to practice his position as head—are often not short of idolatrous. Woman is asked to please man rather than God, and it is easy to see how the typical feminine vices of vanity and pettiness come of serving this false god.

Flowing from the definition of the married woman as wife and mother only is her position in the parish structure. Legally her parish citizenship is inferior to that of her husband. And although the distinctions may be small, the attitude these foster in the mind of the average pastor is strong indeed. Complaints range from the not extraordinary cases of women who go to the pastor to discuss school problems and are dismissed with the statement that 'I will

[1] Von le Fort, p. 6.

speak only to the head of the family on things of this sort' to the relatively unusual problem of the woman who refused to change her legal name at the time of marriage and later has difficulty registering with her pastor at a new parish.

The discriminations in membership are of the same sort as often occur in national laws, sometimes under the guise of making things easier for women, and are there opposed because they make the citizenship of a woman of lesser importance than that of her husband. Canon law provides that in cases where the husband and wife are members of different rites the woman may change to the rite of her husband without any special permission, but he may not change to hers that easily. This is not at all surprising when we consider that the legal parish domicile is imposed on three classes of persons: wives, children, and the insane. The wife thus becomes a member of the parish through her husband.

Unfortunately one of the more imaginative solutions to our contemporary problem of the lifeless impersonal parish has also identified the married-woman parish-member completely with her husband and forgotten her own individual intellectual and social needs. Many families who belong to 'professional parishes'—such as university ministries—have discovered that the husband is wildly enthusiastic about the intellectual community it provides and the apostolic orientation it gives to his whole life, and the wife slowly becomes more discouraged and withdrawn from the parish life. A solution is difficult to find. Few women, for example, are willing to accept a status in their parish as 'faculty wife' (even if the image conjured up by that term were not so dismal) in which their only bond to the community is their husband, and the peculiar apostolate of the parish is not their own. Devoted homemakers, on the other hand, in a territorial parish of much more varied texture, will often be happy to be considered 'wife and mother', as vocational a term as mechanic or teacher. For the husband and wife to belong to separate parishes seems impractical and in most cases even unhealthy.

With all this consignment of woman to a minor role in the functioning of the Church it is difficult to see how we can continue to refer to the Church as mother, as *she*. The analogy of the Church as the nurturer and teacher as opposed to the authority of Christ cannot hold when all the acts of the Church universal are governed and directed by males who see their function as to rule.

The analogy is complicated by the fact that each bishop, and in practice each priest, is taken to represent Christ, and the laity assume the passive female role. The laity who are beginning to rise into minor policy-making positions on the lower levels are, however, for the most part male. For although spiritual and popular writers have tried to romanticize homemaking and child-rearing as the most demanding of all professions, the clergy at least remain unconvinced. Lay people on parish and diocesan boards have too often been professional men with no special competence in the area, or successful business men. We are still awed by the man who makes money, assuming he can apply his golden touch to religious matters with magical results. But the wife who has shown unusual competence in running a home, educating children for leadership, and integrating her life is instead asked to report for bingo duty. Even on the boards and staffs of seminaries, where men are being formed to serve the needs of a population over half female, women are seldom found.

Part of the reason for this is the equation of woman with 'the heart'. Definition of 'the heart' varies considerably. In the earlier days of the Church it merely meant that woman, confined to her home and uneducated, did not think well and tended to be governed by her emotions. Sometimes today it means that women, accustomed to working with people, especially with children, tend to bring more warmth and humanity to their work and relationships with others, an approach which surely would be no small contribution to today's Church. But too often, like other imagery and symbolism which has been superstitiously ossified by religion, it has been set up as a norm. We are now told that a woman is 'queen as long as she asks humbly; but should she presume to command or *reason*, then her influence evaporates'.[1] This same author tells us that the humility and passivity of woman's position are a

[1] Alberione, p. 85. The italics are mine.

'blessing in disguise since it makes things easier for her and by staying in her place she will be loved, venerated, respected'.[1]

Our whole approach to symbolism has been incorrect. We must not discover that an object is a natural symbol for a truth and then proceed to perfect the object by making it conform more closely to what we think it represents. Just because the birds of the air are a natural symbol of the complete dependence of the creature upon the creator it does not follow that bird-feeding stations are evil; it is just as ludicrous to discover woman's role in gestation as a natural symbol of man's passivity and acceptance and then to educate and form each woman toward this ideal.

It has long been clear that any major movement toward equality for woman parallels other movements for equality—the abolition of slavery in America was the real source of the impetus for legal rights for women in America, and the pain which a good many Catholic women feel today when they see non-Catholic men permitted to share in the Catholic liturgy in a way that they themselves are denied is undoubtedly leaving its impression. Since Vatican II especially, our whole emphasis has been toward seeing other people as individuals and toward loving and accepting others for what they are, even if that differs radically from what we are. This is the real meaning of brotherhood. As Jacqueline Grennan summarized it, the key drives of our time are integration, internationalism and ecumenism. The Church is involved in trying to break down many walls, and there seems to be no fear that Burmese, Negroes or Presbyterians will be unable to keep what is good in their culture, thought and life-patterns—and perhaps teach what is excellent in their own tradition to the rest of the world—simply because each is now thought of as an equal and welcomed openly by those in other groups. And yet the status of woman as perpetuated in the Church suggests that woman's differences must be legislated lest they disappear; at the same time we are taught that these differences were ordained by the creator.

This is doubly unfortunate because at this particular time the official approaches toward other nations, races and Churches are

[1] Alberione, p. 223.

clearly progressed far beyond the attitudes of the average individual member, and it is the personal relationships which must now be fostered. These depend heavily upon spontaneous gestures and informal social life rather than official meetings and dialogues, and in this area it is the women who dominate the scene. Yet because they have not yet been trained to openness, because they are still taught a falsely lady-like reticence and narrowness in their social circles, symbolized by the concealment of their own given names in correct social usage, the social life of the average Christian tends to build up rigid social structures rather than to contribute to the brotherhood of man.

One solution to this many-faceted problem, often proposed by liberals of both sexes, is to merge the lay groups on all levels from the parish to the international. It is significant that this proposal is far more acceptable to the male groups than to the female. The men will, if pressed, admit that the women are probably not yet prepared to assume their rightful place, but the more perceptive women wonder whether the men are yet prepared to receive the women as equals.

An example from the American scene is illuminating. In practice the National Council of Catholic Men and the National Council of Catholic Women are not considered equals. The Jesuit editor of *The Documents of Vatican II* is typical when, in his list of commentators to the volume, he describes the executive director of the NCCM as 'recognized in the United States as the Catholic laity's most official spokesman'. Anyone knowing the executive directors of the two organizations—and I do not—could undoubtedly find many ways of comparing them: one is probably more intelligent, one more personable, one may even be better looking or more pious; in fact, about the only thing that cannot be said is that one is *more official* than the other.

And yet the Jesuit editor was perhaps right: the NCCM director *is recognized* as the most official spokesman for the American laity. The NCCM, for example, is nicely subsidized by the American bishops to produce a television series; the women are not. Such favoritism, which runs through every level from the national to the parochial, can no longer be dismissed as the natural limited perspective of a celibate male clergy and hierarchy. Most Catholic liberals would not dream of serving on a committee or performing a church function from which the Negroes were all automatically excluded; yet it is only seldom that we hear of a parish (much less diocesan) schola cantorum or liturgical or ecumenical committee which refused to function until a representative number of women were included. This kind of integration is not yet fashionable.

Another insufficient solution is the talk in some quarters about the return to the use of deaconesses. When we consider the tremendous change in the life of woman from the time of the earliest Christians to the present—a shift from the state of slavery to full citizenship, from ignorance to college education, from physical confinement in the home to world travel—the suggestion of a return to the use of the biblical deaconess as a symbol of a new confidence in the Catholic woman is rather unimpressive. The use of the English form deaconess is also disappointing, suggesting as it does that the deaconess is not the equal of the deacon. Employment of married women deacons would be a more proper first step at this time.

Some way must be found to provide spiritual guidance for the contemporary woman, and the use of women deacons, and later women priests, is the logical solution. Within the past few years women working for a female priesthood have suddenly discovered that all the recent scholarship on the question has had a cummulative effect; the problem is no longer theological, but merely sociological. This means that it is only a matter of time until the Church gets around to ordaining women. But in the meanwhile, it will be necessary for the male clergy to make an attempt to focus some of their attention toward the problems of contemporary woman. It is rather disconcerting to find that panels and lecture series planned by religious groups to clarify the problems of modern women draw no participants from the clergy or seminarians, and that those who do ask permission are refused it with the terse statement that 'this is none of their concern'.

Here is the reason that women have been so adamant on the

birth control issue, and will continue to question the Church's stand on abortion. As long as men of intelligence and obvious good will oppose the Church's position, today's faithful must constantly experience the Church's intense love and concern for the well being of *all* mankind in the moral decisions it promulgates; mere abstract principles are not credible. Many Catholic women of intense religious conviction fail to discern such a love. They ask whether the position of the Church on sexual matters radiates concern and sympathy for mankind—or half of mankind.

The idea of the official Church calls up only the unusually strong opposition to civil rights for women, the weekly humiliation of being barred from assisting at the altar or perhaps even from singing in the choir in favor of ten year old boys, the old, repeated arguments about letting the mother die even if the fetus dies with her, the decisions on nuns' fashions made by men in Rome. To sensitive women the Church is no longer able to present herself as a loving mother. The great contribution of a Jewish Golda Meir and a Hindu Indira Gandhi cancel out all the traditional talk of how the Church has consistently raised the level of woman above that in other religions.

The Church must first show as much concern about the women who are victims of violence as it does about supposed victims of insult among the hierarchy. It must focus its attention on the illiterates in emerging nations—and these illiterates are mostly women—rather than on just potential seminarians among those peoples. It must care for and protect the widow and orphan rather than just those who have a man to fight the enemy—if it expects its laws to be seen as expressions of Christ's love.

The only solution for the woman problem, as for the less pressing lay problem, is to junk the molds. The vitality and eagerness of today's woman cannot be contained in the ideals and style of gentility, decorum and subordination left from her grandmother's youth. The clergy, like good parents, must teach and guide those intrusted to them until they reach maturity; then, like any loving parent they must rejoice to see some of their children mature far beyond them in love, in knowledge, in responsibility. And to women, whose role has been too long described and circumscribed by a rigid tradition, the Church owes special help.

Women, like ordinary people, must not be confined to one role and one place. Just as the contemplatives have been invited to re-orient themselves to service to the world, women must have two worlds. Each woman needs a private world of warmth and acceptance in which her spirit and personality can unfold, in which she can live as an artist, creating and working for the joy of working; and each woman must find herself sent forth into the public world to respond to its painful demands, to give part of herself to its impersonality, to be Christ. The rhythm differs from woman to woman. For some it means devoting herself to raising a family and going out only a few hours a week; for others it means a full professional life and a few quiet rooms to retreat to. For many it means trying to fill both professional and family demands adequately. Each of these patterns brings its own problems.

Life is difficult for anyone, but for women brought up to please men rather than God and now subject to pressures from clerics on the one side and feminists on the other, the situation is grossly unfair. And the Church which teaches the need of both the quiet interior life and the mission to the world, must show women that each must determine for herself the balance of personal and public. Only if women feel free to discover their own path to salvation with the warm and sympathetic approbation of the Church will they finally be free to discover just what they really are.

Today the Church must supply the means for women to grow in both these facets. We must find ways to help mothers establish real family life; we must send reading materials and constructive projects for children into the home. Now that the long-resented churching ceremony is so seldom used we might request women to draw up a new family-oriented liturgy for use at baptisms. We might experiment with our retreats and missions, perhaps inviting Montessori teachers to lead conferenes and discussions for parents.

For the mother who finds herself completely limited by the needs of the family the Church must present genuine opportunities for service for a few hours each week, providing nursery service and transportation if necessary. The woman who has been encouraged by us to bear more children than her abilities and energies warrant will especially need our aid in developing a balanced life. But the mission must be a valid one; no adult may be told to clean out the attic for a white elephant sale as her part of the apostolate. Each woman must be given the opportunity to accept a real responsibility according to her talents and desires—becoming a friend to someone lonely, visiting the sick, teaching or organizing an apostolic project. It must not be anything which can just as well be bought: she should not be asked to leave her home to clean or sew or cook or type. Woman's contribution is not to raise or save money for the parish; she must confess Christ by serving people, not structures.

The most imagination will be needed in finding ways to create small intimate communities among women who are alone. In schools and universities we will have to find ways to help girls to learn how to create a community so that they will be able to form families or circles of friends later. But the greatest need right now is for someone to bring the elderly, who too often live close to poverty and in fear and loneliness, into a warm circle of friends. The Church must be willing to experiment, even to the extent of sending retired sisters out to live alone or in pairs and build up communities to give warmth and security to the lonely.

If the Church will reach out to women as it does to separated brethren and Negroes, acknowledging its omissions in the past and providing them the means and stimulus to grow into mature and responsible Christians, it will find itself repaid many times over. Its women will grow into service in every area and it will be unnecessary—after Vatican III—to address one charge to rulers; another to men of thought and science; one to artists; another to the poor, the sick and the suffering; one to workers; another to youth; and one to women alone, as though they formed a monolith to be treated separately.

Schism, Heresy and a New Guard

FREDERICK D WILHELMSEN

A writer contributing to a symposium of this nature must define his position at the very beginning of his essay. It is of the very nature of the crisis that Catholics today are deeply divided on the meaning and destiny of their Church. This American Catholic defines himself as a radical traditionalist, as a Catholic faithful to the historic creeds and as a rebel within contemporary secular society.

In a word, I am a papist, proud of the Catholic inheritance in history and grateful to God for the faith I received at baptism. This Catholic does not believe that the Church ought to adjust itself to that euphemism known as 'the world' nor does this Catholic feel the slightest repugnance towards the history of his Church, be it from Constantine to Trent or from Trent to today. I am a triumphalist, convinced that Christ's Church is the only guaranteed road to salvation and the only hope for civilization.

That a crisis grips the Roman Catholic Church at this time in history I take as evident, a fact not needing demonstration here. The modernism of the turn of the century was, Jacques Maritain insists in his *The Peasant of the garonne*, 'a mild case of the measles' in comparison with the doctrinal deviations sweeping the Church today. I would like to explore this crisis but first it is necessary that it be defined.

In the bluntest of theological terms the Church of the post-Vatican II era is racked by internal schism; in terms more comfortable to current schools of psychology, the Church is suffering a grave inferiority complex in the effort of many of its leaders, clerical and lay alike, to adjust the Bride of Christ to contemporary secularist society. The causes of this malaise lie deeply embedded within the nature of modern Western society. Therefore, I address myself, in this study, first to establishing my theological and psychological propositions; secondly, to exploring what I consider to be their causes.

Schism can be understood abstractly in two senses. Formally, schism comes into being and disturbs a Church when a body of men leave that Church in order to found another because they differ on matters of faith, morals, or discipline with the mother organization. Formal schism can also be ratified publically when the mother Church itself expels dissidents from its body because of doctrinal, disciplinary, or moral deviations. When the differences between the two ecclesiastical bodies are more doctrinal than disciplinary, schism hardens into heresy, each body excommunicating the other. But before schism is formalized juridically, it must exist really in the hearts of men. Men formulate and express heretical doctrines long before they act on them and separate themselves from a mother Church they consider to be in error on the meaning of Christ's teaching. It matters not at all that the term 'heresy' is in disrepute today. Those who chastize others for using the term consider *them* to be heretics, even though they eschew the word. Hard thinking, unburdened by sentimentality, demands that the philosopher, meditating on religious doctrine, use the term. This is offensive to the pious sensibility of the times, but only Oscar Wilde could have taken seriously the proposition that a man who calls a spade a spade ought to be forced to dig with one.

I suggest to the reader that the Roman Catholic Church today is already in schism in my second sense of the word. This schism is concentrated within the Western world, rampant in Holland, widespread in Germany and the United States, but present everywhere in diverse degrees of virulence. The disease tends to abate its fury as one moves away from the centers of the Church and out towards its periphery, in mission countries and in diaspora. Only the Church itself, through its hierarchy, can act authoritatively in dealing with schism. Thus far the Church has not so acted.

Nonetheless there is a kind of authority which belongs to the human reason itself and which ought to permit any educated Catholic to determine for himself whether or not the People of God is wounded by heresy. Let us distinguish, therefore, between an authoritative and an epistemological criterion for discerning the presence of schism in our midst. The juridical pertains only to the *Magisterium* but the epistemological pertains to good sense. If two or more Catholics do not believe in the historic creeds in the precise same way, then schism exists between them and brother is in arms against brother. This civil war actually exists today in the Church.

Can any intelligent man, be he Catholic or not, seriously believe that Cardinal Ottaviani believes in the same body of substantive doctrine entertained by Cardinal Alfrink of Holland? Can such a man—I assume here that he is a fellow marked by intellectual integrity and not prone to weasle when called upon to judge— upon reading *Commonweal's* celebrated editorial attack on Pope Paul VI's encyclical *Mysterium Fidei*, an editorial in which the progressivist editors of that journal accused the Pope of being a bad theologian, seriously entertain the proposition that the Roman Pontiff and the editors in question hold the same substantive position on the sacrament of the altar? Can my intelligent observer assent honestly to the proposition that many contemporary theologians, talking a variety of tongues but talking all of them with a Dutch accent, believe what I believe when I recite the words of the Creed: '*Et exspecto resurrectionem mortuorum. Et vitam venturi saeculi. Amen*'? Can these theologians who begin now to question the immortality of the soul be said to maintain what the vast bulk of us Catholic faithful have believed since the dawn of the Christian era?

Can the Bishop of Cuernavaca in Mexico, who recently declared at the National University in the capital of that nation that Marxism is the only possible road to actualize the Christian message, be said to hold the same series of judgments concerning Marxism and Catholicism that are entertained by the Cardinal Prince Primate of Hungary in his self-imposed exile in the American Legation at Budapest? Does His Excellency of Cuernavaca *react* to Communism emotionally as does the Cardinal when he peers out of his window at the booted and uniformed killers who maintain a constant watch lest Mindszenty fly the coop and embrace a martyrdom for which, we have reason to believe, he yearns?

Or, to select a humbler and more academic instance involving myself, can Leslie Dewart who recently denied the existence of God, his Being, and the Blessed Trinity in *The Future of Belief* and who was rewarded for his rosary of heresies by his fellow Canadian Catholics by having his book declared the Catholic Book of the Year, believe what I believe about God's existence, Being, and trinitarian life? Now the difference between Professor Dewart and myself is measured precisely by the fact that I believe in the above doctrines and he does not. This puts him in schism so far as I am concerned and, if he be consequent with his position, I must be in schism to him, or, to comfort his own rhetoric, I must be out of tune with the contemporary consciousness which is the only heresy he seems to recognize. One cannot walk both sides of this street. If Dewart is a Catholic, then I am not. And if I am a Catholic—the weight of an ancient tradition would seem to assure me that I am—then Dewart most certainly is not.

The most elementary textbook in the philosophy of religion has always marked out Catholicism as the archetype of an *exoteric* faith in opposition to an *esoteric* one. Whereas esoteric religions permit contradictory formulations of their doctrine to be entertained within the total sweep of the gnosis, exoteric Catholicism has always insisted that the humble Irish washer woman (remember Newman's example!) believes exactly what the pope in Rome believes. Differences look to a profundity of insight and not a shift in content. The fact that this is no longer true marks out, tragically and as would a wound, that the Church of God is internally disturbed by the gravest of schisms in all of its history.

The evidence is legion. I have made my own list but my readers can make their own. Together they would fill volumes and they would spell out the tragedy within which the Church lives in our time. And this tragedy is not confined to conceptual and propositional differences concerning Christian doctrine as though the latter were some kind of celestial geometry. Doctrinal propositions are not the faith, of course. We do not concede this to the progressivists because we learned it long ago from a Doctor of the Church who is not, as the Spaniards say, a 'saint of their devotion': Thomas Aquinas. But although not formally identified with the living faith of the People of God, defined doctrines are the articulation, the flowering into speech and reasoned coherency, of that secret and inner treasure conferred upon a Christian at baptism. The slightest alteration in the expression of true doctrine works to the wounding of the prayer life of the least of all the faithful. Impoverishment of doctrine is both produced by, and in turn produces, spiritual impoverishment in the deepest recesses of the heart where God talks to man in the wordless mystery of grace.

Our crisis in the post-conciliar Church is fundamentally doctrinal and to say so much is to say everything that can be said. If the heretics in our midst succeed in altering the substance of the faith; if they reduce infallibility to some vague response of the entire Catholic people, a response today engineered incidentally by the mass media that make do for the inspiration of the Holy Ghost; if they continue to rub out the sacrificial aspect of the Mass until it drains away into a familial *agapé*; if they succeed in so blurring doctrinal differences with dissidents that the unique character of the Rock which is Peter is lost behind a cloudburst of false ecumenical expediency; if they implement their liturgical reforms in the direction of ever more noisy Masses that simultaneously hide God in a corner and then offer him to be handled sacrilegeously by laymen, as in Holland; if they continue to permit the 'marriage' of homosexuals while they piously write theologies condoning sodomy, if they bully Rome into silence or partial silence—and this is their tactic today: they are buttressed by the world press in their efforts—the Roman Catholic Church as we have known it will disappear.

Continuing to exist as a despised and often persecuted sect (we have Christ's promise that the Church will last until the end of time), the Church will no longer occupy the center of that civilization which she created and which has been, in the immortal words of Hilaire Belloc, 'the standing grace of this world'. The mass exodus today of priests like Davis and Kavanaugh hell bent on heresy and the marriage bed, will be followed by a truly frightening phenomenon, a quiet and unheralded exodus of millions of traditionalists, who will not deny the faith but who will have found it impossible to worship any longer, led by a new breed of priests that simply does not believe in the things or in the priorities that we have inherited from our fathers and from civilization itself.

Possibly the most hideous crime of all will be the confusion of the old, of men and women on the verge of death when faith is often tried to the point of despair in that supreme act of facing a destiny whose name is either God or Nothing at All. An uncle of mine died last Christmas. He kept repeating in the last few days of his agony, as the life was rushing out of his heaving and over-worked heart, 'There is nothing over there for me. I shall never see my father and mother again. Now they tell us there is no afterlife.'

Do not try to comfort such men—you and I, dear reader, one day or another!—with talk about building the secular city; with fantasies about omega points; with illusions about a human Church; with lies about a heaven that is this world. In that ultimate moment in which the soul traverses the Calvary of despair and is tested therein, all the modernist theologies are so much straw. It is the tradition that sees a man through, neither more nor less. 'If Christ be not risen, our faith is in vain,' says St Paul and today it is insinuated in seminaries everywhere that he be not risen, that the resurrection was an 'event' that 'happened' inside the apostles. If this is so, then why any Church at all? Why not the despair of the pagan who at least ate, drank, and was merry before he tumbled down the abyss into nothingness? It is the dying who suffer the cruelty of the new Church. Their faith is stolen from them and this robbery of the only gift that ultimately means anything to man is something we shall never forgive the heresiarchs in our midst. For this crime against charity they merit every punishment ever dreamed up in ages past by the Holy Inquisition for they have done the last outrage to the human spirit: they have taken away hope at the moment of death. In so doing they crucify again the God in whom they no longer believe and who also was forsaken by his Father when he hung there on that cross.

A purely human Church at the service of secular liberalism, its liturgy swept clean of grandeur, its prayer life imposed upon the faithful by a vernacular liturgy whose proletarian flatness is only equalled by its artistic banality, for a time might linger on in history. It would look pretty much the way the Church looks today in Oklahoma, like that Church there that displays the photograph of a woman modeling a foundation garment (a peculiarly ugly woman, to my taste) taking the place of the Station of the Cross that remembers the women of Jerusalem who wept upon meeting Christ with his cross. A purely human Church would buy completely Roger Garaudy's Marxist-Catholic dialogue and would sink, more rapidly than slowly, into the morass of that network of international organizations dedicated to soften up the West for a final occupation by the Soviet Union. In that same church in Oklahoma a photograph of Karl Marx represents our Lord Jesus Christ. Such a human Church might command the allegiance of the peaceniks among us, of the hippies, of the New Left. It is doubtful whether Marines returning from Vietnam would care to worship in it.

At best such a Church, the dream of the Left, would not last more than a generation or so. Totally the chameleon of every last twist of the secular mind, real men would soon sicken of its lack of personality. After all—once again—what do we need a Church for, if its principal destiny consists in serving the city of man? We can do that altogether without a corps of priests who would serve the city better by becoming social workers. In a word, unless Rome can clean up this mess, unless Rome can find in the Catholic world a power structure willing to back up its every command (I shall return to the issue), I predict three consequences for the Church:

1. A continued exodus of the Left and especially of progressivist priests impatient with the 'institutional Church's' reluctance to move fast enough in the total de-catholicizing of Catholicism.

2. A subsequent drift away from religious practice by millions of traditionalists in disgust at the failure of the Church to check its own enemies from within and due to their inability to worship at the new liturgy.

3. The subsequent rapid humanizing of the Church, now purged of its conservative and traditionalist elements, until it ceases to be either a force in the world or a danger to the mythology of secular liberalism.

And, although not given to apocalyptic visions, I conclude that should the above occur we would have reached the razor edge of the precipice dividing us from total barbarism and the end of civilization. Let us repeat the proposition; it can never be repeated too often: the Roman Catholic Church created civilization and should that Church abandon its civilizing role in the world out of a desire to placate the forces of secularism, there would be left not one moral voice in all the West, not one authority capable of keeping the standard of human dignity aloft.

Saint John the Evangelist urges us 'to harden ourselves in hope' and therefore no Catholic worth the name can simply acquiesce in the above prognosis. He must look upon it as a kind of Dickensian Christmas Future which will come about only if we fail to reform from within. This reformation of our very sick Church ought to come from the following sources: our elementary and secondary Catholic schools; our universities; our seminaries; the religious orders. I suggest that these avenues are closed to us for reasons which I shall advance. The only other possibilities are reactions from the national episcopacies and from Rome. I hope to demonstrate that we can hope for little from either quarter unless there is a massive reaction from the laity itself which will take the form of what I am going to call 'Catholic Power'.

1. Our primary and secondary schools, especially in the United States, are still largely staffed by nuns, by women. They have inherited, within the English speaking world, the tradition of Irish clericalism and this prohibits their reacting in favor of orthodoxy today. A word first about Irish clericalism. As a result of the bloody Protestant persecution of Ireland by English Protestantism, first under Cromwell and later under the Whig Establishment that dominated England in the late seventeenth and throughout the eighteenth centuries, Ireland suffered the 'Flight of the Wild Geese', the loss of its natural aristocracy that sought an outlet for its energies in the service of the French and Spanish kings. The cultural dominance of the Irish clergy was guaranteed by the priest's assurance, as he mounted the pulpit, that nobody out there in the congregation knew as much as he did about anything under the sun with the exception of farming. A kind of reverential awe surrounded the person of the priest, not only in his spiritual but in his political and social roles. Not unlovely in itself—did it not bespeak Ireland's love for the priests of God ?—this awe left Ireland and went east into England and west into America. The tradition has lingered on.

Our nuns believe anything anybody wearing a Roman collar tells them. In so doing, they reiterate, in a heightened fashion, the reaction of the Catholic laity in both England and the United States. Outside of a handful of old families, descendants of the recusants in England and of the colony founded by Lord Baltimore in the United States, the mass of English speaking Catholics take the word of the priest on everything as being the voice of God. This situation possessed its advantages as long as the clergy was orthodox. Today the New Breed, despite its vaunted rebellion against the dead hand of the past, is cashing in on the clericalism that it publicly deplores. The congregations of nuns, once the strongholds of orthodoxy, are today fields of heretical mischief. Their hysterical mobbing of doubtful and dubious younger theologians such as Hans Küng is symbolic of their total dependence on the Roman collar (on the gray tie in the future, perhaps) and the male psyche. This spills over in their enthusiastic adoption of religion textbooks that systematically 'demythologize' scripture, emphasize the social aspect of Catholicism to the detriment of doctrine, compare—in one case at least—Christ with Martin Luther King and Buddha, and spread a sentimental humanism well suited to the feminine temper.

The results are already upon us; a new generation of little religious monsters whose religion bears small resemblance to that of their parents and whose grasp of the fundamentals of the faith is buried in a sea of ecumenical marshmallows. Cases are multiplying of parents protesting to no avail, and of then withdrawing their children from Catholic schools in order to better preserve their faith. At this particular juncture in history, we can expect nothing from the elementary and secondary system of schools staffed by nuns. They would do an aboutface tomorrow, by the numbers, if ordered to by their male superiors in religion: such is the nature of their servility. But they will institute no reform on their own initiative in favor of orthodoxy. We can look for no hope *there*.

2. Our universities (I refer to the American Catholic universities) were formerly a bulwark of orthodoxy. Built by the pennies and quarters of a proletarian people bent upon assuring a Catholic education for their children, the typical Catholic Liberal Arts College of the past gave its students a mediocre education in the sciences; a vision of our literary tradition that emphasized the Catholic revival in England from Newman to the Chester-Belloc; a splendid discipline in Latin and often in Greek; a somewhat dry but basically sound training in scholastic philosophy; apologetics; and religion courses that did not pedantically pretend to the dignity of theology. Little science; much Latin and some Greek; Church history; scholastic philosophy; dogma; a healthy fear of hell and sex; a weakness for the bottle—this made for a sound education, vastly superior to anything found at Yale or Harvard. The system produced gentlemen, somewhat rough around the collar because these men were largely the sons of working stiffs and immigrants. But they could follow the Mass in Latin and in so doing they were firmly within the large inheritance of Western civilization. They

G

could write good English because their Catholic models wrote the best English of the last hundred and fifty years. If they read anything at all after graduation besides the morning newspaper, it was likely to be an essay by Belloc or a poem by Hopkins. Our graduates were rapidly integrated into the commercial and financial life of America where they have been astonishingly successful despite the dominant Calvinism surrounding them. Spiritually and culturally, however, they were distinct from their fellow citizens because they were Catholics with a specifically Catholic education.

We owe to them the vast machinery of higher American Catholic education today. They paid for it, the old grads. They were far better educated men than are their sons today who can talk about Bultmann, but cannot read a page of Augustine in the common tongue of Christendom; who often know Harvey Cox but not Aquinas; who tend to be corrupted spiritually to the degree of their exposure to theological training. Their teachers today are the sons of poor men, eager to scramble out of the Irish and Italian ghettoes. Truculantly nationalist, even in their liberalism, they despise their own origins. They do not glory in being Catholics but in belonging to the National Association of University Professors. Academic freedom has become a god for them. Their excessive professionalism bears little resemblance to the dedication of an older and shabbier generation of Catholic college professors. I would dissemble were I to suggest that I liked them at all, even though I live among them.

The massive desire to secularize our universities and make them typically American at the expense of their Catholicity has already been juridically successful at Webster. Notre Dame has publicly announced that it is no longer a Catholic University. Saint Louis's invitation of the French Communist theoretician Roger Garaudy to lecture before a crowd estimated at some two thousand, laced with clerical black, plus Santa Clara's invitation to Apteker to participate in a Marxist–Catholic 'dialogue' indicates that not only are our universities secularizing themselves, but that they lack the common decency that prohibits men to sit down with the murderers of their brothers in the faith. Garaudy, after all, publically defended Russia's re-entry into Budapest in 1956. He has blood on his hands, Catholic blood. We can hope for very little from universities with such a massive lack of common shame. Catholic University of America's show of defiance to the very episcopacy upon which it depends in the Curran case (the Reverend Father was caught guilty of teaching artificial birth control out of his own textbook) demonstrated that the press and television will back any insubordination by university professors against the teaching authority of the Magisterium. They have ceased to be Catholic. I gravely doubt whether there are enough dedicated scholars available with a thoroughly Catholic vision of life to staff more than two or three modest colleges in all the United States. There is no hope for us *there*.

3. The religious orders are in deep trouble all over the world. Vocations have fallen off and most orders tend to be split down the middle between traditionalists and progressivists. One older Jesuit in California reported to me tearfully that, as he sits down for meals in common with his fellow Jesuits, an abyss separates him from them, that the soldierly unity in the common cause of the defense of the Faith that has always knit into one the Companions of Jesus has simply ceased to exist. A similar spirit wounds the erstwhile soldiers of Ignatius in the Latin world where, for instance, a number of them went to the American Embassy recently and protested the giving of a loan to the Autonomous University of Guadalajara on the grounds that it is run by 'Fascists'. These 'Fascists' in fact are the survivors and sons of the men who raised the banner of Christ the King some thirty-five years ago in the *cristero* rebellion against the religious persecution of Calles in Mexico. Yet Jesuits are offended by their lyrical and militant Catholicism. An American Dominican predicted to me that the Order of Saint Dominic would disappear within twenty years. It was a bleak and probably overly pessimistic prediction but it fingers a universal disease. Precisely those very orders that owe their existence to the perpetual war against heresy are today most willing to sit down with the enemy. Obviously they are ceasing to attract militant young men to their banners. Who

wants to join sinking ships whose skippers lack the courage to blaze away at the enemy ? No hope *there*.

4. The seminaries that train the diocesan clergy are in comparable trouble. Although there are many laudable exceptions here and abroad, the seminaries of the Latin rite are turning out young priests who lack sufficient linguistic training to say a decent Mass in Latin even if they wanted to. Despite the repeated exhortations in favor of the language of the West in seminary teaching by Pope John XXIII and by Pope Paul VI, but most especially by the former, our seminaries are producing young men cut away from the majesty of the Catholic intellectual tradition. Badly trained in apologetics and often not trained at all, seminarians frequently abandon their vocations in disgust because of the foreign and dangerous doctrines to which they are exposed. I know one ex-seminarian, a Mexican, who had to take turns with a friend at standing guard over a painting of the Virgin of Guadalupe in order that the iconoclasts of his seminary, professors and students alike, would not rip it off the wall on the ground that Marian devotions are today *passé*.

These young men enter seminaries because they believe they have a vocation to serve God. This not very original but certainly quite noble intention is often subtly corrupted by professors, the substance of whose teaching consists in attacking the history of the Church and the Magisterium. Too many young men who persist tend to become little prigs who despise the popular devotions of their flocks, who are contemptuous of their traditions, who whore after every liturgical fancy in the name of a specious 'relevance' that finds, however, little or no resonance out in the pews. It is instructive to talk to such priests. Almost totally ignorant of Catholic letters, they try to be painfully in touch with the last shift of wind within the contemporary consciousness. Many of these young men confuse their priesthood with social service. They would have been better off as playground directors.

Yet it is indeed a miracle that so many turn out decently despite the overwhelming influences working against their very priesthood. I salute these young priests because they have rarely been helped in coming to know the meaning of their destiny as priests. As one of these men hurries from early Mass to religion classes, from confessional to the death bed where the Sacrament he administers stiffens and sends the Christian soul to God; to rosaries said before coffins by mourners who glimpse—if but for a moment—the truth that priests are given us in order to usher us into the Promised Land of the Lord, that they have no other destiny within the economy of salvation; as he baptizes infants and seals in matrimony the young; as he mounts his pulpit Sunday after Sunday and faces the faithful who expect from him neither politics nor the social Gospel but Christ and him crucified, the priest comes to learn that he is not like other men, that he is marked by God himself, that his vocation is fingered mysteriously by eternity. Unbuttressed by the triumphalist education of the past, forbidden crusades and warned against making converts, often ignorant of the giants of our own inheritance who could shore him up humanly in his daily going down into the world; altogether without that pride in the past that marked the older priest; incapable of decent rhetoric because good prose is always triumphalist; not even knowing that civilization is simply a byproduct of Catholicism, these young priests of whom I speak are heroes.

Crippled spiritually and intellectually in their education, bombarded towards mediocrity by the vast bulk of the Catholic press that comes their way, these men—in the very exercise of their sacred office—are undoing the pusillanimous character of their formation. They do not escape into the crowd as does that Jesuit philosophy professor at Fordham who dresses in mufti because he enjoys anonymity—and then advertises the fact in the *New York Times*. These young secular priests—the best of them—out there on the firing line of birth and death often come to know that a cross is too big an affair to carry around without being conspicious. They look like what they are: priests—men burnt by God and no jesuitical nonsense about sport coats and coloured ties. But it is Christ that makes them good priests. Their seminaries, taken in the large and by the handful, lack both the will and the intellectual brilliance needed to pull off a successful reform.

5. Can the rank and file of the Catholic laity hope for reform from our bishops ? My answer to that question, as suggested in my early remarks, will be a cautious yes . . . if. Our bishops are not simply shepherds of souls. Within the highly industrialized Western world, they are successful business men whose vast diocesan machinery not only cuts across but also weaves itself within a financial and commercial world having little in common with the transcendental claims of the Roman Church. Our bishops are civil leaders as well as religious pastors and this dual role, forming not altogether the most felicitous of marriages, constrains the hierarchy to seek respectability and to live at peace with the dominant secular society surrounding them. The bishops notoriously do not want 'trouble' and they are reluctant to criticize one another.They would have it that everything is well in Peter's Barque.

This passion for respectability within the community, wedded as it must be with the image-making power of the overwhelming liberal mass media, renders bishops reluctant to take stands which must be condemned by the world as harsh and reactionary and obscurantist. Few bishops want the public crucification of Cardinals McIntyre and Ottaviani. Burdened by an inferiority complex, even conservative bishops yearn for a good press. (They will never get it, for the enemy of the Church knows *his* enemies!) We have not entered into the decline of late eighteenth-century France when the King, upon being presented with a candidate for the See of Paris, exclaimed: 'But the Archbishop of Paris ought at least to believe in God.' Our bishops today in the world are largely orthodox (an exception: the Bishop of Cuernavaca, Mendez Arceo) but they suffer, most especially in the Anglo-American world, from an excess of caution which disguises itself as prudence. Perhaps it would be fairer to say that the bishops suffer from the disease of professionalism, the arch-type of which is found in the medical profession. Just as it takes a cosmic explosion involving outer space to get one medical man to even hint in public that another might have been remiss in his duties, so too does it take an even vaster cosmic explosion, invoking worlds upon worlds, to get one bishop to criticize another publicly or even to comment on liturgical or doctrinal scandals taking place outside his own narrow jurisdiction. These bishops often comment bitterly in private but their remarks are always, once again, 'off the record'.

But the hierarchy in the United States at least does seem to be stirring, at last. In a 25,000 word collective pastoral, written in a prose that recalls Newman, the Bishops here have broken their silence and have issued an epistle described by them as a 'major doctrinal statement'. More than two hundred bishops have set their signatures to a document which proclaims what we members of the party of tradition have been proclaiming for a long time now: the Church is in danger. Reaffirming the infallability of the pope and the uniqueness of the Roman Church within the economy of salvation, calling upon priests to shoulder the burden of their vocation and calling those who fail to do so 'defectors', this last episcopal statement gives heart to the defenders of the Catholic tradition. But this document must be followed by deeds.

6. The first deed looks to the restoration of our liturgy from the chaos into which it has fallen. There are those Catholics, fewer in number than we are led to believe, who do seriously prefer the new vernacular liturgy, who do find more spiritual sustenance in it than in the older Latin Mass. With such men we traditionalists cannot quarrel because the question is one of testimony. Each side can only give his own testimony and let the chips fall where they may. Nonetheless, the fact that Catholics today—after a scant three or four years—are rent into two factions, one at home in the new liturgy and the other loathing it bitterly, reveals that the innovators have succeeded in doing in half a decade what the Church's professed enemies never accomplished in four centuries of opposition. They have split the faithful and they are succeeding in creating a new sensibility at war with the old. They have broken us into a high Church and a low Church whose respective members scarcely speak to one another any more. They have artificially reproduced Anglicanism within the Body of the Church.

Traditionalist objections to the new liturgy are sufficiently well known, so that it suffices here merely to list them. The vernacular unveils that awe and mystery which is bound up with the very essence of religion, stripping it thus of the dimension of the holy and of the sacred. This leads to the fashioning of a religious sensibility from which both fear and awe have departed and this reminds us that a common pagan master, Aristotle, condemned men with no sense of awe before the sacred as being something less than human. The vernacular at best can never match the splendor and majesty of the Latin, the common tongue of the Patriarchate of the West, the visible sign of Catholic unity according to Pope John XXIII. But the vernacular offered us, especially in the new English Canon, connives to produce banality and flatness, as well as working towards an egalitarian religiosity which is hostile to the essence of Catholicism. This liturgy destroys those moments of silence when men can enter into communion with their God. It substitutes a fake communal 'togetherness' for true worship and works altogether against any lived awareness that what is taking place on the altar is the sacrifice of Christ to his Father. The busy coming and going of lay readers—those new Mickey Mouses—with their rude instructions to the faithful to get up and sit down, with their nasal intonations of badly translated scriptural passages, violate Pope Pius XII's warning that men worshipping their God should be left at liberty to follow their own dispositions in the matter, that what is abstractly preferable—such as following the Mass with the priest—is often existentially deplorable, that the Mass is as many-mansioned as is heaven itself.

Our bishops could settle the *liturgical* differences between traditionalists and progressivists, for a time at least, by offering us a choice. In so doing, they would fulfill Vatican II's insistence that, whereas the vernacular is only permitted, the Latin must be preserved as the language of the Church, and, we might add, as the last sign of the unity of the West. An effective reaction in favor of orthodoxy can hardly be mounted if the most orthodox of Catholics, those who prefer the Latin liturgy (can there be any serious doubt about *that*?), are left without any effective instrument for their life of prayer. There are tens of thousands of Catholics, possibly millions, who agree with William F Buckley Jr, that the non-Latin Mass 'is the triumph of Philistinism', who have

simply ceased to pray in Church, who fulfill an obligation placed
on them by the Church, but who grit their teeth as they suffer—
Sunday after Sunday—through services which to them are
merely the ape of Protestantism. They watch the Mickey Mouse
flitter back and forth as he flutters pages. They suffer the indignity
of interfaith services in which heresiarchs lord it over Catholics in
our own temples. They sicken at the silly hymns and they rebel
down in their very guts at God being called 'you' instead of
'thou'. This new hate hour for us often produces the scandal of
Catholics turning away from what was once the communion rail
because they refuse to receive their God standing. Such situations
are intolerable and the blame must be laid squarely where it
belongs; on that knot of doctrinal revolutionaries that pass for
liturgical experts and who sold the hierarchies a mess of pottage
along with the Mickey Mouse. A sound reaction within the Church
can hardly set in unless our liturgy is restored to us by our bishops.
7. Ultimately, of course, the reaction must come from Rome and
it can come from Rome only if the Holy See is obeyed. There are
signs that Pope Paul VI might just as well drop his encyclicals in
the Tiber as address them to the Catholic world. As I have
insisted elsewhere, Rome today faces a deep *political* problem
which is has thus far not solved. The Magisterium of the Holy
Father is purely moral as is all authority. And authority is only as
good as the response that it encounters in centers of power willing
to listen to authority itself. The philosophical and political
distinction between power and authority, blurred in modern
times, is evident to anyone who attends to the modes through
which authority exercises itself in all walks of life. A physician
has the authority to tell me to take a long vacation or suffer the
consequences, but I have the power to accept or reject his com-
mands. An automobile mechanic has the authority to advise me
that my car needs a major overhaul, but I possess the power over
my own purse. Now on this earth there is one supreme authority
competent in the things of God, the Pope in Rome. His authority
is so vast that what he binds on earth, God binds in heaven and
what he loosens here below, God loosens above. But his authority,

H

cascading down from dogma through morals to ecclesiastical jurisdiction, is existentially only as good or as effective as the response it encounters in men and institutions who possess power. When Pope Pius IX needed a power to back up his authority he created his own army which, however, did not prove powerful enough. But in normal times, Rome has no power but seeks it in the faithful just as all authority seeks an answer in power in order that it might work its message of truth in the world.

The political helplessness of the Vatican was sealed in 1918 with the disappearance of Austria-Hungary, last Catholic power in the world. From then on, the words of Rome—be they words spoken on the social order or on matters more purely spiritual—have only been acknowledged ceremoniously by the political powers of this world. Nonetheless, Rome did command the allegiance of power *within* the Church itself. Pius XI and Pius XII were obeyed by the whole Church. Today the brutal truth is the reverse: the Pope is not obeyed, not even within his own Church. There can be no doubt but that Holland is a schism and that the Dutch, taken in the large and by the handful, are not going to heed the Vatican on matters liturgical, doctrinal, and moral. An interdict would look silly today only because no one would pay it heed. Paul's insistence, to take another example, that the prohibition against artificial birth control stands, that the entire body of teaching on the subject through to and including the teaching of Pius XII, binds all Catholics in conscience, has been defied. Priests everywhere grant couples permission to use 'the pill' and some theologians teach its licitness openly in books and classes. The Jesuit magazine *America* has proclaimed the traditional teaching impossible for our time: so much for that journal's obedience to the voice of Rome. Paul's subsequent command that the subject be discussed no longer until his long-awaited encyclical has been published has been arrogantly dismissed by Catholic journals that continue to print tons of words on the subject, thus disturbing the conscience of millions of married Catholics who literally do not know whom to believe.

Now the question does not look to who is right on these doctrinal and moral issues facing the Church. Obviously the Pope is right, to any orthodox Catholic. Although that proposition can be aired intellectually and questioned, such airing must take place *outside* the context of a common adherence to the Catholic faith. It pertains to apologetics between Catholics and non-Catholics. It has nothing to do with discussions between Catholics in communion with Rome. That 'Catholics' do in fact question the Holy Father simply buttresses my contention that they are literally in schism, that the heretics among us have substituted the Protestant principle of private interpretation for the Catholic authority of the Magisterium. Given that Rome is more often than not, *not* heeded; given that the religious orders are in plain decay where they are not actually shirking their duty; given that the seminaries are infiltrated by heterodoxy; given that the bishops tend towards timidity, the only possible power-response to the Pope's Magisterium can come from the laity.

I suggest, therefore, that the time has come for the Catholic laity in the West to take matters into its own hands when these matters are one with a positive response to papal authority exercised independently of the bishops in allocutions to the faithful and in encyclical letters, when exercsied through the bishops, or by the bishops in communion with the Holy See. What I am calling for, in a word, is the creation of a Catholic *Power* in the West, of a guard of the Church that will move against the Church's internal enemies on all fronts, intellectually by throwing all the weight of its scholarly authority in the breech in the service of the faith, placing this task at the head of its list of priorities; financially, by squeezing off funds from universities and other institutions that do not toe the papist line; physically, by preventing 'Underground Masses' and other sacrilegious profanations done the sacramental Lord.

Such a power structure, fortified from within by a deep spirituality and annealed from without by a militant and lyrical loyalty to the Holy See in time, could supply Rome with the troops it badly needs if it is going to pull the Church out of the morass within which it finds itself. My suggestion is truly radical for this age because what I propose is a kind of Catholic Power, analogous to other kinds of 'power' that have recently sprung up in our midst. But although radical for our time, my proposal has many precedents in history. It was only the formation of the Holy League in the France of the sixteenth century, when the Duke de Guise organized the Paris rabble—Catholics to a man—against the money power of the Huguenots, that saved France's defection from the faith. It was a mob plus Athanasius that saved orthodoxy in the fourth century from an Arianism that was buttressed by all the worldly power of the imperial court. Catholic Power, manned by laymen who do not yearn after worldly respectability and who glory in fighting odds, is the only effective way, to my mind, to clean the Church of heresy today and to restore to Rome, on its knees, effective control of its own house.

Not only would such a movement produce the above but its very need fingers the deeper psychological causes for the collapse of the faith in our time. These causes must move any thinking man towards meditating upon the nature of the Church within the modern world. That world is hostile to the Church because that world is secularist and the Church must sacramentalize the whole of existence. A sacral world is one with the faith's perpetual rejection of Manicheanism and of any dualism that sharply divorces the sacred from the profane. Just as man is a unity in being and not a duality, *pace* the rationalists among us; just as creation includes the social and political institutions men have fashioned in order that they might live decently and decorously in harmony with one another, so too are these institutions destined to be transfigured by the charism of grace. And they were so transmuted when Christendom came into its own in the Carolingian flowering of the eighth century that looked forwards to the High Middle Ages.

The point is grasped when we see that Catholics, but especially Catholic laymen, had an enormous field upon which to expand their energy in that long thousand years that hammered a civilization out of the forests of Europe. The counterpart to sacralization, secularization, dates from Marsiglio of Padua's *Defensor Pacis* in the fourteenth century, but secularization really began a toing momentum only in the eighteenth century, due to the exhaustion produced by the religious wars of the previous two hundred years. The rapid secularization of society, aided in our day by theologians such as John Courtney Murray, has progressively removed the Church from the marketplace, first isolating her from the civilization she created and then attempting to absorb her very energies into the same civilization, now drained of its Catholic blood. The apostles of a human Church or of an open Church would make of her a fifth wheel in the axis of secularism. Thus they preach a world totally stripped of the sacral and they preach a humanity totally dedicated to building this world. For these reasons they gut the faith of its supernatural center. Their Jesus is not the Christ of the Creeds but a pale precurser of secular humanism. Their Church is not the dispenser of the sacraments, of grace, and of salvation but a progressively egalitarianized instrument in the service of a purely human society.

Thus it came to pass that Catholics, from the eighteenth century on, were progressively robbed of what T S Eliot would have called an 'objective correlative' for their energies, for their masculinity, for their civilizing drive. Many of them escaped into a crippling religious individualism that effectively divorced their spiritual from their secular lives. Whereas a crusading Calvinism filled a new capitalism pumped with the Protestant ethic that flooded northwest Europe and the North of America with its nervous genius, Catholics were left defending an ever shrinking sacral order. Tens of thousands of Catholic lads marched to their deaths in that defense, but we lost the war.

In part, the crisis of our time in the Church consists in the tragic truth that we Catholics have nothing to do in history as Catholics. We have been stripped of our civilizing role. We cannot sacramentalize the real any more. It is against the law! Although a handful of red-blooded Europeans took their rosaries and rifles off to Angola in order to defend the Catholic presence of Portugal in Africa, they were the last embers of a once great fire that exploded in the past into cathedrals and crusades, colonies and new provinces quickened by missionaries, an entire world of Catholic men on the march.

Given that our youth today has been denied by history an 'objective correlative', it has sought to fashion one of its own in social service, racial justice, international garbage cleaning, anti-war-in-Vietnam demonstrations, and other decent, dubious, and damnable causes. Religion is forbidden to go crusading. That is what is wrong with the Church today. This explains, in part, the divorce of militancy and masculinity from our youth *precisely in its role as Catholics*. The root of the cry for 'relevancy' and 'meaning' is this failure to have a dominant and leading role in history. Due to the spiritual exhaustion into which we have fallen for having fought on the defensive for so long, our progressivists would have us join a world we could not conquer. They would find 'the relevant' by linking hands with all of our traditional enemies, by trimming our doctrine to the modern consciousness and our liturgy to the contemporary sensibility, by enlisting our forces in every secularist enthusiasm. This effort, if successful, will signal the defeat of Catholicism as a world religion.

Any salvation for the Church as a force in time rather than as a pitiful remnant waiting on Apocalypse ultimately depends on the Church's encountering a network of power—both institutionalized and private—that is willing to risk all in forging a new sword at the service of the authority of Rome. Not only could such a Power clean house at home, but it could prepare for the final collapse of western, secularist, humanist society. Although it is a well-kept secret among our brethren of the Left, their exciting big world—heavily industrialized, technocratic, slick, materialist—is on the verge of dying within the West. The presence of Black Power in our midst, the drop-out of a generation of youth drunk on drugs, bespeaks a massive abdication from a secularist society whose panaceas do not warm hearts hungering after the justice of the ultimate things. By a curious irony of history, larded with the parochialism they deplore, the progressivists in the Church would adjust the Bride of Christ to a world in full decay, to a world that has played out its three-score and seven and that has no place left to go.

When the President of the United States recently noted a 'restlessness' in the nation on the occasion of his State of the Union address, he suggested more economics as the answer. His Republican critics, given equal time on television immediately after his speech, simply challenged the President's economics and offered more of their own. But the Black Brother—our society's conscience—will not be satisfied with economics. The spiritual bankruptcy of our world could not be more obvious. Secularism has nothing left to offer the world but a handful of extra years after a boringly comfortable life, a new Buick, and a relaxed sexual code. It offers Sweden, in a word. But Sweden—that hellish society that has made a reality out of the dream of secular gnosticism—cannot grip the eternal adventure of youth, not for long. Youth demands risk, unequal odds, a glimpsing of the eternal hills, a cause bigger than itself.

Crusading Communism is not satisfied with Mr Johnson's and Mr Laird's economics, nor can it be bought off with Harvey Cox's Secular City. This Communism goes down into the sweaty jungles of Bolivia and Venezuela. It holds up the most splendidly equipped army in the world in Vietnam with sheer courage and cunning and, we must add, with the conniving of men who sense that the West has nothing more to give the world. This Communism asks nothing for itself but the sheer delight of serving a cause whose horizons seem to its followers, as they free physical indignity and perpetual danger, to be bigger than the world. Secular humanism, dying of hardening of the arteries, cannot answer this challenge. But a militant reborn Catholic Power can.

I mean a Catholic movement, quickened from within by the love that Catholic men have always known for the Mother of God, Christ the King its banner, a movement dead certain of the justice of its cause and annealed in loyalty to the See of Rome, capable of any adventure, any sacrifice in the name of the Lord of Battles. Such an elite might just make possible a new flowering of Christendom. This flowering will come, this or its contradiction.

An old world once called 'modernity' is now dying. The world ages, as St Augustine insists, and the times hurry us on. We have no time, literally, to adjust to forms and to a mind already in their agony. They will be gone as are dunes in the Sahara after a great wind. As ephemeral as are men themselves, their absence— guaranteed by every sign of the times—would leave the Church with its eyes riveted on a recently dead past, as remote as the Renaissance from which modernity sprang.

But Christ is our Future, insists St John the Evangelist in a remarkable passage in which the Evangelist states that we do not now know who we are because we are what we shall be and what we shall be is Christ. Let us, therefore, prepare for a new civilization to come. Let us not penetrate it from without but rather let us let it grow up within ourselves. It will then be Catholic. Anything less is not worth the dignity of the Catholic name that we have inherited from our fathers.

American Catholic Exodus

JOHN O'CONNOR

Imagine a scene out of Parkman: groups of emigrants, with their
tents and wagons, encamped along the banks of the wide and
muddy Missouri. Long-haired hunters in buckskin. Pioneer
women in calico and denim. Shaggy ponies and mules tied nearby.
Men crouched around campfires, their rifles across their knees,
their axes slatted to their wagons, the smoke of their fires rising
above the din and rattle of children, dogs and cooking pans.
Beyond the river is the mysterious future: tall prairie grass,
buffalo trails, uncharted creeks, then—the mountains: stony, dark
and massive against the westering sun.

Between the crackling warmth of this riverbank campsite and
the emigrant's promised land are wild cyclones that moan across
the plains and bend the cottonwoods; roving, hostile savages whose
screaming war cry and glinting tomahawk will chill the emigrants
to their marrow; mountain cloudbursts and rockslides; fever,
wagontrain tensions and jealousies—and the bitter desert. Yet,
for those ready to push on, ahead lies opportunity, as well as
ordeal. The emigrants expect both: look at their squints over the
campfire; look at the determination in those hard faces. There is
apprehension here, and restlessness, and hope—for they see
something beyond the prairie dust, beyond the glacial snows, and
beyond the howl of desert coyotes. A feeling for adventure—
unplanned and risky, but promising all the same—pervades the
emigrants' camp. This is the American Catholic Church landscape
today—but at its most advanced staging area.

Only a tiny, spearhead minority, these emigrant parties, push forward the frontiers of the liturgical, ecumenical, social action, biblical and theological fronts. As you'd expect, these are the restless ones, unsatisfied with old forms and old structures—which rumbles within the earth tell them are crumbling—and around them swirl tumult, turbulence and a tense excitement.

But let me assure you, this riverbank tableau is a very small part of the company of strangers we call the Church. Let your eye now pan the landscape that has been left behind, and here you will find the bigger part, the overwhelming majority, much more satisfied with things as they are, conscious, perhaps, that one must move with the times but, if move we must, then let it be a return and a restoration, not an Abrahamic adventure into an unknown land. No man who has it made packs up and leaves, pushes on, searches for new frontiers. The man who has it made sits back, rocking on his porch, husbanding what he has, proud of his full barn, his rick of wood, his sheaf of credit cards and his club memberships. A tremor of fear moves through him at the thought of change. This is the bulk of the American Catholic Church, enamoured of the past, led by necrophiles in magenta, bent on shoring up the threatened monuments their forefathers built.

Two spirits wrestle within the American Catholic Church today: one, the spirit of odyssey, of return to and restoration of the Church of our childhood with its proud sectarianism, its efficient clericalism and its glorious triumphalism; the other, the spirit of exodus, of bold venture forward according to no clearly drawn map, of let's dump, demolish or drastically re-do the institution and move ahead. These two spirits grapple with one another inside the American Catholic, literally tearing him apart, as they tear apart communities and dioceses. No area of the Church escapes the strain of the struggle between odyssey and exodus. Families find themselves divided. Old friends come to the parting of the ways. Rectories and convents—despite tranquil facades—are split right down the refectory table. There is a powerful undertow that tends to polarize the Church at two extremes—go ahead, and stay put. The Church the immigrants built is feeling the pull of the emigrant. Some people of no little sensitivity and concern feel that this pull will snap beams and braces, and that a great crash will follow.

And there is reason to be concerned: the inheritance from the past makes an imposing picture, and what will Catholics of the future say if we of this generation let the demolition squads do their work? It was only yesterday that the immigrants came, cap in hand. They built an institutional marvel, a miracle of organization—didn't travelling clerics always comment appreciatively on our parochial school system?—and a quake-proof monument to the newcomers' success drive. Steeples spot the horizon where the immigrant Catholic musked his neighborhood: from the dismal port ghettoes of the Atlantic seaboard across the country to the Pacific coast where lacy pepper and eucalyptus cascade over red-tiled mission roofs, Catholic culture was part of the American scene. The institution grew fat; its members became furry fat cats. It all became very snug—the warm tranquility of vigil-lighted side altars, the certitude of cassocked classrooms, the gold dust of success on domes and spires.

A snug feeling of security wrapped us comfy in the sectarian ghetto with its special saint's day holidays at the school and the savory dinners at the parish hall. We acquired a feeling of supremacy, too, at being a member of a supremacist group. It was not a supremacy of money or blood—indeed our forefathers were poor and most often unlettered. Somehow, by God's design, we Roman Catholics were, by birth, made members of a private club of God's special friends, inheritors of all the privileges attendant to being a follower of Jesus Christ. We enjoyed a supremacy of grace. Any journey today through this crisis of our own making must be a return. The bickering and criticism will pass; the uneasiness and uncertainty will disappear; the irreverence and disrespect and rebelliousness will be overcome and everything will be all right again. Some of us have staunchly maintained, all along, that, despite the furor of the Council, when it was all over with, things would be quite the same again—the loyal sticking with the Church, and the weak shearing themselves off in a kind of great self-castration process. Odysseys always wind up back home again, where things are snug. And for the American Church, things have been snug, thanks to the generosity and docility of generations of simple faithful and the bent backs of long-serving, hod-carrying Monsignori. Any odyssey through this new crisis will only lead back to where it started, to warmth and safety within mother Church's great womb, from which we were popped by the progressive physicians of the Council, who snatched us squawling and kicking, in a great caesarean section.

What has been left behind, for now, that will be restored in even more grandeur once the ordeal of renewal is over? The Sunday Mass of our childhood: the candles flicker against the carnations, the bell tinkles and a hush falls over the rustle of the worshippers, the organ pumps out 'Holy God We Praise Thy Name' and we file into the bright sun, nodding at familiar faces, pick up the paper, and go about our lives. The sermon was dependably dull, but now and then it would fortify our personal piety or re-fire our will to obey or keep us from a dirty movie. It seldom asked us to risk our comfort, though, except for some mild Lenten admonition. And it never asked our personal *involvement* in the world; merely support of the institutional system.

But since the Council, with the stress on liturgical up-dating, have things really changed very much? There is some participation now, more hymn singing, and the Mass is celebrated in English— but things are not too much different: the sermons remain dull, the large parish churches are as impersonal and unfriendly as ever, and the small ones retain their flavor of rural pieties. The Mass, as central to the worshipping community, may even be less warm and cozy for some as it has become more distracting from individual devotions.

What else shaped us? The parish school. Concrete play yards and statues of Mary and Joseph. Report cards from the hands of the pastor, the portrait of the bishop hanging in the principal's office, long skirts on girl cheerleaders making them look like hoydenish postulants, May processions, and the smell of wax at Friday afternoon stations of the cross. Here the elite were formed, here future vocations to the religious life were planted, fertilized, shaded from too much sun, freshened daily with overhead mists of piety. Here pagan babies were redeemed through a little cardboard box. Here the evils of communism, freemasonry, Luther and Cromwell were told in stories that told, too, of Lord Baltimore's vision, Marquette's courage, and Rockne's imagination. Here the story of our little band of Catholics was recited, from Peter to the modern popes, whereas in the state schools, sad to say, scant attention was paid, and often men, movements and martyrs were passed over in the rush to educate for American democracy while canonizing the lily-white forebearers of modern secular America. Any journey here must be towards bigger and better schools.

Back home, too, was the devotional life: novenas in honor of Our Lady of the Miraculous Medal on Tuesday evenings, novenas to St Jude, St Anthony or some other wonder-worker on Thursday nights, and benediction of the most blessed sacrament on Sunday. But heading all was the rosary—during May and October, at grottoes and on country radio stations, at wakes, and for many of us every Sunday before benediction. The hymns were tender and child-like: 'Bring flowers of the fairest', 'Hail Holy Queen enthroned above' and 'Mother dear, O pray for me'. Devotion to the mother of Jesus was sustained through the generations by mother-worshipping Irish priests and no less devoted Italian clerics. And we drew great consolation from them.

And it was to this devoted clergy, men of military regimen and mysterious powers, that we looked not only for consolation, but for guidance, for formation, for correction, for certitude and paternal benediction. We depended on them; they were always there—early in the morning, before the Mass, the pastor meditated upon his knees, hunched in the darkened sanctuary; in the evening, or late at night, when the town was asleep, his light was on. He rallied the immigrants around him to worship the Lord and salute his law—the Lord's law, though some thought it was the priest's law. (The priest was occasionally caught in this error, too.) He studied the sacred sciences, was drilled in pious practices, worked as an administrator of a parish plant—and kept his hands clean. Poets were always writing about the clean hands of the priest. Friend, counsellor, consoler in the time of trial and bitter sorrow, he even treated affairs of the heart. The Irish immigrant wrote, not to Dear Abby, but to Father Con.

And somewhere behind these sacrificing priests, and above them, were the bishop and the pope—guarantors of orthodoxy, united, certain, descendents of the Twelve, vicars of God.

This was the system—pope, bishop, pastor, school, church. Whatever travail the *aggiornamento* brings, whatever adventure the odyssey pursues, the system that holds together the edifice must be restored in renewed beauty and efficiency and security. Isn't this what an odyssey portends? The ancient Greeks tell the story well: Ulysses sets out on his adventure, but after much peril and sweat comes home again. Maeterlinck wrote a variation on the theme: the bluebird of happiness is right back where you started. Some of the Church's escatological prognostications are similar: death is a return 'home' to the bosom of our Father.

This seems to be the goal of the system-keepers and the great bulk of the Church in America today: to restore the pre-Council calm and quiet, to consolidate and amalgamate in some instances, to decentralize in others, to allow for more variety in some cases, to sharpen efficiency, and over all to secure and embellish the institution—as we have known it.

Even for the weary, this is an inviting prospect. A new triumphalism, a more militant clericalism, a super-sectarianism, all are possible, if we will just cut out the criticism and the carping, pay little heed to self-appointed prophets among theologians and writers, and rally round the petrine structures that identify, with eternal certitude, the company of the saved.

But if all the foregoing is true, if the immigrants built well and their pastors slaved like Yeat's old priest Father Gilligan, '. . . weary night and day', then why all the disturbance? Where did we go wrong? Something must have happened to unleash this tornado of activity that is shaking the Church from St Patrick's Cathedral to Mission Dolores.

Historians some day will describe the cataclysm as the Johannine revolution, but simply to write it off as Pope John's singular responsibility is not quite accurate. For some time preceding John XXIII's call of the Church to Council, a yeasty activity was bubbling under the surface of the regimented world Church. Bible scholars among Catholics had been following the lead of Protestants and looking closer at scripture. Their pens became shovels, and they dug up new meanings to old stories. A worldwide network of vernacular enthusiasts found focus particularly among the Benedictines of Minnesota, and the liturgical renewal's preparations were begun. The call of Pope Pius X to the laity was echoed by Pius XII and broadcast by such continental names as Congar, Cardijn and de la Bedoyere, while in America priest-revolutionaries like Hillenbrand and Putz sounded the lay apostolic trumpet. The Jesuit Gustave Weigel began talking before the public with Protestant authorities—notably Robert McAfee Brown—and Pius XI's slight ecumenical opening became a breech through which rushed all kinds of people genuinely interested in Christian unity. While Franklin D Roosevelt was bringing about a social revolution in the United States, down the street at the Washington, DC, headquarters of the National Catholic Welfare Conference, Msgr John Ryan was promoting a social consciousness among churchmen and readers of the Catholic press. When the currents of modernization, in some cases sprung from the pontificate of Leo XIII, began to flow through the worldwide Church, they joined, in America, with the emergence of the immigrant Catholic from his ghetto, and together this confluence formed a strong tide rushing along a reform course. The scattering of people, the mixing of energetic elements long confined by ghettoes, the exposure to European ideas by the publishing explosion—such scattering, mixing, and exposure being by-products of World War II—prepared the Church for John XXIII's green light to reform.

But when I say prepared the Church, I do not mean the whole American Church, only a portion, but that a spartan and determinedly prophetic one. And, to be sure, an activist portion. The great bulk remained unaware, as, for all the *braggadocio* about the marvel of the parochial school system, the average Catholic, by virtue of a tightly-controlled indoctrination system, remained, as he still is, a religious illiterate. And leading the flock, sad to say, were men caught theologically napping when the Vatican Council bugled them to Rome and to the shock of a world Church plunged into revolution.

Everyone knows the American bishops' contribution to the Vatican Council. The Yanks were hardly super stars. Yet for all the silence—doubtlessly we should be thankful—and the timidity of the majority, brilliant exceptions included such names as Ritter, Cushing, Wright, Hallinan, Primeau, Levan and Meyer. It became clear that the American Church had few scholar types among its official teachers. We were a Church led by administrators— business managers of huge construction companies, ill at ease among the erudite, proud of their own pragmatism, clever enough to see which way the wind of the Spirit was blowing (and to vote progressive), but anxious to get home and resume control lest the revolution get out of hand.

And a revolution was going on. The changes in worship, the loosening of the fast, the ecumenical hand-holding were all evident and publicized. Changes manifested itself in other ways: in church architecture the church as meeting hall, or better yet, as auditorium for spectators at a lone ritual, became more community-conscious, bringing the participating people closer to the altar, surrounding it in some cases, with the baptistry brought out of hiding, and the altar as banquet table definitely in. The sticky devotional art of the pre-Council Church began to fade before more modern stuff demanding a viewer's involvement, occasionally, with its representational meaning. A more open and honest policy was adopted by portions of the Church press, notably the portion not owned by the bishops, which, though changing somewhat, remained apologetic and catechetical, yet often improved technically. Moreover, the laity was invited into more responsible positions, particularly as aides to the religious and the clergy in the Confraternity of Christian Doctrine's vast instructional program, and here and there a key office within the college system or as a chancery bookkeeper. The Council gave impetus to these changes, although many had begun within the decade before the Council was called, and in some places, as under Sister Maria de la Cruz in San Francisco with a snappy and updated CCD program, they were well on their way by the time John XXIII asked for reform.

Moreover, the openness of the Council was reflected in less narrowness towards the world. Catholics have not exactly said farewell to Queen Victoria—far from it; she occupies an influential mantle place among the American Catholic's household gods—but there is less nervousness about human sexuality and only the rear guard rightists carry on crusades against certain novels, plays and movies, whereas a decade ago pulpits were being mounted regularly as bishops rode like Paul Revere crying 'The corrupters are coming!' This is not to say an awful lot of concern is not occupying the Catholic mind about pornography and the skin-press, but the hysteria of the Legion of Decency days is no longer as widespread, I'm sure.

What has happened, then, since John XXIII? What has happened is that, in the United States, the *absolute* control of a brick-and-mortar mentality on the American Catholic has had its grip broken. This does not mean that the excesses of the edifice drive are past. By no means. Building committees still carry the most weight among bishops' advisers, I'd surmise. School officials appear to be as concerned as ever over blueprints for new wings while the Confraternity of Christian Doctrine flounders as the underfed step-child of the Catholic educational system. But having said this you still must admit the palpable evidence of a break with the past.

Perhaps this example will illustrate what I mean. San Francisco's red brick cathedral of St Mary burnt down in 1962, not too long after the arrival of the new ordinary, Archbishop McGucken, who had succeeded to this lovely see following the death of Archbishop John J Mitty, the personification of the brick-and-mortar prelate. Before the charred bricks could cool, the new Archbishop had surrounded himself with money raisers and public relations men and a drive for a new cathedral had begun—along with expanded diocesan services to the aged, school children, and archdiocesan welfare expansion. The drive was a whopping money success. San Franciscans of all faiths and none rallied behind the Archbishop and responded generously. But the wraith of dissent also emerged from the ashes: aesthetic minded members of the Catholic Art Forum raged at the chancery's choice of architects—not known for anything stunning—and an echo was bounced back from the community. In response to this vocal public opinion, led by a downtown daily, not the Church's official paper, the archdiocese sought out more acclaimed architectural minds and the plans proceeded. After an agonizing wait, while plans were drawn, submitted, redrawn, and all that, the first steps were taken to clear a hilltop and plant a foundation. Meanwhile, however, the waves made in Rome at the Council began to lap at San Francisco's shore. A long smouldering discontent with the institutional Church's shuffling pace towards helping solve the Bay Area's racial and poverty problems—connected like Siamese twins—resulted in a desperate public outcry against the continuation of the new cathedral's construction. This outcry came not from war-on-poverty workers, but from the Bay Area's own priests, twenty-seven of whom signed a public letter begging that the cathedral's foundation stand as a monument to the deprivation of so many of San Francisco's poor, and that the monies collected in the $8 million drive go to alleviate this blight on the city.

Of course, the protest and the searching questions of the dissenters have caused no more than a ripple across the pond of policy within the archdiocese. The archbishop's plans have not been deterred. He has called the protest an act of disloyalty, and the priests, along with their agitator, a woman theologian at Jesuit-operated University of San Francisco, have been scathingly denounced within the pages of a neighboring diocese's official newspaper. But the point is, ten years ago public dissent would not have occurred. Five years ago priests' participation in any kind of protest against the action of any chancery would have been unimaginable. Today it is a fact, and is among several husky straws in the ecclesiastical wind.

What has happened is that dissenters from the system are taking courage—slowly, and certainly in very small numbers; but a revolution in thinking, in structures, and in direction of mission is slowly taking place. If this is good—and I, for one, believe it is—then the credit, if you will allow that credit is due, must go to a hardy few. It is to the credit of this hardy few that any progress is being made at all—not, certainly, to the credit of widespread chancery immobility, institutional prudence, and cautious administrative personnel. What progress is being made within the Church in the United States is being made in spite of official gradualism, and the obstructionism of nine out of ten pastors whose careers found them unprepared for the coming of the revolution of the Holy Spirit.

To describe the agony of the American Church in terms of a generation gap is to over-simplify it, I think, and to nurture the erroneous idea that it's only a matter of time until a younger wave of bishops and pastors come along and everything will be all right, Jack. To be sure, there is a gap between the generations—those largely in power among the clergy over forty-five, say, and the priests ordained since Vatican II; between the laity disciplined to private devotions, and those eager to march for fair housing. But there is much more to it than that. First, to assume that with the rising of younger men into positions of power and responsibility, with the elevation of a new Establishment succeeding yesterday's, all will automatically change, is, I am convinced, wrong. Among the younger diocesan priests I know, few appear to have courage or vision; most, I fear, are career conformists who will go along, like the good Germans, with the command of their superiors, or with their superior's non-action. This may testify to the spirit of obedience engrained among American priests, a holy obedience that has much going for it, and that has served the Church, at times, but that all the same has produced still another generation of system-functionaries, goose-stepping with out-dated canon law, and silent in the face of any number of injustices within the church and within the world.

If among the younger priests there is only a slight glimmer of hope, among the laity things are even more disappointing. Few care. Why should they ? More and more are writing the institution off as an anachronism. What percentage still owe to hard-working religious their early preparation as Christians, soon discover that the Holy Name society is hardly a satisfying team, and since their understanding of the Church's mission is limited to perfunctory sacrament participation and institutional expansionism, they soon tire of the dullnesses of it all and are lost to the Church in all but envelope number. Among the young laity who care, and they are distressingly few, there is a built-in conviction that, to recall Sir Walter Scott's epigram, the further from chancery, the closer to God. The red-hots among the laity who might be counted on to step into their father's shoes as leading Catholic laymen, are, for the most part, Che Gueveras, carrying on guerrilla warfare against the stick-in-the-mud institution. Let me repeat: they are very few. Most young Catholics, I'd observe, have neither zeal nor vision. Those with zeal and vision lack patience, as who doesn't these days. But the vast majority of the up-coming generation have been lost to the Church, as I see it, because we have offered them neither romance nor challenge, but stone tablets and the example of a medieval oligarchy in a parade of narcissism and pretense.

And who leads the parade ? Sons and grandsons of immigrants, the American bishops. Here are the steeplejacks of the structure, the nightwatchmen of the institution. You say—but the bishops come from the clergy; it is the priests who are responsible for the way we are. But the priests have been, for the most part, only the functionaries and *volkstrummers* of the system. True, we have a personnel problem here. Some of it is tied to celibacy, but I think there's more to it than that. And the question is not whether or not we shall have married priests, but when. The priests themselves will work this out, probably sooner than most people think. Celibacy is the priests' problem first, though it is the concern of the whole Church insofar as this discipline helps or harms those called to the ordained ministry, or prohibits others, perhaps well-qualified, from seeking ordination and the ministerial career. Certainly competent priests, celibate or not, are needed. Perhaps, as the idea of the priesthood of the faithful is developed, we shall have men called by the people from the people to serve as Mass celebrants. Many indications suggest that tomorrow's priest will be first a competent worker, teacher, artist, medic, then a priest. The idea of a priestly class, set apart and coddled in privilege, has worked many hardships on the Church, not the least of which is the frankensteinian clericalism which has frightened the people away from their responsibilities. Moreover, such a class system has often eunuchized good men, turned them into monitors of womens' meetings and deprived them, for many years, of their civil rights within the Church.

Now the formation of priests' associations proposes to do something about the problem intramurally, whereas scholarship, a modernized recruiting and seminary system, and an increased people's interest may bring reform before it is too late.

Still, we must return to the bishops as the key men in our problem. You say the bishops come from the clergy, and state further that the clergy come from the people, and then everyone is reminded of that old clerical joke about how the people get the priests and bishops they deserve. Let us admit that: the immigrant Church was served diligently by men cut out for the job of serving an immigrant Church. But we are past that stage now, despite the hard-dying ghettoes of the urban centers that keep Irish, Italians, Poles and Puerto Ricans strutting about in tribal self-consciousness. The immigrant age is past, and the diaspora has begun. Yet the bishops seem hardly aware of this. On the contrary, the system that has worked so well in the past, that has protected the immigrant, nurtured vocations to the religious life, inculcated a spirit of generous financial support to church works, and enhanced the institution's power and wealth beyond anything imaginable elsewhere, is not to be jettisoned lightly. You don't kill the goose that lays the golden egg.

Yet, somewhere the bishops went wrong. It is not hard to

discover where. Precisely in building such a powerful and wealthy institution did they construct the false god. Precisely in over-protecting the simple faithful did they prove derelict in their task of preparing the people for the present crisis. Precisely in commanding such stern mosaic obedience to organizational authorities did they cripple the people for assuming adult Christian responsibilities. The erection of institutional shelters took priority over the social mission of the Church.

The bishops arrogated to themselves the gifts of the whole Church. They have acted, and continue, for the most part, to act, as if they held a monopoly on the Holy Spirit, as if truth were not truth until they stamped it with their official stamp, as if you could substitute a medieval institution for a living and loving community. The bishop as one-man-Church is the rule in the United States.

True many have sought community, as many, in bursts of what must be campaign oratory, claimed to be 'your simple father in Christ', while as an example they drove around in Cadillacs and Lincolns, were inaccessible to their people (in many cases even inaccessible to their priests), listened, apparently, only to what they wanted to hear, deceived the public, including their own flock, with cleverly managed news and the control of opinion, and erected a vast potentatedom that cast fear and trembling into the bones of teenage seminarians and small children and which relished, tolerated, and promoted pomp and bluster right out of times long dead.

It would be grossly unfair to admit of no exceptions to this rule, for here and there you can name men who have for some time sought the participation of the whole Church in the mission of the Church, who have had to ride hard on some very difficult administrative problems, particularly personnel problems, within their own dioceses, who have remained priests of the people—not flannel-mouthed politicians—and who have tried, earnestly, to put the decrees of the Council to work among their flocks. But these are the very rare exceptions, and even in their cases, institutional phoniness has not been entirely relinquished.

Most bishops have acted as if the Holy Spirit spoke solely to them, as individuals, or, safer yet, to the body of bishops assembled at a national conference or to its committees. Moreover, the idea of equating the Church with the hierarchy—a logical outgrowth of clericalism—has not only been swallowed by most of the Church's people, it has been gobbled up too by the public which has been pretty well victimized, in this regard, by the collusion of chancery public relations officers and toadyish metropolitan news desks.

Whereas Christ called together a people to do a job, Churchmen have substituted their own private club, bureaucratized and bolstered against public scrutiny or accountability. Troublemakers, agitators, and incendiaries who call too much attention to certain aspects of the institution, are silenced, curtailed, neutralized or dropped over the side as quickly as possible. Every diocese has its graveyard for the corpses of dissenters. What happened to Daniel Berrigan, SJ, a couple of winters ago, has happened many times over to lesser personages, men of fewer gifts and no contact with a sympathetic element in the public press. Only the DuBays, Coffields, Hafners and O'Reilly's rise to the surface as signs of wreckage on the deep, but vast numbers go unnoticed, unheard and undefended—priests, for the most part, but laymen too, not necessarily nuts, but men who have tried to help, in many cases, only to be rebuffed, denied their rights within the Church—the right to participate in decision making, that is— and their reputations tarnished with the brush of disloyalty.

Not only have the Catholic people bought this patriarchal one-man-Church idea, so has the public—through the defaulting journalism of the daily press, which, for the most part, lives in fear of mass circulation loss if they offend sensitive elements within their circulation area. The daily newspapers, though often responsible watchdogs of local government, have long treated the government of the Church-institutional with kid gloves. Maybe some of this has to do with the long-held American reverence for men called to the ministry. This is partly a by-product of clericalism, and Protestants must share with Catholics the blame for this aura of privilege and immunity with which a portion of the respectable public surrounds men of the cloth. But there is another reason, and it is practical: chancery office cooperation is needed on many stories and the city desk that is blacklisted through indiscretions of some reporter or the stubbornness of some editor, soon hears about it at publisher level. It is well-known that Catholic institutions often boycott certain publications; it is not so widely known, but understandable, that chancery officials cultivate certain friends in the city room—not always Catholics, as they may be the most untrustworthy when it comes to swallowing institutional handouts—and through this agent the public is fed a steady stream of official bunkum.

You must allow, too, for the pragmatic mind of harassed city editors: the Church-institutional is a source of certain tried and true human interest features, cliches, perhaps, but as dependably popular as apple pie: pictures of young *ordinandi* prostrate before the altar at ordination time; old ladies with arthritic fingers telling their beads at rosary rallies; children having their throats blessed on Candlemas Day or the husky worker with a daub of ash on his forehead and the caption that always reads, 'Remember, man, thou art but dust. . . .' If Church officials clip off some sources to the press, or throw such a scare into the nuns that school news has to be filtered through the office of the superintendent—in some cases, even parent-teacher news—then you can see how, in dread of such havoc, a newspaper would seek an arrangement with the local chancery office, wherever possible, out of which would come a policy mutually protective. Exceptions there are, but the hard fact is that many of the hottest stories within the Church-institutional have never been touched by newspapers, or even high-powered magazines which have come to enjoy a respectable circulation among Catholics. It would be erroneous to attempt to make a case for a possible conspiracy between the lords of the press and the lords of the Church-institutional, but much evidence exists for a kind of mutual agreement to let sleeping dogs lie.

What has developed in reaction to this institutionalism and the absolute power of the bishop, is a dump-the-institution move-

ment. There are good men inside—in key positions, priests for the
most part—who are working towards changing the institution
from the inside. They have no intention of going off the Talla-
hatchee bridge. They're staying in, letting Davis and Kavanaugh
jump, if they insist, but staying and working intensely for reform
from within. 'I'm screwing the institution: I'm staying in' is the
way one clandestine reformer puts it. These men are diligently
preparing the way for reform by piling coals under the renewal
pots. They may not be able to stir, as the radical on the outside,
but they can stoke.

Although there is this reform element working from within the
institution, and though there are many bishops committed to some
degree to just such a course while their neighboring episcopal
brother may be dragging his feet or even, as in most cases, obstruct-
ing or resisting the reform, an even more dramatic and revolutionary development has occurred. A big walk-away is happening.
Men are just walking away from what all their lives they've been
taught was duly constituted Church authority. Raised to respect
the bishop and to conform to his wishes, they are now discovering
that the bishop has over-played his hand. Men are turning to the
authority of competency and the authority of observable holiness
and charity, wherever it is found—and too often it is not found in
the local bishop. Men schooled to expect true leadership from their
bishop are turning to leadership wherever it is found—and too
often it is not found in the local bishop. Rather, the expert—the
theologian, biblical scholar, or charismatic priest, or minister,
becomes the bishop-substitute, for he seems to show a grasp of
what it means to say 'Church', and he restores the romance of
religion to tired but baptized blood.

These men who take a walk: their road often leads from
disillusionment to contempt, for they looked to hierarchical
authority for leadership—first in faith and in love—yet found, too
often, the bishop's faith was in the certitude of canon law or the
apostolic delegate's *bel paese* smile, while his love was a narcissistic
projection of the institution. The Church's mission was equated
with expansionism; inertia rather than enthusiasm greeted each

new problem; even the popes seemed johnny-come-latelys to the needs of the world. For many, therefore, the bishops became the pall-bearers of God.

A portion of the Church has already gone underground. It has its laity and its priests—hiding, in new catacombs, not from Roman legionnaires, but from chancery officials. It is only a matter of time until this underground also has its bishops. Perhaps it already has. As yet no Archbishop Roberts has popped up on the American scene, nor any Bishop Simons; indeed the American hierarchical pattern is one of almost phalanx-like conformity. But it would be rash to suppose that so many good priests and laity could feel the call to go underground, and even more to strike out for some kind of emancipation from the regimentation of the one-man-Church system, without a bishop sensing the same urge. If just one bishop would resign his comfortable see, turn in his medieval insignia of power, and go—like Leger—to serve the lepers of the Church, the married priests, the peaceniks and conscientious objectors, the front-line social actionists, and all those who join them in the underground catacombs below the respectable surface of our middle class American parishes, he would be making a most remarkable contribution. He would also be called a nut.

Perhaps, on second thought, the people are better served without such a volunteer ex-ordinary. Bishops have a way of becoming killers of the dream, unfortunately, as in their administrative training they somehow, in so many cases, lose sight of the vision, allow the romance to dry up in their souls, and set about organizing to protect the *status quo*.

If the revolution to reform the Church in America is allowed to be directed by the hierarchy, then the revolution will sputter out, like a dead fire—for the job requires men of raw courage, men to match the mountainous mission. And few dioceses have heroes heading them—though there may be saintly men, men of patience, wearied by the fight, and men of some gifts. But most of them are where they are because they were branded early as solid yet diplomatic conservatives, watchful and cautious. The years which

Amleto Cigognani (now the Cardinal Secretary of State of the Vatican) and Egidio Vagnozzi (now Cardinal Prefect of the Department of Economic Affairs of the Vatican) spent as successive apostolic delegates to Washington profited the cause of reaction well, for their influence is evident in the pattern of conservative episcopal appointments in this country. Cronieship and like-thinking have played their part in establishing a hierarchy as cohesive as the US bishops. Not even the Green Bay Packers have displayed such defensive strength.

Some slight hope might be taken from the action early this year of Cardinal Shehan of Baltimore, who wrote to the priests of the Diocese of Wilmington, Delaware, saying he would entertain their suggestions about a successor to their late bishop. But he did not include the laity in his offer, and his offer did not come until an independent priests' association of the Wilmington diocese had publicly suggested that the whole Church in that area be permitted a chance to recommend candidates for the vacant chair.

No, the revolution of Christian expectations has come to the stage where leadership has passed from the hierarchy as we have known it. Demolition crews are already at work stringing out their fuses. Meanwhile, the American Catholic Church has arrived at a crossroads. Whereas up to now we have had pretty much a 'religion without decision' as Hoekendijk puts it, now we must decide if we want to stay put or push on. The overwhelming bulk of the people have been criminally retarded in their sense of Church, their grasp of mission. They have been deprived of a truly Catholic education by a hierarchy that has preferred to protect the system and embellish and strengthen the institution through indoctrination of a subjugated class—in a word, the bishops have brainwashed the people. They have turned the Church-institutional into a private club worshipping an image of itself. If heresy and schism were words that had any meaning today, they would have to be applied first to the bishops and their lieutenants who have split the Church from the Spirit, who have raised the false god of institutionalism, and who have permitted themselves to be made, in many cases, into little gods.

The portion of the Church that has gone underground will spearhead the thrust of the future, which will be open, ecumenical and communitarian, rather than closed, sectarian and authoritarian. Whenever this movement gets strong enough on the local level, it will elect its own bishops, if we are to have bishops at all in the diaspora, and I suppose we will—though perhaps not elected for life. It is a joke within the 'in' and clerical circles of the Church that nothing could so quickly cure so many of the Church's ills as a number of episcopal funerals. It is sad to admit, but true, that the flaming pyres of a number of anti-reform bishops would doubtedlessly ignite the hopes of the more cynical elements within the Church's renewal camp. But this must be dismissed as a joshing, though wicked, thought, only temporarily entertained. Retirement is the answer, but so far machinery has not been constructed that will ease the replacement of aged, infirm and over-weary bishops who deserve honor and respect for their years of service, yet who obviously hold back renewal because, grown set in their ways, they no longer bring vigor, imagination and daring to their jobs.

One of the saddest tales to be told within the American Church today, and it is a tale that can be told more than twice, concerns the tired and battle-scarred bishop, now gibbering in his senility, shuffling through ceremonies and snoring through meetings, surrounded by ambitious courtiers and defenders of the system that has kept them comfortable, finally giving up the ghost when the last ounce of holy endurance is exhausted, his waxen bones now laid out in princely finery while children who never knew him are marshalled for a public demonstration, while priests who had barely a whit of respect for him file by dressed in lace, and official news accounts prattle the expected reverences—and all the while the institutional jackals gather to see how they are going to take care of themselves should the new man be not of their faith. Is this any way to guarantee the dignity of the office, to enhance the authority of the teacher, to instill a sense of the Church's mission into a people or underscore the Church's concern among those who look on and note the phoniness of it all?

It is this phoniness that the pathology of the body is rejecting; we're puking it all out.

Although a yeoman effort at Church re-organization is being made at Rome—witness Paul VI's Curia reform beginnings—and throughout the United States—witness Archbishop Dearden and the struggles of the National Conference of Catholic Bishops, still progress is at a snail's pace. And central to the pace problem is the matter of personnel: as many Roman Curia members were extremely advanced in years, and their replacements themselves beyond peak productivity, so the voting members of the NCCB include many who deserve to have the burden of administrative and teaching responsibilities lifted from their shoulders.

Is there a chance that the American Church-institutional will catch itself in time, purge itself of its reactionary elements in leadership positions—including pastors and bishops—bravely call what amounts to constitutional conventions in each parish that can be free from clerical manipulating, overcome its conditioned tendency to nurture narcissism and pharisiastic legalism, and shake off the fear of being fully Christian—is there a chance? I am by nature an optimist. But I don't think there's a chance.

What chance we have, I believe, is the opportunity, now, to move forward swiftly and pioneer new territory, leaving behind old forms where they no longer are satisfactory, and allowing those who want to stay behind to do just that—but not to let them get away with thinking, and preaching, that they, alone, are the Church. The fact is the people are the Church, and the institution is almost hopelessly behind. And a portion of the people are ahead, and there lies the romance. For they are the new Hebrews, called not to the restoration of a clerical empire, but to the pain and promise of living for the development of men.

Can this be done without violence? The frontier is always the scene of violence. And let those who whimper recall that the institutional Church has tolerated a good deal of violence— violence to consciences, violence to the truth, violence to personalities, violence to the mission. Let us hope the violence that comes can be confined to eye-sore structures and crumbling forms.

We cannot wait for mitred leadership; it's back there muttering about authority. We must push ahead with the exodus—suffering with those who choose to exit; suffering with those, too, who choose to remain where it is safe—but push ahead, all the same, being grateful for our gifts and our disabilities, getting on with the enormous reclamation task against hunger, disease, illiteracy, poverty and war, through which task we can—unworthy as we are —discover a new sense of community, refire man's hopes, and renew a lovable world.

Notes on Contributors

PHILIP BERRIGAN, SSJ, is a Josephite priest from Baltimore, Maryland. He is a member of CORE, SNCCZ, NAACP, co-founder of the Catholic Peace Fellowship, author of *No More Strangers*.

EUGENE BIANCHI, SJ, is a Jesuit priest, who is assistant professor of theology at the University of Santa Clara, California, director of the university's Center for the Study of Contemporary Values, author of *John XXIII and American Protestantism*, and a former staff member of *America*.

WILLIAM BIRMINGHAM is general editor of Mentor-Omega Books for the New American Library, and editor of the quarterly *Cross Currents*. He contributed to numerous journals, including *Thought* and *Commonweal*. He is editor of the symposia *What Modern Catholics Think About Birth Control*, and *Cross Currents of Psychiatry and Catholic Morality*.

ROBERT MCAFEE BROWN is an ordained Presbyterian minister, a professor of religion at Stanford University, co-author (with Gustave Weigel, SJ) of *An American Dialogue*, of *Observer in Rome*, and numerous articles in such publications as *Christian Century*, *Commonweal* and the *New Yorker*.

DENNIS CLARK is a member of the staff of Temple University's Center for Community Studies, a former director of New York's Interracial Council, and author of several books on race and urban problems, including *The Ghetto Game*.

A V KREBS, JR is a free-lance writer living in San Francisco, is west coast correspondent for *The National Catholic Reporter*, and is a regular contributor to *Commonweal*.

SISTER MARYELLEN MUCKENHIRN, CSC (formerly Sister Charles Borromeo) is professor of theology and director of the graduate school of theology at St Xavier College, Chicago, Illinois. She is the author of *The Changing Sister, The New Nuns,* and *Implications of Renewal.*

JOHN MULHOLLAND, a free-lance writer living in Washington, D.C., is the former assistant national director of the National Council of Catholic Men, headquartered at the National Catholic Welfare Conference, Washington.

ARLENE SWIDLER, of Philadelphia, Pa., is the managing editor of the *Journal for Ecumenical Studies,* and has contributed to such journals as *America* and *Commonweal.*

FREDERICK WILHELMSEN, a professor of history at the University of Dallas, Texas, is one of the editors of *Triumph,* a contributor to the *Saturday Evening Post, Catholic World* and *The Wanderer,* the author of four books on Spain, has taught at the University of Navarre, Spain, the University of Al-Hikma, Bagdad, and the University of Santa Clara, California.

JOHN O'CONNOR is the founding editor—now former editor—of *The Delmarva Dialog,* of Wilmington, Delaware, a former editor of *The Monitor,* San Francisco. He has taught at the University of San Francisco and contributed to such journals as *America, Commonweal, Catholic World, Lamp* and *Sign.* At present he lives in Chadds Ford, Pa.